Contents

Acknowledgements

My thanks are due to the British Library (Bloomsbury and Colindale), the London Library, Manchester Central Library, Birmingham Central Library, Lowestoft Central Library.

The Public Record Office, Leicestershire Records Service, Lancashire County Record Office.

The libraries of the *Illustrated London News*, *Yorkshire Post*, *Staffordshire Sentinel*, General and Municipal Workers' Union, Transport and General Workers' Union, General Federation of Trade Unions, University of London History Department, the House of Commons.

The Imperial War Museum, National Army Museum, Corps of Royal Engineers (Chatham).

The Manchester Ship Canal Company, Caledonian Canal Company, Port of London Authority.

Above all I would like to thank the Rev. Hereward Cooke, former Director of the Industrial Christian Fellowship, and Kathleen Campbell, the Fellowship's hon. librarian, for their unfailing help.

Pictures still in copyright are reproduced by permission of: Manchester Ship Canal Company, plates 2, 13, 15, 21, 36; BBC Hulton Picture Library, plate 5; *Illustrated London News*, plates 25–35; Leicestershire Museums (Sydney Newton Collection), cover, plates 1, 3–12, 17, 22–3, 39–41, 44–5; Islington Public Libraries, plate 20.

Foreword

My father became a navvy around 1903. *His are the words in this typeface throughout the book.* He was born at Riddlesdown in Surrey in the early 1880s. His father was a settled man, a road-mender and labourer.

My mother was born a navvy-woman at the Elan Valley dams in mid-Wales in 1900. Her father was also born into navvying, in the 1870s at Appleby-in-Westmorland where his father was a navvy on the Carlisle-Settle line. Their name was Jewell, which is Cornish.

Dick Sullivan
London, 1983

Chapter 1

The Chew Valley Dam

In 1908 we were boring in the gutter trench at the Chew Valley dam and it was a very cold winter. I lodged at Upper Mills at one time but was such a rough old place I shifted and went down to Rough Town in Mossley. The crowd where I lodged was Nick Docker, Scan Williams, Curly Williams, Snatchem, and London Snowy. They all worked up the Chew Valley, landlord Offland and all. He was a gangerman and his missus was a knockabout as well.

We were getting good money there, until the walking ganger come along and says, 'You men are earning too much money' and knocked a ha'penny a foot off. We'd been getting a tanner an hour until then. We were knocking out twelve shillings a ten-hour shift.

The contractor was Morrison and Mason and the dam served Stalybridge, Ashton-under-Lyne and Dukinfield. The dam was right on top of the moors at the end of a gorge and it was too steep and high to get materials up an ordinary railway. We went to work in small railway carriages, roofed with tin, with back-to-back seats. At the end of the route we got out and walked up the cart road up the gorge.

The puddle and muck for the dam come from Mossley and when that got to the end of the route the wagons were uncoupled and dragged up the mountainside by a winch. On the top-yard an ingine pulled them to the dam.

There were two gangs of men boring with jumper drills in the gutter and two men in the sump hole. In one gang was Geordie Owens, me, a feller they called Taff and one big lazy old bugger. Old Shoebury was filling peat wagons. The men in the sump were Tommy Tucker and his brother.

Well it was a very cold hard winter and we were seventy foot down by December and there was ice half way down the trench sides. We went back to work after one dinner time and Tommy Tucker goes into the sump hole with his brother. We'd blasted just before dinner, but one of the holes had misfired and when Tommy struck it with his pick, it blew out. It blew half his face off and caught his brother on the head.

We needed a round-bottom skip to get them out of the trench but the skips on the derricks were square ones with doors in the bottoms. Eventually they got hold of the right skip and wound them out. They carried them down the mountainside and put them on the paddy train but Tommy died just before they got him to hospital in Manchester.

His brother was hurt bad as well. He was laid up for a long time but he did get better eventually and I worked with him in the Lunedale tunnel later. They were navvy people, like us, only they were tunnel tigers by rights.

Chew Valley Reservoir, Greenfield, Dec. 4th. T. Arnisson (38) killed owing to fuse accidentally exploding. – *Navvies' Letter.*

Chew was a hard place. You could die of exposure in sight of the smoke of Manchester and Sheffield. The mills and all the houses smoked up to the moors. Usually the wind from Lancashire blew the smoke into Yorkshire.

The dam is one of the highest in England, so high there are no hills on either side of the lake: only low flat banks, like a fen. Within a few feet of Chew Brook's source another beck rises and flows the other way into Longendale. Chew Brook flows into its lake through black mounds of earth, like miniature tips around a colliery.

On the moor it is bleak and black. The moss – the bog – is more water than earth. The ground oozes black water, stained prismatically like oil. Grass humps up between patches of bare black earth. Up there is nothing but the moss. Each step opens up more black patches and bright green holes. Lost curlews cry. Hares are big as lambs. The wind always blows.

Old Shoebury was filling peat wagons up there. He belonged to Shoeburyness in Essex and he used to go fishing at one time. He looked old for his age. I first met him in Portsmouth. I never see him no more until I see him working at Chew, then we jacked and went on tramp together. He left me at a place called Crych in Derbyshire. I never see him no more.

I lodged with Offland at Hirwaun in South Wales, next time I lodged with them. I see them again in Ewden after the war. Walt

Offland was his name.

I come out of a pub, drunk, and it was raining. I slept under a hedge and woke sopping. I got to Hirwaun and was give some of landlord Offland's clothes. I asked how I was fixed for going to work. He said the night shift only so I had to put the wet clothes on again.

The job there was mining. You put in a dozen holes and Offland came and charged them and fired them. We had to take eighteen inches off the roof and the bloke striking for me struck me on the temple. I fell into the invert among the water. I told Offland I got a clack aside the head. He bathed it, bandaged it, and I stopped the night in the hut until daylight.

Snatchem he got crippled up, he did. He fell down a coal pit in South Wales. They were sinking it.

I don't know what happened to the fat bugger. He always wanted to be sitting down turning a drill. We got fifteen-foot lengths of hexagon steel and used them as jumpers. That's how we come to be using them. He had to work then.

Scan Williams was boring with three other men. His little boy got suffocated in cement in Ripponden. Someone shouted to poke the cement through the chute. The boy got on top and fell through. Scan's wife had left him. A Welshman. It was a long time ago.

Chapter 2

In Brief

Navvies built canals, railways, dams and their pipe tracks, the big nineteenth century sea-port docks, and the Manchester Ship Canal.

Navvying began suddenly in 1760 on the Bridgewater Canal: it ended around 1940, after a twenty-year fade-out. Along with the rest of Britain there was a kind of kink in the navvy's history in the 1870s when things began changing, generally for the better.

At first they were just skilled earth shifters digging canals at prodigious speed. Later they were skilled in tunnelling, mining, timbering – skilled enough to set up as one-man contractors employing local unskilled labourers to shift their muck. You could set a gang of prime navvies down in an untouched valley, they said of themselves, and they'd build you a dam without aid of an engineer. At times they slotted into the pay scales at twice a common labourer's wages, though they never equalled apprenticed craftsmen like masons.

It is easy for the urbanised and pensionable to romanticise them. They seem free, fearless, above the humdrum conventions of shopkeepers, clerks, factory workers, vicars, and the legally wed. Perhaps we glamorise cowboys, blue-water sailors and the hell-bent navvy for the same reasons.

In reality, isolation was the biggest thing in a navvy's life. They were perpetual outsiders: a people apart. Sub-working class. Sub-the-bottommost-heap of English working society. Sub-all, almost.

The navvy never called a spade a spade, always a bloody shovel. Everything he shovelled he called muck. Earth, blasted rock, clay, all were generically and indiscriminately muck. With the muck he created new landscapes and changed old societies. It was mass transformation by muscle and shovel.

To do so navvies worked in geographical and social isolation: crude, muck-caked men on a helix spiralling down from prejudice to more isolation, isolation to more prejudice. Eighty per cent were English, most of their work was in England, yet they lived like aliens in their own country, often outside its laws, usually outside its national sense of community. They were their own country's non-belongers. They belonged to themselves only tenuously. Mostly they lived apart in navvy settlements. New habits of life, thought, dress, speech, and a tightening of the ring against outsiders came out of their isolation. Their own countrymen were terrified of them, and despised them. Heavy drinking was normal, death by alcohol common. Drink was a common cause of riot, along with an unhesitating hatred for their own Irish minority. Their accident and death rates were higher than any other group in Britain, including colliers, including soldiers fighting nineteenth century wars. Often they were nameless, known to each other only at second-hand by nickname. They were a homeless, wandering itinerant people belonging nowhere except to the island as a whole.

They survived the Great War as a separate community, but not for long. Navvying was killed by a lack of large scale public works (worsened by the Slump), by bureaucracy and by the petrol engine. Probably in that order. By the mid-1930s they were quietly ending as a recognisable separate community. Individuals did live and work on. Their descendants still do (at their height, just before the Great War, there may have been as many as a hundred and seventy thousand of them).

In one way the navvy's is a story of a long taming as things got better for them (mainly from bestial to bad), chiefly because the country changed (from bad to better), but also because of a few individuals, events, and institutions.

To begin with there was the Select Parliamentary Committee which sat for a few days in the summer of 1846, alternately dismayed and appalled by the way the navvy lived and behaved. The Committee got none of the things it asked for, though perhaps that mattered less than the fact that Parliament had taken the trouble to be shocked.[1]

1 It all began when Edwin Chadwick sent copies of a pamphlet printed by the Manchester Statistical Society to MPs and the press. The pamphlet was about the way men lived at the Summit (or Woodhead) tunnel between Manchester and Sheffield. Edward Bouverie, member for Kilmarnock, chaired the Committee as it questioned its way through navvies and truckmasters, contractors and clergy, doctors and the police. It asked for a public works Truck Act, more public works police, and accident insurance.

Sir Edwin Chadwick (1800–1889): journalist, barrister, social reformer, civil

In the 1850s Katie Marsh, a vicar's daughter, wrote a book about navvies which was very widely read and *very* influential in changing people's perceptions. From the late 1870s they had their own Mission to tame and christianise them. It, too, was dominated by a vicar's daughter (and a vicar's widow) – Mrs Elizabeth Garnett. The Mission reached the heathen navvy through resident missionaries and its quarterly magazine, the *Navvies' Letter*. From the 1890s they had their own trade union, which they ignored in vast numbers. After 1906 they had an MP in the House of Commons: John Ward, one of the Union's founders. It all helped, but nothing ended their isolation. Navvies remained a people apart.

'In the making of the canals, it is the general custom to employ gangs of hands who travel from one work to another and do nothing else,' Peter Lecount, a railway engineer, said of them in 1831. 'These banditti, known in some parts of England by the name of "Navies" or "Navigators", and in others that of "Bankers", are generally the terror of the surrounding country: they are as complete a class by themselves as the Gipsies. Possessed of all the daring recklessness of the Smuggler, without any of his redeeming qualities, their ferocious behaviour can only be equalled by the brutality of their language. It may be truly said, their hand is against every man, and before they have been long located, every man's hand is against them.'

'The women shun us as lepers are shunned,' Patrick MacGill, a navvy, said in the 1900s. 'The brainless girl who works with a hoe in a turnip field will have nothing to do with a tramp navvy. The children hide behind their mothers' petticoats when they see us coming, frightened to death of the awful navvy man who carries away naughty children, and never lets them back to their mothers again.'

What they said about navvies was often true (true perhaps more often than not) yet it was also often exaggerated and sometimes undeserved. In the early 1840s the Bristol and Exeter railway was being laid along the Culm valley below the fat red hills of Devon. At one point the river swirls around Killerton Clump, a remnant of a volcanic cone. Tucked into one side is Killerton House, then home

---

servant. Involved in one way or another, with the Poor Laws, the factory inspectorate, the Ten Hour Act, pensions for servicemen, the Employers' Liability Acts, setting up of the new Civil Service with public exams for would-be bureaucrats, registration of births/deaths and – and above all – public sanitation.

to Sir Thomas Acland who spent his life landscaping his estate. Around 1843, three hundred navvies intruded unexpectedly into this deeply rural place ahead of their materials. Terror stained the entire countryside. Landowners in panic barred their windows, armed their servants, prepared to repel, or kill. All except Sir Thomas, the tenth baronet. He hired them to make a road from his house to the highway, the sunken Devon lane about a quarter of a mile away. When they tapped into a spring, he hired them to pipe water to the house.

Eighty years later, in 1924, navvies again worked in Killerton Park, laying a pipe track. The Great War was safely over. Killerton Clump still overlooked the long views of Devon: woods behind hills, hills beyond woods, all misty with damp and distance. Sir Francis Acland, fourteenth baronet, now owned Killerton and in 1924 his ten-year old daughter Ellen was killed on her bicycle outside the park gates.

'I am a perfect stranger,' one of the navvies wrote to her parents, 'but I shall never forget the bright little angel who used to greet me with a smiling face and a cheery good morning when I chanced to meet her while working the pipe track through Killerton Park. I feel as though I would have given my useless rough old life to have saved that little maid, and may God comfort you, Sir and Madam, for this great trial he has put upon you.'

There was a place coming up out of the bottom and a little boy got struck and killed by one of these carts off the works. His little sister ran indoors shouting, 'Look at Tommy – his head's all jam.' She didn't understand, you see.

They think rough fellers like me have got no heart, but I could see that little boy for years after.

Chapter 3

Strangers

One day a man, not a navvy, went down to a dam asking for Mr Millwood. Nobody knew him. 'Hang it,' then said a stringy woman, taking a gum-bucket pipe from her mouth, 'tha means my feyther. Why didn't tha ask for Old Blackbird?'

It was part of a paradox: navvying was a community, but a community of strangers. People were isolated from each other partly by nicknames, partly perhaps because they were rarely sober, but mainly because they were so footloose. Theirs was a community in permanent flux, river-like in its constant flow. Men sometimes worked only an hour or so before drawing their pay and tramping on.

Well, I jacked at Stony Stratford and went on tramp. I had enough money to take a train to Nuneaton and I walked from there. Leicester, Burton, Derby, Matlock, and up to Chatsworth. Went to work laying a pipe track from Derwent to Leicester. I didn't stop long and then I went on to Mexborough on the railway there. Trimming the batters to make them look a bit decent. I lodged there with Big Arm Jack, a navvy.

After that I went to Penistone, over Woodhead into Manchester, on to Ramsbottom and Scout Moor. Worked on the puddle at Scout Moor, putting in puddle clay. Two weeks there and we was froze out.

So winter come. Went away to Otley. Froze out. Couldn't work at Masham. Nothing for you but to walk. On to Lunedale. At Lunedale the gutter hadn't been sunk deep enough to stop the dam leaking. We drove seventy foot shafts down the sides, then drove a tunnel under the dam itself. They lowered concrete in skips and ran it under the dam in barrows. They were still winding the muck out of the hole when I got there. I says to Jack Petty, the gangerman; 'How are you fixed for miners?'

He says: 'Get agate tomorrow.'

8

The isolation wasn't always broken even by marriage. Husbands went on tramp and were lost – killed, crippled, too careless to bother. If the woman had no children it wasn't too bad. If she had, she was usually in trouble. If on top of that she were a hut-landlady, it was often worse. Only a man working on the dam could rent a hut. If the landlord left, the landlady had no rights to it at all. What she did have was the power to hand on the tenancy. She couldn't be queen in her own right but she could pick the king. When the timekeeper next called for the rent she had a few simple choices: the workhouse, skivvying in another woman's hut, or creating a new landlord from among her lodgers by inviting one of them into her big iron-bound bed.

In the middle of so much movement (and death) children were often handed along a line of foster-parents like small inheritances. Little Rainbow was the hero of one of Mrs Garnett's novels, but a boy taken from life. Boys like him were not uncommon on public works. His father was dead, his mother ran away, and he was brought up to the age of twelve by an old woman (until she died), by her widower (until he died), by Big Rainbow (until he went on tramp), and by Long Slen until Little Rainbow himself was killed by a wagon on the dam. The book opens with Little Rainbow dressed only in boots (too big), torn trousers and ragged coat. 'I'm cock o' this dock,' he boasted, challenging anybody roughly his size and weight.

Childhood in any case ended early. Pre-puberty boys often ran away, hidden on other works by nicknames. If they ever met their mothers when they were men they might shake hands in a restrained kind of way. Girls were often mothers, more rarely wives, in their teens.

Latter-day married navvies usually hauled their families and belongings about the country in railway wagons and furniture vans, but single men *always* tramped, sleeping rough in cowsheds, haystacks, hedges, kip-houses, pubs or using the workhouses like coaching inns, strolling from one to another in a leisurely sort of way. Navvies, along with sailors walking from port to port, were the casual wards' commonest inmates.

Similarities with the sea didn't end in the workhouse, either: navvying and the Navy paralleled each other in several ways, particularly public works and the 18th century gundeck. Both the sailor and the navvy were isolated, hard-worked, short-lived, and wild with it. Both lived dangerously but in the end monotonously.

When the larboard watch was ended, the day shift done, there was not a lot to do either in a frigate or on a dam except get drunk, and the navvy and the matelot met in a ready greed for drink.

Rum and the sea ran together, like ale and earth. The images are harsh and salt-scoured: a gunner, his chin clipped away in battle, pouring rum down a speaking-trumpet into his stomach; Sailors tapping the cask carrying Nelson's corpse to drink the blood-thickened alcohol which pickled it.

On public works it was whisky and ale. Buckets of it.

Buckets of it. You could wash your head in the buckets of beer we had. I wonder a feller wasn't ruined altogether. You come home half-lunified, get up stupid and go to work, work all day and stand up all night pouring beer down your neck.

In Scotland, where the drinking was harder, whisky was graded by the devastation it caused: Sudden Death, Fighting Stuff, Over-the-Wall, Pick-me-up, Knock-me-down. Sudden Death was nearly pure alcohol. One mid-century observer thought most navvies averaged thirty gallons of booze a week. Another thought a thousand pounds was spent on drink for every finished mile of track: twenty-five thousand pounds, perhaps, in today's money.

Even navvy society, unconventional as it was, had its own conformities, one of which was to drink. A society relying on its own generosity to itself has no place for personal meanness. Mean people were called 'near'.

'And you know, ma'am, to us navvies to be called near is as bad as murder almost,' a navvy once told Katie Marsh, explaining how Red Neck Henry Hunns came to be drunk after taking up religion. Red Neck had been lured into a pub by two young navvies. 'Henry,' said one, 'treat us to a mug. You've grown rather near of late.' The publican, a mischief maker, gave him a mug of drugged ale. When he came round Red Neck was devastated. Almost unmanned. A massive dose of Bible-reading and self-recrimination helped, but in the end his misery was ended only by the cholera which killed him when his regiment, the Westminster Militia, was drafted to the Crimea.

I was lodging with Granny Tinsley at Llangyfellach the night the bog broke through and didn't I get some black looks from her when I went teetotal? It was a farthing a mile on the Great Western then

*and I went up to London to my sister's wedding. When I got back I
called her up and called for beer.*
'I've broke teetotalling, landlady.'
'I knew you would, my boy.'
She was a navvy person, but respectable. Some of them were.

'How is it you go back to your old ways so soon after leaving me?' a
lady, the author of a book about navvies called *Life or Death*, once
asked a navvy in the 1840s.

'Well, ma'am,' said the navvy, 'it mostly comes of breaking the
teetotal.'

'Why, then, do you break it?'

'Well, ma'am, it's only in a public or some low place a navvy can
get lodgings and his tommy cooked: and the landlady won't say
thank ye to cook your victuals for you if you don't have no beer.
And when a chap's been keeping teetotal some time, the first pint is
about sure to get into his head and make him want more, particular
if it's public house beer.'

That drink was made easy to get, was one problem: grocers in
bowler hats sold it from carts; wandering vendors carried casks of it
– on yokes, like milk-maids – on to the works; most landladies sold
it – it was almost the only way they could cope with high rents, bad
debts, and the household bills – and neither big fines nor police
raids could stop illegal liquor sales in the huts.[1] Either the drinkers
swore the stuff was a free gift from a caring landlady or the police
were shamelessly bribed with a bucket or two and sent home drunk
as navvies.

'Another cause', said Mrs Garnett in 1881, 'is piece work. When a
man says he has "made ten days in a week", who can wonder that
being tired out, his pocket full of money, no fear of God nor respect
for himself before his eyes, he goes and gets drunk? The first glass
"picks him up", and if he ate a good beefsteak and two or three
pounds of pudding with it, he would be all right, he would go and
have a sleep and wake strong as a giant ready for "cricket" or the
"tug of war". But, no! He turns from his lump of cold meat and
cold pudding: for the landlady in a full drink selling hut has no time
to make things nice, as she otherwise would, (and can get more

---

1 In 1889 the police raided the Moore settlement on the Manchester Ship Canal in
a furniture van. It stuck in mud. Navvies hauled it out. Unsportingly, the police went
on to arrest four hutkeepers.

profit drawing beer to wash down cold tommy, than making you comfortable) so her lodger says, "another pint," and then "another", and then "one for Jack", "all round, landlady" is next; and when night comes – perhaps after a fight in which he has made himself look a brute instead of one of the finest Englishmen in the land – he snores in drunken sleep on his bed, every now and then muttering foul oaths, or lies sick as a dog under the summer sky, with God looking down on him; God who loves him, Christ who died for him! Think of it, brothers!'

When a man died there was, customarily, a gathering – a money collection – to bury him. What was left from the funeral was called the back-money and was spent on a wake. A ganger on the London-Birmingham railway once raffled a navvy's corpse, it was said, to raise money to drink to its demise. A fortnight later the parish had to bury the still unburied and now rotting navvy. Pre-1880, up to fifty pounds was sometimes spent on funeral parties. The drunker the mourners, the greater was the respect for the dead. One ganger is said to have jacked in protest at a teetotal funeral – it was, he growled, against all navvy custom.

In the 1830s (and perhaps earlier, but probably not much later) money collected to throw a welcoming party for newcomers was called a colting or a footing and was generally given by the newcomers themselves. On some jobs they saved the coltings till they had enough for a proper randy which always entailed a certain amount of riot, as Miss Tregelles found when she came on one unexpectedly in a South Wales village. Blackbird and The Miller were happily pounding each other while the police did their duty by keeping the natives out of harm's way.

'Are they fighting *really*, Sam?' Miss Tregelles asked a ganger.

'In course, ma'am,' said Sam. ''Tain't no randy else.'

Generally, women on public works are vague grey figures flitting into the printed record only every now and then, usually as insubstantial as souls in the Greek afterlife. Many who lived in the huts as 'servants', some of them *very* old, were prostitutes, while at least one contractor in Worcestershire in the 1840s or '50s ran a truck-brothel: women or girls in lieu of wages. Around the same time the asking price for the loan of a wife at the Summit tunnel, where syphilis was endemic, was a couple of pints of cheap ale.

But having said that, the abiding impression is that many, perhaps most, navvy women were extraordinary, more extraordinary than their men. Many were as sober as their men were drunken. Their own rough respectability didn't always extend to marriage but cruelty to children was unheard of and an extraordinarily high percentage seem to have worked hard from early morning to late at night cooking, cleaning, washing, mending: sweeping and scrubbing huts inherently dirty, feeding gangs of men inherently hungry. 'I've known nothing but work and wickedness,' a navvy woman once told Mrs Garnett.

Women got on to public works in two ways: either they were navvy-born, or they were seduced into following some passing, strapping buck-navvy, free, carefree, careless, and well-paid.

Navvy-born girls became small women when they were still very little. Mrs Garnett remembered one twelve-year old called Polly scrubbing the brick floor of her mother's hut one Saturday afternoon. Her lodgers got under her feet and she ordered them out.

'But, Polly, where are us to go?' they asked her.

'Go for a walk, it's Saturday afternoon.'

The big men ambled away, all except one who teased her by taking his time tieing his boots. Polly drove *him* out with a dish clout.

One day Anna Tregelles, who wrote about navvies on the South Wales railway in 1847, met two girls from Wiltshire. Both married navvies when the railway came to their village. Both wore the navvy dress of the time: black bonnets and bright ribbons, ear-rings, necklaces, short muslin frocks and thick leather boots. Caroline was older and more anxious, always fretting over the health of her children and mourning those who died. Sarah married Chimley Charlie in 1842 when she was sixteen. They had no children ('they're the ill-convanientest things that ever was to a navvy women,' she said).

At first Chimley was brutal, beating her with his belt until she knocked him down with a poker ('he come sich a bang,' she remembered, 'I thoft I'd a-killed en') after which he only hit her with his hands. 'Us was main comfortable for a year,' Sarah went on, 'and then 'twas winter time coming, and they was working nothing but muck. Charley was tipping then, like he is here: and 'tis dreadful hard to get the stuff out of the wagons when 'tis streaming wet atop and all stodge under.' The stodge ripped the soles off his boots, *and* they cost fifteen shillings a pair. In the end he could stand it no longer and took her on tramp into Yorkshire where he said the ground was all rocky and beautiful for tunnels. She'd never been more than twenty miles from her Wiltshire village and didn't even know where Yorkshire was, but: 'He took his kit, and I had my pillow strapped to my back: and off us sot, jawing all along. Us walked thirty miles a day, dead on end: it never stopped raining, and I hadn't a dry thread on me night or day, for us slept in such miserable holes of places, I was afeard my clothes'd be stole if I took them off.'

In Leeds she would never forget, not ever, the pleasure of a fire and supper in a pub. 'But,' she said of Leeds, ''tis a filthy, smokey place and when I seen it by day, I says, well, if this is Yorkshire, us had better a-stopped where us was, dirt and all. And what a lingo they talk!'

And there was no work. They tramped another three days until Chimley got a start in a tunnel. 'They was a rough lot there,' said Sarah, 'and then us seen and done all sorts o' things I wish I'd never heard on.'

They were a rough lot in Wales, as well, as she found when colliers from St Fagans challenged navvies to a Great Fight, or brawl, open to a dozen men a side but otherwise rule-free. Sarah heard about it from a navvy who ran up to her lodgings the evening of the Fight.

'Missus, they're fighting up to St Fagans,' he told her, 'and they've sarved your man very bad, and somebody's been and stole his clothes, so he can't get home.'

'I axed where he were,' Sarah told Miss Tregelles, 'and I up with his other shirt and slop and runned for my life to the place. There he was under the hedge, most dead with the cold; his things was all stole, and his money too.'

She half-carried him home and put him to bed where he stayed all Sunday. Monday morning he went to work but never came back. Sarah sat up all night, waiting, and at six o'clock next morning ran down to the line. Nobody had seen him. Perhaps he'd sloped, they said, on account of the fight: one Welshman was dead, two others were in a bad way, and the police were looking for navvies who'd been there.

Sarah traipsed all over Cardiff, town and docks, before she thought, 'He must have gone back into England.' In a pub a mile out of Cardiff she heard her first news of Chimley. He and two other navvies had stopped there, but only for a pint apiece. That night Sarah stayed with navvy people on the railway. Chimley had slept there the night before, they told her, and had gone on to

Sedbury where the line crosses the Wye at the Chepstow gorge into the deep rock cutting that ends abruptly at the crag's edge. (Sea birds swooped below the working navvies, close to the crinkled brown water.) Sarah followed in the morning. 'My shoes was all rags,' she told Miss Tregelles, 'and my feet a-bleeding every step.'

But she found Chimley. 'Poor fellow, he were dead beat, sure 'nough.'

'But why,' asked Miss Tregelles, 'didn't he go to the police? The Welshman was killed at ten o'clock: Chimley was in bed by nine.'

'He couldn't, Miss,' said Sarah, shaking her head, quietly stitching pillow lace. ''Tain't possible. They dodges so dreadful with their questions, there's no matching of them.' Besides, the Welsh had been worsted and that would have gone against Chimley with the Welsh police. Right or wrong, navvies got the blame. ''Tis so bad, you know, to be clapped up in prison, and their hair don't hardly grow proper again for a year, when they're out.' (So navvies wore their hair long as a mark of respectability.)

Well, they were a bad set of buggers, there's no doubt about that, and it was a bloody dull sort of life any how, but it was a fraternity, was navvying.

Perhaps all societies which live hard, isolated, and uncertain lives tend to open-handedness among themselves. Navvies did. In a way their hospitality was self-help at one remove – you helped strangers because essentially you were a stranger in need of help yourself. Contractors like Peto relied on it and never subbed money to new men, who had to live for a week off their fellow-navvies. 'There's a feeling amongst all those men exceedingly creditable to them', said Peto. 'Any man who comes there, and is at all in want, his brother navvies will take care he shall have plenty of tommy: they'll divide their dinner with him.'

Hospitality was even half-ritualised in one or two 'ways of the line'. Men injured at work were entitled to help from their gang. Men on tramp were at least *half*-entitled to money from men in work. They called it the navvy's shilling.

From the Somerton tunnel I went to Fishguard and started in the tunnel and lodged at Rosy Slen's shant. She sold beer. All these old landladies sold beer. Well, we were froze out at Fishguard and I went on tramp again.

*Walked all day and all night. Had a mug of cocoa and bread in
Gloucester Workhouse. It was crowded, and all. I had to sleep on the
floor and then you had to wheel stones around for your keep.*

*Then I went to Winchcombe and got down on to the railway but
there was no chance of a start. Devon Tommy gave me a shilling and
Old Church and Greaseley Scan, the ganger, he gave me a shilling.
That was the custom among navvies in them days. They called it the
navvy's shilling, any how.*

In effect the shilling was a crude kind of dole which worked as long
as people kept up the payments and which lasted till the Great War.
In no way was it token: a man could make as good a living
scrounging as he could by working, though more often than not
giver and getter got drunk as navvies and ended penniless together.
Some non-working navvies (on canals they were often maimed men
with names like Hoppity Rabbit and Dai Half) did offer the latest
news and scandal for the shilling but others were little more than
professional beggars in navvying clothing. 'Beware of William
Grime, *professional moucher*,' the *Letter* warned of one such in
1900. 'He is an old soldier and has bad eyes. He shows a hospital eye
ticket from Nottingham.' He'd begged on public works for twelve
years calling himself a navvy though he'd navvied only once, for six
months, in Hull.

'If you would not give them the shilling and the tommy,' said Mrs
Garnett, 'we should soon see the last of these liars and thieves, who
go about the country calling themselves navvies, and bringing
disgrace on our honest name – for the kind people who are deceived
by them do not know the difference between cadgers and real
navvies, though you do and I do, and then we all get the blame – and
no wonder.'

A cadger called Lincoln told Anna Tregelles his wife was ill.
'She's a weakly body, and up in years, and we tramped from
Gloucester, and are very bad off, my lady.' Their lodgings were a
long way off, too far for Miss Tregelles to visit. But Miss T went
anyway and found Mrs Lincoln dead drunk, swaddled in a coverlet
like a mummy with a gin bottle. Miss Tregelles left no money – just
a Bible, which Lincoln wanted to pawn, except his landlady
wouldn't let him.

In the 1850s Katie Marsh knew of only one navvy-beggar: a
gigantic, glib-tongued man who doctored a letter she wrote him
(about his drinking) and used it to beg money from genuine navvies.

But after the 1880s sham-navvies – professional beggars – began swarming, battening on the navvy's generosity. Large moving bodies of navvies carried hordes of them, like lice: slow-moving, mis-shapen, fluttery with rags.

'We bring in a tremendous number of good-class navvies for these public works,' the Chief Constable of Lanarkshire said in 1906, 'and they are followed by a regular horde of tramps who live on them. They are an absolute curse to the whole country. They come in and take away the character of these good-class labourers. People come and say: "We want extra policemen. We have navvies, and they are playing the mischief with the whole countryside". I say that the navvy is a poor, harmless person who gets drunk every Saturday like other people. It's these people who follow him who're the nuisance.'

'Could the vagrants be dangerous?' he was asked.

'I don't think they have the pluck.'

'Do they frighten the women and children?'

'There's a good deal of exposure of person before decent people,' said the Chief Constable, 'but there is very little assault.'

Tramps following navvies to the Manchester Ship Canal were kept in specially rented warehouses. A few years later the Corwen Board of Guardians, plagued by beggars battening on men tramping to the Alwen dam, tried to get rid of them by making the workhouse even more loathsome than usual, mainly by increasing the weight of rocks casuals had to break and at the same time decreasing the mesh size of the riddles so they had to break the stones even smaller.

Yet begging *was* a navvy tradition, as well. They called it mooching. Usually they begged from door to door, rather than from people in the street, and they mooched food as much as money.

(Another time Old Hereford was in some place in Yorkshire where they wouldn't give a navvy anything to eat. He took a brick up to one house. He says: 'Can you spread a bit of butter on this?' The woman looks at him. He says: 'It'll go down better with a bit of butter.')

One day in 1906 Moleskin Joe, Patrick MacGill and a navvy called Carroty Dan left Burns's Model Lodging House in Greenock to tramp to the Blackwater dam at Kinlochleven. Since it was a hundred miles away, Moleskin reckoned on a six day tramp and six days' mooching to keep them alive. Outside Greenock they split. Moleskin went ahead, followed by Carroty Dan, then MacGill.

'Whenever I manage to bum a bit of tucker from a house,' Moleskin told them, 'I'll put a white cross on the gatepost: and both of you can try your luck after me at the same place.' (A circle with a dot in its centre meant unfriendly police. The haft of a fork scratched in the dirt showed the best of two roads for mooching.) 'If you hear a hen making a noise in a bunch of brambles,' he told them in those free-range days, 'just look about there and see if you can pick up an egg or two. It would be natural for you, Carroty, to talk about your wife and young brats, when speaking to the woman of a house. You look miserable enough to have been married more than once. You're good looking, Flynn.[2] Just put on your blarney to the young wenches and maybe they'll be good for the price of a drink for three.'

At the first white cross MacGill asked for a slice of bread. 'Don't give that fellow anything to eat,' a woman called from inside the house to the girl who answered the door. 'We're sick of the likes of him.'

'Poor thing,' the girl pitied him. 'He must eat just like ourselves.'

But MacGill was now too proud to take anything: he'd heard servant girls talk like that about pigs. He walked on until he came upon Carroty cuddling a withered whore by the roadside. She was blemished, aged by vice, yet it was a small comfort to MacGill that at least one woman took pleasure in a navvy. It was the last he ever saw of Carroty Dan.

He was turned away empty handed from two more white crosses before he met Moleskin again. Moleskin was milking a cow into a little tin drum he carried strapped to his leg. He filled MacGill's drum and they drank their milk and ate their mooched snap dappled in sunlight by a beck. They took a dog-sleep in the sun and then crossed the Clyde in a stolen rowing boat, steering by the great crag of a rock with Dumbarton Castle on top.

Beyond Dumbarton they split again, Moleskin promising to

2 Flynn is MacGill's name for himself in his autobiographical book *Children of the Dead End*. MacGill writes in the Foreword, 'I have endeavoured to tell of the navvy; the life he leads, the dangers he dares, and the death he often dies. Most of my story is autobiographical. Moleskin Joe and Carroty Dan are true to life; they live now (1914), and for all I know to the contrary may be met with on some precarious job, in some evil-smelling model lodging-house, or, as suits these gipsies of labour, on the open road.')

wait for him in the dusk along the Loch Lomond road. Now MacGill was luckier. An old lady gave him twopence, and his pockets were crammed with bread, his pipe with tobacco. Along the road in the wild country he heard Moleskin ahead of him singing in the twilight:

> Oh! Fare you well to the bricks and mortar!
> And fare you well to the hod and lime!
> For now I'm courting the ganger's daughter,
> And soon I'll lift my lying time.

Moleskin had a stolen hen. ('When you're on the road as long as I've been on it, you'll be as big a belly-thief as myself.') 'Now we've got to drum up,' said Moleskin, 'and get some supper before the dew falls.' They plucked the hen and washed it in a spring of clear water. Deer came down to drink in the moonlight as they baked the fowl in the fire's embers.

Next day Moleskin had an argument with a ploughman who refused them a chew of tobacco. 'I'm a decent man and I work hard,' claimed the ploughman, 'and hae no reason to gang about begging.'

'You're too damned decent,' said Moleskin. 'If you weren't, you'd give a man a plug of tobacco when he asked for it in a friendly way, you Godforsaken, thran-faced bell-wether, you.'

'If you did your work well and take a job when you get one, you'd have tobacco of your own,' came back the decent man, unabashed. 'Forbye you would hae a hoose and a wife and a dinner ready for you when you went hame in the evening. As it is you're daundering aboot like a lost flea, too lazy to live and too afeard to die.'

'By Christ,' bellowed Moleskin, 'I wouldn't be in your shoes anyway. A man might as well expect an old sow to go up a tree backwards and whistle like a thrush as expect decency from a nipple-noddled ninny-hammer like you. If you were a man like me you wouldn't be tied to a woman's apron strings all your life. You work fifteen hours a day every day of your life,' Moleskin accused him. 'If you look at another woman your old crow goes for you. You bring up children who'll leave you when you need them most. Your wife will get old, her teeth will fall out, and her hair will get thin, until she becomes as bald as the sole of your foot. She'll get uglier until you loathe the sight of her, and find one day that you can't kiss her for the love of God. But all the time you'll have to stay with her, growl at her, and nothing before both of you but the grave or the workhouse. If you are as clever a cadger as me why do you suffer all this?'

'Because,' said the ploughman, 'I'm a decent man.'

Next day Moleskin and MacGill stood above a great glen in the rain, tasting the dye from their caps as it washed down their cheeks.[3] They spent the night in a field. 'It's a god's charity to have a shut gate between us and the world,' said Moleskin, pulling the gate shut. What they'd mooched had to last until the next night when they reached the Kingshouse, an old inn with dormer windows breaking out all over its grey slated roof, standing alone in the yellow ochre and heather-coloured wilderness between Rannoch Moor and Glen Coe.

Moleskin prised off his boots by the heels, then broke bare-footed into the inn's chicken coop (he always carried a steel bar for snapping off locks). He groped about in the restless darkness, among the roosting hens making small unhappy clucking noises, touched and grabbed a rooster and padded back to the road where the cock got away, flapping awkwardly, clattering his wings and crowing. Moleskin threw his boot but missed. The cock zig-zagged away. 'Holy Hell,' said Moleskin.

'Who's there?' a man called from the inn. A light went on, a window rattled up.

'Can you get hold of it?' Moleskin half-bellowed, sweating into his whiskers.

'I can't,' MacGill told him. 'It's a wonderful bird.'

'Wonderful damned fraud,' said Moleskin. 'Why didn't it die decent?'

MacGill caught the fowl by the neck and they made off, chased by the publican, Moleskin alternately clumping and padding, one foot booted, the other foot bare, up the smooth black trough of Glen Etive towards Glen Coe.

'If you come another step nearer,' Moleskin stopped and roared back at the publican in the blackness, 'I'll batter your head into jelly.'

The publican slunk away, unseen.

3 MacGill mistakenly calls it Glen Coe. It might be the glen above Loch Tulla. Similarly, perhaps misremembering, he calls the Kingshouse the King's Arms.

They plucked and roasted the rooster by a burn in the small hours of the morning. Dynamite crumped in the mountains above them. Navvies on the night shift blasting rock at Kinlochleven. 'There's a good time coming,' said Moleskin, picking on chicken bones, 'though we may never live to see it.'

Those good times, though, never did roll for the navvy, while the *better* times which had already arrived were doing the navvy's character no good at all, according to some. By Moleskin's day, things had been changing for thirty years, both nationally and, for the navvy, domestically. Most people were at least semi-literate because of the Education Acts and every man could vote in Parliamentary and local elections. The navvy's railways, like draw-cords, gathered the country together, making it less parochial. Navvies changed the country, then the country changed the navvy, softening him, educating him, making him less wild.

Public works changed, too, and changed the navvy in the process. Contractors were bigger and more respectable. They paid their men regularly, in coin, every week, in pay offices, and not irregularly every month in pubs. They were not cheated (so much) and not made drunk before being paid. A lot of their work was now on docks and dams which were inherently more civilised than the mobile squalor of the railways – they lived in semi-settled villages, for one thing, with all the restraints of a half-settled life. The Navvy Mission was bent on loving them, if nobody else was, so the sharp feeling of being totally rejected was slightly blunted. The works themselves were more mechanised and if the navvy still shifted his twenty tons a day, at least he was now surrounded by better educated mechanics, less brutal than himself. Because of mechanisation, as well, navvies were relatively less well paid than in the hey-day of the railway mania when their image of unhuman wildness was last imprinted on the public mind. At the same time, many non-navvy people thought they'd lost some of their finer qualities, their compassion and unthinking generosity to each other. As early as 1887 Mrs Garnett thought their moral fibre was becoming unravelled. 'Now, friends,' she said that year, 'I dare say you won't like what I'm going to say, but it is the truth, and any old navvies will bear me out in saying, *there is now not amongst the new navvies the feeling of honour there was amongst the old ones years ago*. It now seems the fashion on some Public Works to think when winter comes it is the immediate *duty* of all the ladies in the neighbourhood to give food and soup, and keep all those who drank or tramped about in laziness in summer. I was with a lot of the old sort on Sunday, who would *scorn* to think such meanness, and on Monday I got a letter which told me "I look in vain for a typical navvy on this job – the navvy of today is learning pauperism."'

But by 1911 even the police spoke more kindly of navvies. That year, as the work on the Chew Valley dam was wound down, the local police superintendent said the area would lose some of its most law-abiding citizens when the navvies left. A navvy had been a rare sight in the police dock.

In 1908 they even had official Government praise. It was when the Unemployed Workmen's Act, giving local unskilled labour preference on local public works, was distressing navvies all over the country. 'I say there is no man in the army of our industrials,' said John Burns, President of the Local Government Board, 'to whom we owe more than to the navvy, the mark of whose hands is seen in the Tunnel, the Reservoir, the Railway, and Public Works, that serve our transit, supply our water, and make England the healthiest country in the world.' He went further and asked all public men to 'have that fine, healthy, strong, and clean industrial figure, the British navvy, on the skyline of your foresight, your outlook, your sympathies.'

It was, however, all relative: a tendency, not a break. There was a blunting of prejudice against navvies, not an abandoning. Shop-keepers and trippers from Rhayader visiting the Elan valley dams at the beginning of the twentieth century could still peer into the navvies' bedrooms, exclaiming in amazement that they slept in beds. With sheets. Like *people*.

Well, I was on tramp in Gloucestershire when this farmyard savage stops me. He says, 'Are you a navvy?' Only speaking countrified. He says, 'I'll give you sixpence if you show me your tail.' They thought navvies had tails, you see, like monkeys.

Chapter 4

The Sloping Lodger

Canal navvies, rough and lowering but not yet thought monkey-like, began by calling themselves Excavators, Cutters, Diggers, Bankers, and Navigators (because they made inland navigations). When navigator was shortened to navie or navey, nobody knows. Navvy – so spelt – was first used in print in the 1830s. In the 1850s they called themselves Pinchers and Bankers, as well as navvies and navigators. By the 1870s they were Thick Legs and Blue Stockings, as well as navvies. By the 1890s they were Bill Boys, Tradesmen, Excavators, and navvies. In the twentieth century they were Pick-and-Shovel men, men who followed public works (the posh phrase, that, for polite society) and navvies.

For each other they had a whole welter of nicknames which spanned the entire navvy era. Brindley's proto-navvies on the Bridgewater Canal had them: Busick Jack, Bill o' Toms, Black David, and in 1932 a navvy woman could still advertise for her runaway husband by his nickname of Shakey Joe. Most incorporated place-names, like peers' titles: Cumberland Ike, Lincoln Tom, Nottingham Rags, Cheshireman, Dover Curly. In 1795 North-amptonshire Tom, a man who terrorised every county he lived in, was arrested for rioting in Leicestershire. Cousin Jack was a Cornishman. Geordie came from the Tyne's north bank. Lanc or Lank came from Lancashire, though he could be a lanky man as well. York/Yorkie came from Yorkshire. Less obviously Waxie was from Northamptonshire (from the wax used in the leather trade?). Clanger came from Bedfordshire and was named after a local sand-wich, a convenience meal in itself, beginning at one end with meat and ending in pudding at the other. Veg was stuffed in between.

Moonrakers were Wiltshire men. Once, one night when the water was bright with moonlight, revenue officers surprised smugglers raking contraband from a Wiltshire village pond. The smugglers quick-wittedly pretended to be village idiots raking the moon's bright reflection from the water.

Taff was a Welshman, but so less frequently was Moutainpecker. Herdwicks, like the sheep, came from Westmorland and there were never many of them. Suffolk men were sometimes called Punch after their own big horses, though more usually Punch was a description of size and shape. Wide shouldered, stumpy men, squat like Judy's husband, were Punches. Many names, in fact, described the man himself: his intact bits or his missing bits, it didn't matter which. Peg or Peggy had a wooden peg in place of a leg. Chump also only had one leg – chump, like chump-chop, being the blunt end of something that's been sundered. Wingy was one-armed, and had been on the canals. Gunner, when he wasn't an old artillery man, was one-eyed, so called because he was ready-made for aiming a gun. 'They've got one eye closed already,' said a mid-century navvy, 'and they've no occasion to shut *he*.'

Tweedle Beak had a great parrot-bill/eagle-beak nose, as had Snipe. Duke, too, was nosed like his namesake, the Iron one. Slen, a common name for a slim lean man, was short for Slender or Slenderman.

Some names described character: Scan, short for scandalous, was so common it's a mystery how so many navvies managed to scandalise so many others as to earn it. Some described personal habits, like Swillicking Dick who swillicked himself to death with ale at a dam on the moors above Accrington in 1887. Some were ironic: Primrose who navvied near Kirby Stephen in the late 1850s was a most unflowerlike, scruffy ruffian. Some seemed to go in fashions: Rainbow Ratty, Fatbuck, Hopper, Chinaman, Beer, and Brandy were popular in the '70s but not noticeably so at other times.

Gorger gorged a shoulder of mutton at a sitting. Hedgehog *looked* like a hedgehog (snouty face? spikey hair?). Uncle Ned was forever singing *Uncle Ned*, a minstrel song. Rush, the name of a well-known Victorian murderer, was given to an unknown navvy for no known reason. Cat's Meat had been in the cat's meat trade (presumably selling dead cats, not pet food). Graze-the-Field almost literally grazed the fields for a year when he was out of work, living on stolen vegetables and fruit.

Which is all very well and mostly understandable, 'But why,' asked the Rev Daniel Barrett, 'Skeedicks, Acamaraclous, or Okem-finny Joe?' Unless Okem-finny was a corruption of oakum-fingered and was a nickname for an old lag or seaman, nobody seems to know. Why Pupe, an obscure obsolete word for a kind of snail? Why Johnny-up-the-Steps? Why Standing-up-sitting-down-shitting Scan, a poacher so skilled it was said he could entice rabbits from their warrens on the Westmorland fells?

Food to the navvy was tommy and he carried it to work in a tommy handkerchief, generally red with white spots. Tommy was bought in tommy-shops and the provident and non-mooching carried it on tramp in straw bags called pantries. At work navvies drank tea, either brought cold in a tea bottle or made on site in a can called a drum. A drum could be anything: a biscuit tin with a wire handle, perhaps. Making tea was drumming up.

A nipper was a boy (any boy, all boys) and drumming up was a nipper's job. Usually it involved a dented tea-bucket and a certain amount of ritual. After screwing the half-filled bucket into the flame of an open fire, the nipper circulated among his navvy-clients collecting the tea and sugar which each man brought ready-mixed in his own Colman's mustard tin. The nipper emptied each tin, one by one, into the bucket, following it with a cup of cold water. (An engineer once asked why? 'To tempture it,' he was told).

Tea bottles were usually metal, bottle-shaped, with a metal ring-handle near their wide mouths. They were stoppered with corks, or wads of folded newspaper when they got lost. At work you either drank your tea cold, drummed it fresh, or reheated cold tea by sticking the tea bottle in the fire, in which case the tea bottle itself became a drum. In tunnels, tallow from the candles was often used as a drumming-up burner. On some dams, later, some contractors supplied coppers of boiling water in special tommy-cabins.

To slope was to welsh, do a midnight flit, sneak away without settling your debts or after you'd stolen something. There was a child's song about it:

> I had a sloping lodger, but I don't care,
> But I don't care,
> He left a pair of clogs that I can wear,
> And he won't get them back till he pays me.

Sloping was probably the major navvy-crime against another navvy, and it was never all that widespread (*It didn't pay to slope a lodge, any road. You never knew when you'd meet up with them again*) though there were a few sloping black-spots, like Breary Bank near the Leighton dam outside Masham, a slopers' haunt right up to the Great War, as far as the Mission was concerned. The pay office was beyond the huts, so slopers could collect their pay and slink away unnoticed.

Mrs Garnett particularly scorned slopers. 'Slopers are street corner boys, and such like, who come on Public Works and call themselves "navvies". They are not navvies, but moochers and have no business working with decent men, and bringing disgrace on our respectable class. I wish every one was back and starving where they came from.' (Though she conceded shopkeepers deserved to be cheated for overcharging.)

Some words stayed. Others went. Yorks – strings tied around the leg below the knee to hitch trouser bottoms clear of muck – were known to railway navvies in the 1840s and dam navvies in the 1930s. 'A randy is a drunk frolic,' Thomas Jenour, missionary on the Croydon-Epsom railway, told the 1846 Committee. He added: 'There's every sort of abomination, lewdness and bad women.' As a word it survived into the twentieth century, but only just. As a concept it slowly died away as the navvy settlements were slowly tamed.

What happened to navvying in fact was one long taming. Even dress got less flamboyant, more dowdy.

Except that they wore knee-breeches we don't know how the first canal diggers dressed, but by the early railway period you could always tell a navvy by the brightly coloured clothes he wore: scarlet waistcoats, glowing neckerchiefs, velveteen coats, white felt hats with the brims turned up, breeches buttoned at the knees, high-laced boots.

By mid-century, in the '50s and '60s, they turned out on knock-off days all a-dazzle in yellow and blue, scarlet and flame, waistcoats flashing with glass buttons, shining with mother of pearl, rich with silver watch chains. White duck frocks set off blazing silk neckerchiefs knotted sailor-like around muscle-thick throats. Below the waist they were more sombre: short, smooth, velvety moleskin trousers and huge boots. Whiskers, like explosions of hair, exploded from jaws. Thick curls tendrilled about heads gleaming with white enamelled teeth, better than anything in the mouths of those tiresome Italian ruffians you kept reading about.

In 1907 Mrs Garnett remembered the navvies at the Junction dam thirty years ago.[1] 'They were dressed in white knee-breeches, blue woollen stockings, thick boots, white shirts and sweating caps. Every Class on Public Works then wore its own dress. The

Gangers: brown velvet jackets and vests, and cord breeches tucked into high boots. The Black Gang had shining buttons, stamped with engines, on their caps. The (horse) drivers, in red or blue plush waistcoats, with big rows of pearl buttons. The men, double canvas coats, as well as trousers, white all over, and exquisitely clean from top to toe of an evening, a bright neckerchief tied in a knot – silk on Sundays, cotton on work days. In the south of England the men wore much embroidered slops, and frequently these and even shirts were made by the men. It was the fashion in some places to sew pearl buttons on slops, and I have been told of six dozen sewn on one!'

Knee-breeches survived into the 1890s, usually accompanied by thick blue woollen stockings. Double-breasted waistcoats were now popular, along with smocks like big bags. Moleskin, always navvy-fashionable, was worn right into the 1900s when corduroy started rivalling it. Between the Wars, corduroy was *the* mark of the navvy, as fur is the mark of the beast. *Only* navvies wore it. Navvies wore corduroy almost as soldiers wore khaki or nannies wore starched cotton: as a uniform. Subdued flannel shirts, bought by post from Wales, latter-day navvies wore as well. By now the navvies' former colour-splashed brightness was reduced to the blue, white-spotted snow-storm neckerchiefs they wore around their necks.

Most navvies in the twentieth century bought their clothes by mail-order from George Key's, the navvy's tailor, in Rugeley. (Old George fell out of a window and killed himself soon after the Great War.) Key's also tailored special corduroy trousers called Fork-strongs. 'When navvies meet and talk of clothes,' ran one of their ads. in the 1920s, 'they are sure to mention Keys' cord trousers. Their fathers thirty years ago nicknamed them "Forkstrongs" because they couldn't split the Forks no matter how hard they wear.'

There was no real navvy-lore as such, just twists on old country wisdom. 'It won't rain if there's enough blue in the sky to make a navvy a waistcoat' (instead of a sailor a pair of trousers). Irish navvies in Brunel's Rotherhithe tunnel believed that if you blinded flood water by dowsing the lights it couldn't see you to drown you. Navvies on the Calder Navigation chipped away Robin Hood's gravestone at Kirklees, thinking it cured toothache.

1 Now one of four lying in line astern near the headwaters of the Tame in the Lancashire moors. Both the village of Denshaw and the dam were called the Junction because five roads cross there. More properly it is the New Year's Bridge dam.

But navvies always expected each other to be cool in danger. Being phlegmatic – 'taking misfortune in your stride' – was part of the navvy ethic. Muck from Blisworth, a thatched, two-tone ironstone village (two tones of brown: light and deep), on the London-Birmingham was wagoned to the Wolverton embankment for tipping. At yo-ho and snap time men and nippers rode the wagons back to camp. Derailments were common. One derailment heaped a body of men and lads under a pile of wagons and limestone. A nipper was dragged from under it, his foot squeezed into a mess of flesh and splintered bone.

'Crying'll do thee no good, lad,' said the ganger, taking his pipe from his mouth. 'Thou'dst better have it cut off above the knee.'

A broken-armed man scrabbled from the same heap. 'It's broke,' he announced, unemotionally, wagging his dangling limb. 'I maun go home.' And home he went, striding the six miles to his village.

A rock fall in a tunnel east of Rouen in the 1840s trapped a French labourer and a Lancashire navvy. Rescuers sank a shaft to them at the rate of ten feet an hour, a brisk mole's pace. When they were safely back on top the Frenchman wept. The Lancashire man strolled round the lip of the rescue shaft. 'You've been an infernal short time about it,' was his professional and professionally phlegmatic verdict.

A contractor called Bayliss used to tell a story about a tunnel just north of Bugsworth on the Manchester-Ambergate line. One day its mouth caved in, trapping a gang of navvies. 'Well, chaps,' said one to the rest, 'we shall never get out alive, so we may as well go on with our bit while we can.' They worked on, hacking at the rock face in the flickering candle light, until one by one they fell limp and dying in the heavy, oxygen-drained air. Rescuers reached them as their candles were guttering. (But there *is* no tunnel just north of Bugsworth.)

Late in the 1880s one of the shafts of the Cowburn tunnel, opening into the Vale of Edale in Derbyshire, was nine hundred feet deep. Signals to the banksman were sent by thwacking the iron skips with iron bars.[2] One day a skip was dangling just above the floor, with a man inside, waiting for the shot-firer to clamber aboard. The waiting man slipped and struck his iron-shod heel against the skip which was immediately raised. The shot-firer leaped for the rising bucket and was still swinging outside it as the

2 The banksman drove the winding gear.

shots went off in a flower-like pattern below him.

Another time a navvy on the Central Railway in Scotland lit his fuses at the bottom of a shaft. As he was being raised in the skip, the winding horse fell down with the staggers. The fuses spat and flared in the blackness a few feet below. Faced with being boinged to death like a clapper in a bell or ripped to bits at the bottom of the pit, the navvy vaulted from the skip and calmly began finger-and-thumbing the fuses. The last was a few micro-seconds away from exploding the gunpowder when he finally snuffed it out.

What humour survives is mainly about the two big facts of navvy life: its hardness and its isolation.

Life was so hard even the softness of a bed could kill. A workhouse bed was soft enough to do for Tommy the Gate in the 1870s. Tommy had been born in a Pickford's van and so was on the move even at the moment of his birth. After failing as a pig-dealer he took to following the navvy camps and never slept in a bed for twenty years until he went into the workhouse where the straw-based softness of his donkey's breakfast mattress butchered him.

In the twentieth century, two bedless navvies one night confided to a publican that *they* hadn't slept in a bed for twenty years. The landlord, a jovial soul, gave them a double bed for the night. So delighted were they by its womb-like warmth and flock comfort, they laughed themselves to death.

Getting the better of the non-navvy enemy was a common theme, like the story of the young man who bested a bragging publican's wife on the London-Birmingham in the 1830s. She despised all navvies and boasted none would ever outwit her. One morning a young navvy went into her pub, the Stag and Pheasant at Hillmorton on the Grand Union Canal, carrying a gallon stoneware bottle of the kind they called a greyneck. He called for a half-gallon of gin. The landlady poured it into his stone bottle. He refused to pay. She poured the gin back into her cask. Exit the navvy grinning happily. Before going in he'd half-filled the greyneck with water.

A man on the Manchester Ship Canal told a missionary to go to hell. He'd be sacked if he didn't apologise, he was told. The navvy knocked at the missionary's door. 'Are you the man who I told to go to hell this morning?' he asked the black-suited man who answered. 'I am. Come in, my poor brother.'

'No,' said the navvy. 'I only came to tell you you needn't go now.' (That at least was the story as told by the *Navvy's Guide*. Reality was perhaps less flattering. It was at the time of the Canal's financial and labour troubles in 1891. Sir Joseph Lee, company deputy chairman, questioned a navvy about his pay, hours and where he worked. 'Go to hell,' said the navvy. A ganger advised him to apologise. 'Master,' then said the navvy, 'I didn't know who you were, and I told you to go to hell, and I'm sorry for it, but I didn't mean you to go.')

For a time in the early 1890s the Navvies' Union had its own stand-up comic called Brighton Ted to keep meetings amused, particularly along the Manchester Ship Canal. A navvy wrote home to his mother, went one of his jokes. He wrote three big-lettered words to the page. She was a very deaf old lady, explained a nipper, and needed a loud letter.

A temperance man collared a Ship Canal wagon filler. 'Ah, my friend,' said he, 'you shouldn't drink whisky. Whisky's killed thousands. Why don't you drink water? Water never killed anyone.'

'Who are you gammoning?' replied the wagon filler. 'What price Noah's Flood?'

A nipper, mooching from a man who had religion, was given a crust of bread. 'Let us say the Lord's prayer together,' said the godly man. 'The first words are "Our Father".'

'That means my Father as well as yours?' asked the nipper.

'Yes. Everybody's Father, for we are all brothers and sisters in this world.'

'Then you're my brother?' said the nipper, wanting to get it right.

'Yes.'

'Then you ought to be precious well ashamed of yourself,' came back the boy, 'to offer your poor little brother such a hard, dry crust as this.'

In the market square in Lancaster a Salvationist told a navvy to stop smoking. 'Friend,' said the Salvationist, 'If Providence had intended thee for that dirty habit of tobacco-smoking, heaven would have provided thee with a funnel on the top of thy head to carry the fumes away.'

'And, friend,' returned the navvy, 'if Providence had intended thee to lead thy murdering brass band by walking backwards, heaven would have had thy toes where thy heels are.'

A notable navvy was being buried. Six men carried him to his grave. 'Reverse the corpse,' said the parson.

'What's he say?' said the unlettered navvies.

The ganger said: 'Slew the old bugger round.' And they slewed him round quick.

A navvy woman took her son to the surgery. 'H'm, costive bound,' diagnosed the doctor.

'Eh, I don't care if it costs *five* pound,' said the indignant navvy woman. 'The lad's got to shit.'

But then a navvy and his money needed no prising apart. Navvies, like horseplayers, usually died broke, their money dribbled away on drink or gambling even before it was earned. If it wasn't for the beer shop, a navvy told the Rev Sargent in Penrith in the early 1840s, he wouldn't know what to do with his money. He would rather spend it on himself now than let strangers spend it for him when he was dead.

'Wouldn't your wife like a new gown?' asked the parson.

Slowly the navvy shook his grizzled head. 'She's as many as she can use as long as she lives,' he said.

One navvy in the 1880s even professed he thought it was 'the duty and the custom of every navvy to work for his money like a horse and spend it like an ass.' And perhaps on the whole he was right. When life is generally rather short and usually very nasty you can afford to be extravagant with it. Like the old-time lower-deck sailor they had little to lose by burning short candles at both ends. Things were done gargantuanly: living, starving, the hard times, dying.

In 1801 a gang of navvies on the Dearne and Dove canal were given supper in the Red Lion in Worsbrough to celebrate the Peace of Amiens. 'They ate and drank as follows,' reported the *Doncaster Gazette*, '40 lbs of beef, 36 lbs of potatoes, 20 lbs of pudding, 18 lbs of bread, and a quantity of ale equal to 150 lbs weight, which amounted to 10½ lbs to each man.' (In fact, *eleven* pounds per man.)

John Ward always said a navvy could eat a pound and a half of prime rump steak without being too conscious of having done so.

Men commonly swallowed two pounds of red meat, two pounds of bread and ten pints of ale in working hours. One man once drank twenty-eight pints of beer in an afternoon.

Jubilee Day, 1897, was a paid holiday for the Elan Valley navvies. Crowds of them, ribald and raucous, trooped down to the junketings in Rhayader, where in less than an hour they gobbled all the food the Jubilee Committee had laid on for the whole day.

Half a gallon of good cheap ale and two pounds of slab-sided beef always induced deep navvy contentment. Collective navvy opinion considered the Westmorland of the 1850s not even part of England on account of the poor thin cow-meat (as opposed to fat bullock beef) and the beer which was very dear at threepence a pint.

Most navvies smoked hugely too: men, women, lasses, nippers, it made no odds. Tobacco was taken in clay pipes called gum-buckets.

In the 1850s Thomas Fayers, the missionary on the Lune valley line at the corner of Westmorland, Lancashire and Yorkshire, had a theory about women gum-bucketeers. The long-stemmed smokers were better, neater, tidier housewives than short-stemmed women. Long-piped woman sat more alertly (even bolt upright), cupping the elbow of the arm that held the pipe in their other hand. Short-stemmed sluts sat scrunched up, elbow on knees, shortening the gap between pipe bowl and lazy hand.

One woman had a worn face, dark with grime. She was bleary eyed and lank haired, a long-boned woman, loose-limbed like a broken marionette. The stitching of her frock was so badly stretched it seemed it would pull apart at any moment and her dress would drop in a heap from her gangling bones. *She* smoked a two-inch stump of gum-bucket. ''Tis the only comfort I've got,' she told Fayers, taking the ruined black stem from her mouth as she slovened among the ruins of her hut under the rainy fells. 'When I'se upset, and things go 'wry, I get me a pipe, and sets me down, and forgits it all.'

Chapter 5

Bumpsticks

Things *often* went awry on public works, though alcohol was a commoner way of forgetting it all than nicotine. Most sensitive people were terror-trodden, down-trodden with fear, and what the sensitive felt acutely, the insensitive sensed more dully. Pain was public and commonplace on public works, pain-ridden, death-ridden terror-ridden places.

Even the religion instilled by the Mission was doom-ridden – for all its cheerfulness about salvation – and what people remembered most was the threat of hell where somehow the body fats fried on your bones eternally and the malice and spite of the world were moulded together, magnified, and given black-hot flesh as the Devil, an ugly implacable thing with skin so smouldering it would burn the hand of any mortal man who touched it.

The Victorians, any way, seem death-haunted. In old photographs you can see death in many a sunken face – whole families, even the smallest children still in pinnies, identically marked with death, illness or insanity. It was a necro-conscious society.

In navvy huts the dying and the newly born almost shared beds, passing each other in and out of a defiled world. A child growing up on public works was circumscribed by pain and the realisation that suffering had no natural end: it went beyond what the human body could humanly be expected to endure.

To begin with, there were accidents. In 1906, when navvy work was scarce, Patrick MacGill climbed on to a railway embankment near Glasgow straight into a dead man's job. They were carrying away what was left of him, bits of him in a bag. A rail had slipped from a wagon. 'It broke his back,' said a navvy. 'Snapped it like a dry stick.' They heard his spine snap and saw him fall under the loco. A thin slice of flesh, perhaps his tongue, lay near his disconnected fingers. An old man picked them up, grotesquely counting them into a bag. Men fingered bits of the dead man's meat

33

sticking to the loco.

Statistically he was one of four to die on public works that day. Another eight would have been severely hurt. There was, said Mrs Garnett, a death for every mile of finished track, one to thirty deaths a tunnel.

There's little doubt that navvying was the most dangerous job of its day: worse than coal-mining, worse – according to some – than war. More men as a percentage were killed in the Summit tunnel than in the battles of Salamanca and Waterloo. A navvy stood the same chance of being killed as an infantryman in the Boer War. By then actuarists worked on the assumption that every million pounds' worth of contract would kill a hundred men.

A tenth were killed by things falling on them, or by falling of things – into puddle trenches, down shafts, into cuttings. A man killed his brother at the Sapperton tunnel in 1787 when he dropped the muck he was winding out of the shaft. Men were hurt at the Strood tunnel, 1819, when some vandal half-cut the winding ropes.

At Eston, a navvy told Mrs Garnett, there was a place they called the Slaughter House because of the daily accidents and weekly deaths.[1] 'There were the chaps,' said the navvy, 'ever so far below and the cutting so narrow. And a lot of stone fell, and it was always a-falling, they were bound to be hurt. There was no room to get away, nor mostly no warning. One chap I saw killed while I was there, anyhow he died as soon as they got him home. So I said: "Good money's all right, but I'd sooner keep my head on", so I never asked to be put on, but came away again.'

Falling machinery killed Hope and Anchor at Boston dock, 1884. Falling muck crushed Soldier Cobb's legs at Hackney sewage works and held him half-upright in dirty water all day and night. Cumberland Tom, a sun-tanned old soldier, fell into the Fontburn gutter with his horse, 1904. Bingy Daft broke his thigh when a gust of wind blew him off the Howden dam, Birchinlee, 1910.

At Chichester we was laying a pipe track opposite the barrack gates and I got buried there. All of a sudden the blooming side come away. The daft fools started digging down on me. Then two navvies come along and dug down the side of me and got me cleared. When they got me out on top I couldn't feel a thing. I was numb. All numb. I

1 It isn't clear where this is/was. Eston, south of the Tees at Middlesbrough, has no deep cuttings.

34

*was taken to the workhouse infirmary in a horse cab. I was there two
or three weeks and come out and walked all day and all night and all
next day and went to my brother's. Then we stood up in a pub all
night pouring beer down our necks.*

Machinery killed another tenth. Johnny Good Morning's foot was
crushed by a wagon at the Oswestry dam, 1888. A dobbin cart ran
over Hash Harry on the Southend-Maldon, 1889. A stone-crusher
broke Egypt Slen's back on the Ship Canal, 1890. A loaded cart ran
over Crying Nobby at Great Missenden, 1891, the year Hair-oil
Pindar was run over and killed at Bob's Bridge, Ship Canal, and
Mexican Joe lost his big toe to a runaway wagon at Chesterfield.
Navvy Parson's eye was plucked out like a bird's egg on the Princes
Risborough railway, 1903.

Four per cent drowned. Bristol Nobby did when his boat turned
turtle in the Tavy, 1889. Up-the-Tree Nobby drowned in the Kent
at Kendal, 1892. Ann Lovesey drowned in a well at Moreton
Pinkney, Great Central Railway, 1896. Bisbrooke Billy drowned in
sewage in Manchester, 1893.

*We got along one day from No. 1 shaft in the Llangyfellach tunnel[2]
when we got into bad ground. There was peat on top, then gravel,
then four feet of coal, then rock, and then the water began to pour
down. The water did pour down, right enough. There was a bog on
top and the tunnel was draining the water off.*

*Then, one night, the bog broke through. It'd been weeping all the
time, then it come in with a rush. We'd been working in oil-skins all
along. It did come in quick. It was half full of water in no time.*

*The banksman lowered the cage down and took up the ponies
first: next to them came us navvies and then the tigers. The water
was up to your chest and still rising. We got on to the tubs and stood
up. The candles went out. It seemed a long while, but it wasn't long.
It wasn't warm, it wasn't hot, but it wasn't anything to complain
about.*

Another measurable percentage were burned, scalded, or exploded
– generally to death. Devon's arm was blown off and his eyes blown

---

2 The tunnel pierces the massif between the River Tawe and the Afon Llan.
Swansea, like a threat, looms over the hill to the south. The ventilation chimney over
No. 1 shaft is still there, in a soggy hollow on the edge of a golf course.

out at Barry dock, 1885, the year Cyder Tommy was blown apart, charging holes. A year or so later, Bristol took a lit candle to a powder box and lived a few days longer.

I went back to Lunedale, driving a tunnel from there to Baldersdale. The tunnel was eighteen inches out of centre and we worked there blowing the side off, on nights. Hammer and drill work – the drills were thin things like pokers, about three feet long. Micky Mitchell had charged the holes and they hadn't gone off. I went back down the tunnel and I could see the last hole burning. I turned in a hurry, knocked my lamp against the side. Lamp went out and I lay against a tub. About thirty charges went off. The place was full of smoke – all dust and muck. I left there soon after.

Drink, directly or not, was a common cause of death. A train cut off Putsey Bill's arm as he lay draped, drunk, across the railroad track at Cullingworth, 1883. Next year Black Joe's George was drowned, drunk, in a brook and Jimmy Drew was stung to death by an adder one lazy, insect-humming day as he lay, drunk, on Effingham Common. Lady Killing Punch, while drunk, bit a ganger's finger in Bolton. The wound festered and the ganger died, 1891. Rats ate Yorky Fenwick's corpse at Millom breakwater, 1902, where he drowned himself while drunk. 'Such is the end of the ungodly,' said Mrs Garnett.

Then there were the other ways of dying, each too few to make statistic. Bible John gored to death by a milk cow at Leeds sewage works, 1884. John Mornington, a CEU man, killed by a Birkenhead taxi-cab. 'All is well with my soul,' were his last words. Swillicking Dick, frozen to death, alone on the moors above Accrington where the mill chimneys stuck up like black-hot pokers. Bullock's Liver Punch hanged himself at the Moorock, a pub near the Catcleugh dam, 1894. Jane William died 'for fear of thunder', 1895. Owd Lijah fell into an old quarry on an outing from the Saddleworth Workhouse, 1900.

A big sea, breaking over the half-finished Admiralty Pier, Dover, washed away the blacksmith's shop and a group of navvies, 1903. Pyfinch was impaled on a stake, 1904. Soldier Tom was stabbed to death trying to stop a knife-fight between a man and a woman on the Castle Cary-Langport line, 1905. Grimsby Jack overdosed with laudanum at Birchinlee, 1911.

But bad as it was, death by accident was less significant,

statistically, than death by disease: forty per cent, against sixty.

Pneumonia, in fact, was the biggest single navvy-killer of them all, killing a tenth of everybody on public works on its own. Pneumonia, added to other illness of the lungs and breathing – tuberculosis, bronchitis (brownchitis, to the navvy), congestion of the lungs, inflammation of the lungs – killed a fifth, twenty per cent.

Inflammation of the lungs killed Bridle-mouth Punch at the Ramsden dam, 1882. Bronchitis killed Crooked Arm Jack at the Sabden dam, 1888. Congestion of the lungs killed Hard Labour at the Cwm Taff dam, 1889. Bromichem Punch died of bronchitis *and* inflammation of the lungs at Newport dock, 1890. Pleurisy killed Virgin Slen, 1896. Pneumonia finished Unfinished Lank, 1900.

Heart diseases, kidney failure (often listed as Bright's disease), cancer, typhoid, bleeding, killed another tenth. Fighting Sammy died of a supposed heart attack on the Ship Canal, 1888. 'Overflow of blood at the heart and cancer of the stomach' killed William Fleming, 1897. Bumble-Bee Dick died of heart failure *and* pneumonia at the Totley tunnel, 1893, above the River Derwent in Derbyshire.

Billy the Finisher's wife died after a long sickness at the Sabden dam, in the witch country under Pendle Hill, 1888. Sunstroke killed Cheshire George, same year, same place. Hoping Dick broke an ankle that wouldn't set, on the Ship Canal, and died in agony, 1889. Peg Leg had an unhealing ulcer on his stump, Ship Canal, 1890. Old Black Tommy, alias Linky Loo, died of old age in Keighley Workhouse, 1896. Dog Belly was killed by a stroke, 1900, on the Chipstead Valley line.

Even epidemics were statistically significant. On the London-Birmingham, men walked about speckled with small-pox pustules, while cholera killed nearly thirty people at the second Woodhead tunnel, 1849. In the early '90s, scarlet fever, diphtheria, and small-pox outbreaks put part of the Dore and Chinley line into quarantine, particularly around the Totley tunnel where, in spite of the quick, pebble-rolling Derwent, drainage was bad and where, on top of everything else, they had a typhoid epidemic as well. Navvy Smith, missionary, coped with typhoid and whooping cough on the Great Central, 1896. 'The bell is tolling for six to be laid in their graves today,' he once noted.

Solitary graves opened and closed like mouths on public works, but so did the odd mass-grave following the odd mass-accident. In 1891 a nipper working a turn-out on the Ship Canal accidentally sent a muck-train into a siding at Ince. The train hit the buffers and dropped over the edge of the cutting (past a navvy called Sloppy clinging to the canal wall) hissing, steaming, scalding, hot ash and coal spilling from its fire box. Ten were killed outright.

The Mission buried the Protestants in a common grave in the churchyard at Ince, a village on a mound in the marshes overlooking the green saltings and yellow sandbars of the Mersey, all as flat as the river.

Sometimes well-meaning ladies opened hospitals – they did on the Newbury-Didcot in the 1880s – and so, sometimes, did contractors: Enoch Tempest had a hospital of sorts in Dawson City, the settlement servicing the three dams in line astern at Walshaw Dean in the tweed-coloured Pennines. But the only place on public works to run a proper accident service seems to have been the Ship Canal, where First Aid Stations the length of the cut fed casualties into base hospitals at Latchford, Ellesmere Port, and Barton: grim, two-floored places full of pain and starchy nurses in caps like cocks' combs. Casualties had priority on the overland railway and a telegram day or night brought the doctor from Liverpool, a Welshman called Robert Jones, the last of a line of journalists, surgeons, and bonesetters.

But, mostly, men depended on their Sick Clubs for support as well as the navvy custom which permitted an injured man to be kept by his gang until he was better. Often, another man from his gang was detailed to rough-nurse him among the restless bodies in the huts. (It wasn't until the 1880 Employers' Liability Act that anybody had any entitlement to insurance at all, and then only if the contractor was to blame for what happened. The 1897 Act was limited to employers rich enough to be able to pay.)

Illness and accident were not the only affliction to hit the young and able bodied. People starved when frost stopped work. Soup kitchens were not uncommon, particularly on remote dams in winters like that of 1895/6 when flour, potatoes, meat, and clothing were sent to the Yorkshire moors to the Gowthwaite and Dunford Bridge dams. A few years earlier, people were dying of hunger at Vyrnwy and, a year or so before that, bread, bacon, and coffee were doled out at the Bill o' Jacks dam near Greenfield in Lancashire. Soup doled out to navvies working in the Blackwall tunnel in London in 1894/5 was paid for partly by local donations, partly out of what was left of the Distress Fund which was set up when work on the Hull-Barnsley line and Alexandra Dock was stopped in 1884 after the promoters ran out of cash.

Many navvies stayed on at Hull, expecting work to start again. Others sailed to Tilbury docks straight into another stoppage caused by an argument between company and contractor over extra money for working the stiff blue clay of the lower Thames valley. In Hull, work didn't re-start, either. People went hungry. Boots and working clothes were pawned. Men lost weight and strength. As soon as she heard about it Mrs Garnett appealed for help in the newspapers, raising enough money to feed the people who stayed. Katherine Sleight and a committee of gangers spent it on bread and cheese, bacon, meat-and-potato pies, soup-kitchen soup, and fares to other jobs. 'When we started these works,' Thomas Walker wrote from Preston docks, 'numbers of men (walking skeletons) came on at once from Hull. They were not fit for work, they were starved.'

All in all, Mrs Garnett thought the Distress Fund was such a good thing, she proposed extending it countrywide. On one summer's day every year all over England a silver collection would be held on every job. It was to be called the Distress and Self-Help Fund, and it came to nothing. Nobody even went to the meetings she organised. 'I did think,' said a sad and angry Mrs Garnett, 'that the *real navvies* would have taken this thing – which was for their *own good only* – up with *some spirit*. I am sorry that you have got so little *pluck or sense*. You may think I am speaking sharply, and so I want to do.'

Not long after, work stopped on the Christchurch-Brockenhurst and the Christchurch-Bournemouth railways. People were distressed. 'You know I begged you to provide against an evil day by giving to a Distress Fund,' she told them all, 'and you would not do it. Now I ask you navvies all over England, what do you think of your own actions?'

It made no difference. If anything things got worse. In 1907 men earned up to seven pounds a week laying a sewer across Blackheath in London. Within a fortnight they were begging. 'When I think what a class navvies were in the old days,' said Mrs Garnett, 'and then see dirty men in rags adorned with red noses, who say, "I've come for a little relief. I'm a navvy," I feel, and often say, "That is a lie." "Rags outside and rags in" is a just description, but not the noble old name navvy.'

Not that it was always the navvy's fault. There was a time, early this century, when to be young and fit in the summertime was no guarantee of eating. The only overtly political thing the Navvy

Mission ever did, in fact, was lobby John Burns, President of the Local Government Board, about navvy unemployment – in particular about Ramsay MacDonald's 1907 Unemployed Workmen's Bill which was never enacted but which would have given the unemployed the right to either a job, or board and lodging for life. It was meant to stiffen the 1905 Unemployed Workmen's Act which kept respectable people away from the Poor Laws by keeping a register of the genuinely unemployed and by giving Distress Committees power to spend ratepayers' money on relief schemes.

It was these relief schemes in particular that worried the Mission. They saw them as discriminating against the navvy, who was disenfranchised because he had no fixed home, in favour of natives who were both out of work and a burden on the rates. Some councils even put ads. in the newspapers warning navvies to keep away.

Burns gazed at them with intense, deep-set eyes: a slight, lean faced man with short pepper-and-salt whiskers and an untidy tie. A hundred years earlier the mere displeasure of a Bishop of London had stopped navvies working on Sundays: now Burns, the first working man to sit in the Cabinet, had another Bishop of London in the delegation in front of him.[3] What you're saying, Burns summed up, is that the state's recognition of everybody's right to work was hurting the rights of navvies to do work that was theirs traditionally. 'Local work for local men means local jobbery and local extravagance,' he agreed. He agreed, too, that unagile and untrained men meant inefficiency – and what was the point of training natives for public works if they clung to their back streets and refused to tramp to distant parts?

But you are more frightened than hurt, Burns the politician reassured them. Many relief schemes were purpose-invented. Hackney marshes were being raised for no particular reason. What contractor was going to lose money hiring 'industrial inefficients' on real jobs that really mattered? Where there was genuine navvy work, genuine navvies would do it. Out-of-work tailors, watchmakers and tram conductors would never build dams. (Relief

3 In 1803. The Society for the Suppression of Vice took it ill that men worked on Sundays on the London Dock. They wrote to the Bishop. 'If you could find out the pricipal conditions of the work and state civilly to them my disapprobation and your own of this infringement of the rest and sanctity of Sabbath it would probably put a stop to it,' the Bishop instructed an underling.

schemes, on the other hand, delighted many a navvy. It was easy work – planting trees, laying drains, making roads.[4] Relief pay, though poor, was regular and the money never stopped when the weather stopped the work. Hours were short, the living easy.)

There was, however, a darkness about those years. Illness and old age were the things that worried navvies most: both took away the one thing you needed to make a living – strength. Dying young, in a way, solved the problem of living when you were old.

'And where are the old navvies?' Katie Marsh asked in the 1850s. 'Dead,' she answered. 'Every one.'

She had watched hard work visibly age young men. Old Edward on the Beckenham railway, a grey-haired elderly-looking man (pushing seventy you'd have said), was in fact only thirty-eight and obviously not going to get much older. Navvies worked too hard and lived too rough. Men ate their snap sitting in grass wet as a pond. There were no tommy sheds or shelters.

'Where have all the navvies gone?' asked young Lord Brassey, in the '70s. 'Emigrated, every one.'

Reality, however, was closer to Katie Marsh. Navvies either did die young, or died old in dolour in the workhouse. 'I expect I shall die like a lot of the rest of us, in a hedge bottom,' an elderly navvy once told Mrs Garnett.

Come to that it was a recognised thing at one time for old navvies to end up in the workhouse. They used to call it the Spike in them days. Or the Grubber. Horrid places. (And some of them old kip houses were horrid places and all. They were alive. Not lice, bugs. Of course, it was a good thing to get you up in the mornings. Horrid places, even the fourpenny ones.)

Some few (some very few) of the soberest cutters stayed to work the canals. Thomas Telford recommended John Ford – 'an old canal man' – as a bank tenter (today's lengthsman) on the Liverpool-Birmingham, where Benjamin Moffat, gangman of horse-work on the great slipping bank at Shelmore, was also offered a permanent job.

Some maimed cutters with names like Hoppity Rabbit and Dai Half eked out a living carrying news from job to job, not only as limping scandal sheets but by relaying what the wages were and

4 Road-making was *never* navvy work, except in the Crimea.

where the new work was.

Good railway contractors like Walker and Firbank retained men crippled in their service as watchmen. Until he died in 1886 it was said no old Firbank navvy need fear white hairs. Walker's 'Fragments' were famous on public works for their ferocious loyalty to him. Once a geologist carrying Walker's written permission tried to climb into the Eastham lock on the Ship Canal to look at the boulder clay. He was stopped by a Walker Fragment: a man, the canal's historian tells us, with one foot in the grave, the other made of wood. The geologist tried to out-run him. The Fragment whistled down the cutting. A one-armed, but two-legged, Fragment popped out. Between them the Fragments had three arms and three legs. The geologist – out-armed and out-legged – went home.

Walker also kept old but unfragmented Fragments, grouchy to everybody else but loyal to him. 'I'm not paid by my employer to make a collection for myself,' one old watchman on the Ship Canal would say, rejecting tips from the trippers. Sam Hall was no fragment either – he was whole in every limb –he was just old. Ninety-three, in 1889, when he became a watchman on the Ship Canal.

Some few (very, very few) saved up and got out, like one of two navvies engaged to sink a well at Craven in Cleveland in the 1860s. One opened a greengrocery near Chester with the money he saved, the other went his dissolute way. Later, they met in a Cheshire lane: the saver in his two-horse cart, the spendthrift on his two tramp feet. While the greengrocer prospered, the tramp navvy died of drink at the Lindley Wood dam, still carrying his family under his hat.

Mayhew, researching *London Labour and the London Poor*, met two navvies going different routes around 1850. 'Before I come to London I was nothink, sir,' said one, a tall man with sandy whiskers strapped under his chin. 'A labouring man, an eshkewator. I come to London the same as the rest, to do anything I could. I was at work at the eshkewations at King's Cross station.' He came from Iver in Buckinghamshire and had first gone navvying with his brothers who were hagmen with Peto[5] When Mayhew met him he was dressed as a costermonger, selling pickled eels in Chapel Street market. Rat-catching was his sideline (sometimes, for a bet, he bit

5 Hag, hagman, hagmaster – a sub-contractor.

rats to death with his teeth). It must be unlikely he went back to navvying.

Mayhew met the other man in a Vagrants' Refuge in Cripplegate where down-and-outs could stay for three nights at a time, but no longer. They slept in rows of trays, like open coffins, with dressed sheepskins called basils for bedclothes. The navvy, a big flaxen haired man in a short blue smock, yellowed with clay, had first gone navvying as a nipper on the Liverpool-Manchester and had been cheated by truckmasters and hags ever since. A few weeks back he'd hurt his leg on the London-York but, because the bone was unbroken, he got nothing from his Sick Club.

'I went to a lodging house in the Borough,' he told Mayhew, 'and I sold all my things – shovel and grafting tool and all, to have a meal of food. When all my things was gone, I didn't know where to go. One of my mates told me of this Refuge, and I have been here two nights. All that I've had to eat since then is the bread night and morning they give us here. This will be the last night I shall have to stop here, and after that I don't know what I shall do.'

'Ever since I was nine years old,' the navvy ended, 'I've got my own living, but now I'm dead beat, though I'm only twenty-eight next August.'

It wasn't until 1903 that Mrs Garnett was able to revive the old idea of pensions for navvies and do something about it. Even then, only men over sixty-five who could prove they had worked on public works since boyhood qualified. Single men got five shillings a week – married men, seven and six – the barest needed to keep them out of the workhouse and in lodgings in a navvy hut.

Contractors provided the money although, as with most things she undertook, Mrs Garnett had to bully them. 'I am *very grieved*,' she wrote in December, 1906, 'to inform you no more old navvies can be put on this fund – I know it is *very hard* for the twenty who have been rejected, and we were hoping for a bit more fire and food this bitter weather – many of them born navvies and now worn out! The sons who enjoy the positions and wealth earned by their fathers' ability and the men's work, do not (mostly) help, and newer firms forget these old Pensioners who have worked for them in past years. The hard fact is, the gentlemen who so nobly give, helping not exclusively their *own* old workmen, but those of *all* other contractors, cannot do any more.' Nevertheless by 1914 the fund had cared for over two hundred old people and by 1916 had paid out £20,000.

For those who couldn't get a pension, hawking was one of the very few ways to keep out of the workhouse with any dignity, and it was always popular with the elderly and ill. 'Our chaps are very good,' an eighty-one year old navvy told Mrs Garnett, 'and all our landladies would buy a two or three needles and sich.'

In the '50s the wife of an alcoholic navvy on the Lune valley railway in Westmorland kept her family alive by selling paper fly-cages to farmers in the old fortified halls and hill farms between the Lune and Eden. In 1911 the *Letter* told its readers Richard Smith was a genuine case – ill-health had stopped him navvying and he was now an organ grinder. In 1930 Charlie Ward, born and bred a navvy, was sightless and selling matches in Penge until he got a small pension from the Society for the Blind.

Being free was essential to navvies and every old hawker counted himself luckier than people locked in workhouses and asylums. Blind Billy, a quiet and humble man, had one almost sightless eye when he reached the Lindley Wood dam in the '70s. He had become a navvy when he found his wife was a prostitute and he couldn't bear it. Mrs Garnett sent him to Leeds Infirmary where his bad eye was blinded and his good eye damaged. At first Bowers, the works manager, gave him light work around the dam – road-mending, stone breaking, sand riddling – until he could barely see at all. Mrs Garnett then set him up as a tea hawker, walking around the farms and navvy huts, until the dam was finished. Then he was locked away in Henshaw's Blind Asylum in Manchester to learn basket-weaving, something his clumsy navvy hands wouldn't let him do. He was jailed in the asylum, allowed out once a month *if* he could find a guide, until he died some years later in misery.

Mrs Annie Phelps got somebody to write to the *Letter* in 1909. She was blind and in the workhouse and wanted her husband, Gloucester, to fetch her. Gloucester, a man of about forty with light blue eyes, a fair complexion and fair hair cut in a fringe, was last seen in the Rotherhithe tunnel in 1903, the year Annie Phelps went blind. She had three brothers: Giant, Sammy Spragham, Fat Spragham.

Annie Phelps wrote to the *Letter* again in 1912, this time from Gloucester workhouse. Now she was twice-trapped: double-locked in blindness and the blank, blind workhouse, dun and dingy, sharp with the smell of carbolic and institutionalised poverty. She wrote for the last time in 1914 from the same place. Probably she died there, the worst death a navvy could face, blind, infirm, imprisoned.

44

Chapter 6

Beginnings

Navvies, navvying and English canals (it can be no surprise) were exactly coeval: men who began on the Bridgewater as labourers left it as Navigators, tramping away to spend the rest of their lives digging waterways.

'I've been a canal cutter upward of forty years,' said John Walker in 1801, the first professional navvy we know about. 'I worked upon the Duke of Bridgewater's Canal, and since have worked upon several.'

The last canals and the earliest railways overlapped in time and, at a guess, five to ten thousand canal makers overlapped with them. Richard Pearce, who made the crossing, began on the Lancaster canal the year before Waterloo and worked through to the Great Western Railway and beyond. He'd found work pretty easily over the years he said in 1846, though you were better off in the old days.

It's very unlikely canal men worked on the Stockton-Darlington, almost as unlikely they worked on the Manchester-Liverpool (where they were mainly local or Irish), but it's certain they worked on the London-Birmingham where, it was said by Lecount, they were too few to spread their usual havoc.

Twentieth century navvies thought their canal forebears were fenmen, people accustomed to controlling slow flowing water. Some were, probably, though most must have been farm labourers, picked up when the canal neared them. William Mylne, an engineer who worked on waterways into the 1830s, never hired finished navvies but recruited the rawstock from the countryside. His rustics, he admitted, were slow and awkward but he paid them little and when they grew proficient and ran off to the railways (it took a year a turn a labourer into a navvy) he recruited more.

Like the canals, the railways recruited bucolic hard men when the line neared their parishes, usually men too drunken and disrespectful to be hired by farmers. ('They appeared to me,' said a contractor, in the '30s, 'the same as a dog that had been tied up for a week. They seemed to go out of their way to commit outrageous acts.') Farms and the countryside, in fact, were always good recruiting grounds, even after navvying became partly self-supplying, particularly in the great agricultural collapse of the '80s.

By the '80s, as well, Cardwell's army reforms were working through and old soldiers young enough for navvying were being released from the colours. They became quite common on public works with their give-away nicknames like Soldier and Gunner.[1]

A swarthy navvy called Soldier drew his shilling a day pension in a quarterly lump in Gravesend in July 1883 and boozed it away in his regular fashion, ending foodless, moneyless and kitless in Boston a month later. Joe Chapham took him home and gave him tommy and lodgings, until Soldier robbed his fellow-lodgers of £3-3-8d and stole Jethro Bird's jacket, moleskin trousers, handkerchief and waistcoat (all good). Jethro said: 'He turned out respectable in my rigs, and has skinned me.' (Jethro had no room to talk – he was later expelled from the Christian Excavators' Union for buying things on credit and sloping.)

Rarer was the upper class drop-out, generally a drunk, often strangely reminiscent of a failed remittance man: failed in that nobody was going to pay *him* to go to the farthermost colonies and never return. Men like the Oxford double first Mrs Hunter of Hunterston met at the Dalry dam near Paisley. 'Look at that shovel,' said the navvy, a dark middle-aged man, 'I'm actually fond of it, for by tomorrow night it will have earned me ten shillings, and then I can go and have a drink.'

'We have known,' said the *Illustrated London News* in 1854, 'two surgeons (very drunken fellows) working as navvies.' They also knew of a footman who ran away to navvy on the Lincolnshire Railway, only to suffocate in mud at the New Holland Pier.

Before all that, however, there were two other big navvy-making factors, the new Poor Laws and the Hungry Forties. The trade recession which made the '40s so hungry began throwing thousands of mill hands out of work in the mid-'30s, just as the earliest railways were scrabbling about for labour: out-of-work spinners, redundant weavers, it made no odds as long as they weren't too gaunt to pick up a pick and shovel. Up to fifty thousand unwanted.

1 Edward Cardwell, Secretary of State for War, reorganised the infantry into county regiments in which men could serve for six years, instead of lifetime.

mill hands, it's thought, went straight from their mills to the railways: Manchester-Sheffield, Selby-Hull, Chester-Crewe, Bolton-Preston, Preston-Fleetwood, North Midland, Midland Counties. Many stayed with public works, becoming so good that for a long time a lot of people thought only north-countrymen *could* be navvies: if your vowels were soft you must be a labourer.

The 1835 Poor Law was perhaps a less drastic way of creating navvies but it was longer lasting. It was meant to simplify the maze of parish-by-parish relief schemes which had grown up, entwining the whole country like clinging ivy, ever since King Henry closed the monasteries and with them their alms for the poor. Things *had* got into a pretty mess by the 1830s. In 1835 Edward Gulson, who did some prying for the Commissioners in the still un-Unionised parishes of Oxfordshire, reported that rate-receivers lived better than rate-payers. One woman even paid the parish to let her lodge in the poorhouse where paupers ate meat daily. A gang of fit men, paid by the parish to mend roads, played pitch and hustle with the parish's money and took paid leave to go bull-baiting.

The new Poor Law changed all that. The new system was both unified and rigid. At the top it was run from London by paid Commissioners. Locally it was run by elected Boards of Guardians, generally petty tradesmen with a vested interest in being stingy to the poor. Parishes were lumped together into Unions the better to support the new brick workhouses which, like jails, were meant to deter, not attract; to break, not protect. Only the utterly desperate and beaten would live in them.

Some, seeing the game was up, chose to look for work: others were forced to. Many trekked to the new railways. The Guardians in Halstead, in Essex, clashed with their paupers over the winter of 1835–6 when the poor rioted and fired wheat ricks. Some were locked away in the new workhouse, confident that farmers *had* to give them work if they wanted it. Others trod the tread-mill in the House of Correction. Either way by next mid-summer the poor were broken and were trudging away from their homes. Twenty went to the Southampton Railway.

For a time Richard Muggeridge, the Commissioners' migration officer in Manchester, shipped whole families of southern farm labourers along the canals into the cotton towns. When the Hungry Forties set in, he diversified out of cotton into bleaching, paper-making, and railways. Striplings, he wrote, were no good for railway work: budding navvies had to be young, unmarried, but past their unmuscled youth.

At the same time a circular letter sent to the Boards of Guardians alongside the London-Birmingham reminded them that here was a good way of getting rid of their unwanted poor. In response, the Select Vestry at Hemel Hempstead persuaded the railway company to hire a whole gang of its paupers. The Vestry found the tools, but the paupers couldn't find the energy and they all left in a few days. Others, on the other hand, stuck it out, Francis Giles, an ex-canal engineer, was very pleased with his paupers on the Newcastle-Carlisle: with good gangers he'd match them against any navigator. Many became navigators themselves.

At first, when most people thought only north-countrymen were *real* navvies, most navvies *were* from the north. By the 1880s, on the other hand, most new navvies were southerners (more men always became navvies than were born navvies.) Roughly eighty per cent were English. Ten per cent were Irish. Five per cent were Scots, five per cent Welsh.[2]

In 1793 Sir Charles Morgan tabled a motion in the House of Commons which would have banned canal digging at harvest time when navvies were needed to help get in the corn. Most MPs opposed it. 'Mr Dent,' said the *Morning Chronicle*, 'said there were hundreds of people who came from Scotland and from Ireland, for the purpose only of working in canals, and who knew nothing of corn harvest.' Since Mr Dent says 'hundreds' and the canals were built by thousands perhaps the Irish ten per cent was steady from the beginning. It seems to be true of the first railways. 'On these works,' says the 1841 *Census in Ireland*, 'it has been supposed by one of the leading engineers in England, that the Irish labourers did not at any time exceed five thousand or one-tenth the whole.'

In 1854 the *Illustrated London News* made a point of how many Irish soldiers there were and how few Irish navigators. They put it down to the potato eating habit which they thought weakened men too much for navvying.

The Irish clung together so that on a few jobs they were either in a large minority or even a small majority. Missionaries complained about it. Two-thirds of the men on the Cray dam near Swansea in

2 Worked out from names printed in the dead and hurt lists of the Navvy Mission Society, 1880–1914.
    At least three navvies were black. Six-Fingered Jack died in Malmesbury workhouse, aged 79, in the summer of 1902. Another black man, from the Elan Valley dams, died of exposure in the hills above Rhayader in 1897. A third worked on the Ballachulish railway a year or so later.

1900 were Irish. Three-quarters of those at the Alwen dam a few years later were both Irish and Catholic. Even as early as 1851 twenty-six per cent of the men working around the Knaresborough viaduct on the East and West Riding Junction were Irish. (The rest were English. A quarter of all of them were local.)

Statistics about the origins of people on Pennine Railways have been worked out from the census returns for 1851, 1861, 1871.

1851: the second Woodhead tunnel, Malton and Driffield railway, Leeds and Thirsk Railway
1861: South Durham and Lancashire Union, Rosedale branch line, Nidd valley railway, Ingleton Extension
1871: Carlisle-Settle line, Team valley extension

Ninety-two per cent were English. Four per cent were Irish. Three per cent were Scots. Only one per cent was Welsh (and most of them were on the Carlisle-Settle line where they totalled nearly five per cent of the whole. Most, probably, were miners in the line's several tunnels).

Nearly half the Englishmen were northerners of one sort or another. The eastern counties, the midlands, and the southern counties each contributed around 14 per cent of the English contingent. Only 2 per cent came from the far west of England, though again they congregated in sizeable minorities in a few places: 14 per cent of the Englishmen on the Carlisle-Settle came from the south-west – probably Devon and Cornish miners in the tunnels.

Most Irish navvies were English-speaking Ulster Catholics, a fact not always appreciated even at the time. (The Irish Society once sent Irish-speaking Protestant scripture readers to work among them.) They were different both from the Irish who came seasonally for the sheep-shearing and the harvest, and the Glasgow-Irish who in mid-century were about to become Scots. Most Irish navvies tended to stick to the north, fanning out from their ports of entry, Liverpool and Glasgow.

Burke and Hare, the body snatchers, were both Ulster Catholics who worked on the Edinburgh-Glasgow Union Canal for a short time around 1818. Burke was a labourer's son from County Tyrone. Hare came from Newry and worked on the canal at West Port where a man called Logue had a gang of Irishmen and a lodging house. Logue's wife, Lucky, navvied on the canal as well, dressed as a man.

'The land of Donegal is bare and hungry,' said Patrick MacGill who was born there in 1890, 'and nobody can make a decent livelihood except landlords.' His priest, a pot-bellied little man with sparkling false teeth and a taste for good cigars and first class railway travel, put curses on most of his parishoners. Seven curses to begin with, for dancing. 'May you have one eye and it be squinting. May you have one tooth and it be aching.'

He used the people's fear of him, said MacGill, to extort money. He built himself a house with a lavatory when nobody else knew what a lavatory was (a place for storing holy water, somebody thought). 'He wants another pound for his new house at once,' MacGill's father once told his family. 'I'm over three weeks behind, and if he puts a curse on me this time what am I to do at all, at all.'

MacGill was 'sold' when he was still a child to a bigoted Orangeman for five shillings a week wages and the same food as the pigs, only less. In 1905 he crossed to Scotland for the potato picking, lost his money gambling, and was too ashamed to go home to Donegal. He met Moleskin Joe, an English navvy. Together they worked at the Kinlochleven dam where MacGill became a writer and gave up navvying.

The Irish were cast out even by the outcast navvy: they were the minority within the minority, the outsiders inside the outsiders. Although they made up only ten per cent of the whole, the Irish were the common factor in about a third of navvy riots. The Irish put it down to bigotry. In 1839 the *Liverpool Mercury* reported that an Irish navvy called Peter McDonough had been defrauded of his wages at Ellesmere Port by a hagman called Isaac Dean. 'After I was employed by Dean,' McDonough told the newspaper, 'it was often hinted to me that I ought to consider myself a fortunate kind of Irish animal because I was not driven from the place with sticks or stones, as many of my countrymen had been before my coming, for no other reason than being Irish. I witnessed a few of these Irishmen hunts since I came. One poor fellow, who got employment, and began work, was attacked in a dreadful manner; he ran, and was pursued by them with stones, etc. from which he received a severe cut on the head; his coat, after taking from it a case of razors and a comb, they rolled up with hot bricks.'

Prejudice, as well, was the motive the Irish gave for the riot which drove them off the Lancaster-Preston railway in 1839. Michael Donahue, a tall spare man, was eating bread and cheese outside the Green Dragon in Calgate when the mob came. Somebody stole a tool from him and beat with a knobbed ash plant. He tried to run away, he told the magistrates. 'I went over a field, and went into a road, and found Rough Lanc, and I got tally-ho there. There was another with him in a blue waistcoat. They chased me round the house, and tore my coat and took away my pocket, and my handkerchief with half a sovereign in it. They struck at me, and pulled my coat to pieces.'

Donahue, humiliated and shaken, his coat in tatters, crept away, then made his way to what he thought would be safety in Lancaster. Except Rough Lanc somehow got there before him. 'Damn you, why don't you cut?' Rough Lanc shouted at him, beating him with his fists.

John Trainor, a stout man with only a slight Irish accent, was lamed at Calgate and limped into the witness box. 'They beat me over my head and body,' he told the court, 'they hurt me very much. I begged for my life, and they ordered me to get up, and I walked with them. If I did not walk fast enough they prodded me on with their sticks.'

He was pushed into a crowd of Englishmen. 'Pitch into the bastard,' they shouted. 'What fetched you here?'

'I said we came for work wherever it was. They said they did not allow Irish. They asked me if I would be off the ground, when they were leathering me, and I said I believe I must, as I was not able to work. They said they would not have any of us.'

But there was more to it than pure prejudice. Between the Irish and the Scots it was often religious: Reformation v Counter-Reformation, Calvin v Pope by proxy. Money, more often than not, was the reason the heathen English attacked the Irish. The English, said the *Liverpool Journal* in 1839, 'entertained a general opinion that they (the Irish) flocked too numerously to their country, and by accepting of a rate of wages below the English standard, reduced their value in the labour market.'

'We are all starving,' the destitute navvy in Cripplegate told Henry Mayhew. 'We are all willing to work, but it ain't to be had. This country is getting very bad for labour: it's so overrun with Irish that the Englishman hasn't a chance in his own land to live.'

(The Irish did have their champions. In 1846 Thomas Carlyle watched navvies on the Caledonian Railway. 'I have not in my travels seen anything uglier than that disorganic mass of labourers, sunk three-fold deeper in brutality by the three-fold wages they are getting. The Yorkshire and Lancashire men, I hear are reckoned the worst, and not without glad surprise, I find the Irish are the best in point of behaviour. The postmaster tells me several of the poor Irish do regularly apply to him for money drafts, and send their earnings home. The English, who eat twice as much beef, consume the residue in whisky, and do not trouble the postmaster.')

'As far as my experience goes,' said the Sheriff of Edinburgh, also in 1846, 'in Scotland we have not yet any of the class of people called navigators; they are generally merely labourers, who come for the occasion and probably do not return to that work afterwards.' But though few turned navvy, a lot of Scotsmen did labour on public works in Scotland. The Caledonian Canal was built mainly by Highlanders with only a stiffening of regular navvies from the south. In the 1840s Scotsmen on Scottish railways came from lowland farms and highland crofts, where they went back when the job was done. Just before the Great War many of the gangers on the Kinlochleven dam were bilingual in English and Gaelic. The Gaels went home when the dam was built. (Earlier, they were apt to go at any time: for the herring fishing, the potato harvest, peat cutting. 'The herring season has been most abundant,' Telford wrote from the Caledonian canal in 1818, 'and the return of the fine weather will enable the indolent Highland creature to get their plentiful crops and have a glorious spell at the whisky-making.')

The Welsh, too, usually only took to navvying when navvying came to them, one result of which was they were normally less violent. They at least belonged somewhere. A scripture reader on the Holyhead line said he'd never seen navvies like them: they never lost even an hour's pay through drunkenness and paid cash for Bibles, even the five shilling ones. 'I've seen in a common labourer's purse,' said the missionary, 'two and three and more sovereigns, and silver.'

Most, on the Holyhead line, were miners. Many were monoglot Welsh speakers. Few were illiterate. (At the Vyrnwy dam in the 1880s the store keeper sold twenty Welsh-language books a week, against none in English. Three-quarters of the Vyrnwy men were Welsh.)

Not that they were entirely faultless. On Whit Monday, 1846, James Webb was drinking his quart of ale among a crowd of navvies outside a tommy shop near Bangor on the Chester-Holyhead when somebody suggested, in Welsh, they amputate his bloody ears. They should in fact prune the ears of every English bugger to distinguish them from Welshmen. Webb, after being kicked and knocked down, found his ear had been cut, not off, but in two, and he had been stabbed in the head with a pen-knife.

Full-scale rioting broke out there as well one Friday towards the end of May at the beginning of the long sun-dried summer of 1846. Local Welsh labourers, jealous so many Irishmen were employed, drove them out of Penmaenmawr and marched on westwards, clearing the line of Irish until they reached the Llandegai tunnel which runs under Bangor. Half climbed to the shafts, the rest skirted the hill into town, passing the lock-up and the courthouse of the Rev James Vincent, the magistrate.

Vincent, who'd scrutinised the rioters with disfavour as he rode in from his home near Aber earlier that morning, sent a snatch-squad of constables to arrest a ringleader as he marched by his courtroom window. As the police dragged their leader into the jail-room behind the court, the mob turned on Vincent, hitting him in the face, jeering at him as he read the Riot Act. At the same time the ringleader walked out of his unlocked cell and over the wall, climbing a ladder he found in the backyard. The Durham Light Infantry sailed from Liverpool in steamboats. The mob went back to work.

Chapter 7

The Clockwork Shovel

On public works, work began when the ganger blew a whistle and shouted 'Blow-up, blow-up'. It ended when he shouted 'Yo-ho, yo-ho'. Blow-up and yo-ho, the words, probably go back to canals and lasted the distance.[1]

Navvy-born boys began work when they were seven to nine years old, carrying blunted picks as big as themselves to the blacksmith's forge for re-sharpening. Ten and eleven year olds worked as fats or fat-boys – slithering about in mud under the wagons, greasing axles and wheel hubs. ('Fat' from the fat or grease they smeared on the wagons. A fat-boy was normally as lean as a long dog.)

Older nippers looked after the turn-outs, the points on the works railway where wagons and locos were turned in and out of the sidings or to and from the tiphead. Other boys of the same age were spraggers, poking wooden sprags between the spokes of free-running wagons to control their speed, particularly near the turn-outs.

Older boys – tippers – ran the wagons to the bankhead for tipping. Older than that they became full wagon-filling navvies around eighteen.

On top of that, adult navvies had a loose work-hierarchy of their own: miners, timbermen, navvies, muckshifters, and more.

The classic navvy/muckshifter split was best seen among men working in cuttings. Navvies of the kind called getters or pickmen worked right at the muck-face, bringing it down into heaps suitable for shovelling away by other navvies called muckshifters, wagon-fillers, fitters, or runners-out. If they ran the spoil out in railway wagons, then wagon-filler and muckshifter were synonymous. Runners-out, more usually, were muckshifters who wheeled the

1 On canals a horn was sounded at blow-up.

muck away in barrows, usually straight up the sides of the cutting on planks. Who did what was often a matter of chance – what job was unfilled when a man drifted in off the road. The best navvies could do, did do, all grades of work from muckshifter through timberman to tunnel tiger.

Tigers were tunnel miners and they were helped by other navvies called spannermen. Spannermen changed the drills, among other things. Some tigers, particularly in the early days, went straight on to public works from hard-rock mines (metal mines, like copper and lead, more frequently than coal). Others came up from the ranks of pure pick and shovel men. As between pickman and muckshifter (as between sea and foreshore) it wasn't always clear where tiger began and navvy ended, but generally speaking the tiger picked the places where he wanted the shot-holes to be drilled, and the navvy drilled them, working in turn as hammerman and drill-holder. The tiger then packed the holes with explosives, fused and fired them. Muckshifters ran the broken rock down to the shafts for hoisting to the spoil heaps.

Most tigers stuck to their trade if they could (the pay was better for one thing) though some navvies seem to have switched from tiger-work, to pick-work, to muck-shifting without damaging their pride too much. Some men also tended to stick to other navvy sub-trades like concreting and timbering.

Concreting was a semi-skill on its own, calling for quick, accurate shovel-work when the cement/aggregate mix was at its proper semi-sloppy consistency. It became more important as more concrete was poured on public works, particularly after the turn of the twentieth century when whole dams (Kinlochleven, Seathwaite Tarn, Alwen) were made of it.

Timbermen worked the timber which shored up the sides of trenches and propped up the roofs of tunnels and headings. Timbermen chose their timber, sawed it, nailed it, wedged it. They earned more than ordinary navvies but less than tigers. The extra pay bought the knowledge of where to wedge and what shape to wedge with. Once you'd emptied a space of muck, you didn't want to block it in again with baulks of timber and massive criss-crosses of splintery wood. On the other hand you didn't want the timberwork to be so light everything caved in again. A good navvy-timberman let in people, safely, as well as sunlight.

Apart from living apart in their own communities, two things set navvies apart from labourers: extra strength, extra knowledge.

Endurance was basic (it took a year to turn a flabby labourer into a man hard enough to work his shift in a muck-shovelling gang) but knowledge was almost as important. Knowing how to handle your body to begin with: once you bent your back at blowing up time you didn't straighten up till yo-ho. On top of that you had to know how to handle matter, how to mine and timber, how to cope with the geology of what faced you, how *best* to pick, drill, blast, shovel all kinds of muck from rock to sand, clay to loam. Aggression and thick muscles got you there on their own, a few tricks got you there faster, and if you were paid by the piece *that* mattered.

What struck people most was the clock-like precision of wagon-filling. 'As fine a spectacle as any could witness is to see a cutting in full operation,' said one of Brassey's timekeepers, 'every man at his post, and every man with his shirt open, working in the heat of the day, the gangers looking about, and everything going like clock-work.'

Hard soil fell softly away under the shining shovels. Hard men moved smoothly like Wellington's soldiers at drill. Navvy gangs were like burrowing machines, their shovels like cutting blades, fuelled on beef and beer. 'These dissolute men exert themselves so violently in their work,' said Hekekyan Bey an Armenian trainee engineer, in 1829, 'that I have seem many powerful, muscular men with their blood oozing out of their eyes and nostrils.'

(The English navvy, who went abroad soon after the beginning of railway building, was a revelation to the foreigner. 'My God,' said the French, 'these English, how they work.' At first on the Paris-Le Havre railway the English navvy gave orders by stamping his foot, shouting 'damn' and pointing a finger like a pick blade at what he wanted done. A kind of Anglo-French lingua-franca soon grew up offering brief careers to bright young Savoyards who specialised in translating it. In France the English navvy was a creature to be gawped at for his bigness, uncouthness and wildness. They brought the navvy-sized iron tools and money-making barrows, discarding the puny wooden things the French worked with. Where the French ate sparingly of bread and fruit, the English swallowed heaps of bacon and beef).

A 'good hand' among early canal cutters could dig twelve cubic yards of easy earth a day – eighteen tons, or perhaps the space taken up by a large single-decker bus; a place big enough to set up house in. But that was easy compared to what came later. On the early railways a single navvy was expected to fill seven wagons a day. (In fact they worked in pairs. Two were expected to fill a set, or train, of fourteen wagons between them). To do so each man lifted twenty tons over his head.

Sometimes a pair of men filled sixteen wagons a day and even then the best of them were in the ale house by late afternoon. 'The men, who are the finest workmen in Europe,' said Hekekyan Bey, 'dig out twenty-five cubic yards of heavy clay each day – but their desire to run to the public houses and get drunk is so great that many of them perform their day's work in a few hours.'

In the 1870s Lincolnshire navvies in the Victoria Dock extension in London shifted twenty-five cubic yards of peat or eighteen yards of clay every eight-hour shift. On the Manchester Ship Canal, said John Ward, two men had to fill twelve four-yard wagons as part of a day's work – and *that* meant lifting twenty-four tons of muck eight feet, clear over your head. 'I defy any man to prove that any slaves in the whole history of the world were worked to the extent that English navvies are,' Ward added.

So I went to Stratford on Avon and went to work for Scott and Middleton on the branch line there. Filling wagons. Three and fourpence a day and you had to fill ten three-yard wagons. Two men to a gang and you finished when you'd filled them. But you had to buy your own shovel. Eighteenpence out of the office. Well, on all jobs you had to buy your own tools.

A cutting, for a railway, began with a preliminary gash called a gullet, just wide enough for a single line of wagons. As the gullet widened to a full-width cutting an extra line of track was laid. Spoil was hauled away by gravity (if there was a down-slope) with only a brakesman riding each train – juddering, shaking, tossing, jolting his joints apart, his foot dancing off and on the brake.

Once the gullet and the cutting proper were opened, you faced a bare, flat, vertical face called, in fact, the face. You could either slowly hack the face back, slice by slice, from top to bottom, or you could undermine it at its foot and let gravity bring the lot tumbling down. (The column of undermined earth was called the 'lift'.) How men set about it was usually their concern. Often the head-contractor had little interest, other than in issuing a little self-righteous advice now and then. Usually, navvies went for the quick, bigger-money way.

Depending on the stiffness of the soil a face up to twelve feet high is self-supporting. You began by 'holing' the bottom – cutting square holes in the base – but leaving pillars of earth holding up the rest of the mass. At the same time you cut a groove down the sides of the face. Sometimes a watch was set to warn of the ground cracking. The rest of the gang then began 'knocking the legs away' – chopping away the pillars holding up the face. Once the ground on top began moving, dirt was sometimes poured into the cracks which opened. If it trickled away a warning was shouted over the lip.

The skill was in making the right weight of muck fall the right way, and for that the height of the face was critical: too high, and it slumped down, shoving itself away at the foot, lumping up into a huge heap which then had to be expensively picked and shovelled away. Properly done the fall broke the muck into lumps ready for shovelling into wagons, which was then either dumped or, better still, used for embankments.

As well as being shovelled into wagons at the bottom of the gullet, muck was also cleared by barrowing it up the sides of the cutting on narrow planks called barrow-runs. Full barrow and guiding navvy were hauled bodily skywards by horses; empty barrow and navvy then slithered down again under the influence of gravity and alcohol. Sometimes the horses on the topyard walked away at right angles to the cutting, sometimes they walked parallel to it, the rope twisted through a quarter circle by pulleys. Sometimes the barrow-runs ended in platforms next to a line of rails laid along the top of the cutting.

Robert Southey, poet laureate, described something similar at the Laggan cutting on the Caledonian Canal in 1819. 'The earth is moved by horses walking along the bench of the canal and drawing laden cartlets up one inclined plane, while the emptied ones, which are connected by a chain passing over pullies, are let down another.' The Caledonian is a deep ship canal and among the heaps of muck 'men appeared,' said Southey, 'in the proportion of emmets to an ant hill.'

They even had barrow runs on the Manchester Ship Canal, the most mechanised job of them all. Among the Whittaker steam excavators, the Priestman's grabs and Ruston steam navvies, men still scaled the sides of the cutting on planks, balanced by the weight of the barrows. They went up leaning backwards and came down crouching, their boots like brakes, their barrows like rudders. Some barrows were two-wheeled hand carts. More than the immense massed steam machinery it was the barrow runs that were the wonder of the ship canal. On Bank Holidays visitors came in shoals to gawp at the men on the planks.

Muck from cuttings was taken, whenever it could be, to bridge nearby valleys with embankments, a trick learned early by canal engineers. Canal men tipped their muck, dry-shod, from hand barrows or horse-carts, though muck was also floated along flooded reaches and wheelbarrowed from the boats to the tiphead or bankhead, the place where it was shot off the leading edge of the embankment. Railway men trundled trains of tip-wagons to within a hundred yards of the bankhead where each was uncoupled for running down on its own.

The ground between the cutting, or borrow-pit, and the tiphead was called the lead. Railway lines laid on it were called teaming roads. Four were normal, six not uncommon and a thousand tons a day seems to have been teamed over them, on average.

One kind of tip-wagon had a bar sticking out the side to which a horse was hitched. Another kind had a coupling hook, linked by a light chain to the horse's swingle-tree. The tipper, an older lad, ran on the rail in front of the wagon, while his horse cantered outside him, clear of the rails. Near the bankhead the tipsman, or bankheadman, signalled him to slip his horse. The tipper snatched the chain off the wagon's hook and horse and lad got sharply out of the way. Except scores – thousands – of boys slipped on the rails and were killed or crippled, bouncing and bleeding, under the gravid wagons. It happened so often, some horses learned to undog themselves when their drivers tumbled under the wheels.

As the wagon free-wheeled past him, the tipsman knocked up its tail-board catch with his shovel. The wagon was stopped with a jolt by a barrier of earth and sleepers called bumpers or bumpsticks. The jerk flung the bed of wagon over, shooting spoil off the end of the bank. A good tipper got his speed just right and the wagon emptied itself. Otherwise, the tipsman, none too pleased, had to shovel out the residual muck. The tipsman also spread the spoil evenly on the slope.

Pug or tank locos were later used for tipping. Each was handled by a driver and his rope-runner. The rope-runner (or ropey) was the fireman, shunter, guard, and the man who took the place of the tipper. With one hand he hung on to a rail on the front of the engine, with the other he held a long handled hook which coupled the loco to the muck wagon. The driver opened his valve and shunted towards the bankhead, watching the tipsman all the while. On the tipsman's signal, the driver braked and the ropey jerked the hook off the coupling, and away free-wheeled the wagon into the bumpsticks.[2]

At Wolverton on the Birmingham line they tipped greasy, wet, dark clay straight on to turf for days, then weeks, then months. The embankment bulged at the bottom and spread out like a rubber bag of water. In the end they built the embankment backwards from the viaduct in the middle of the valley, carting material on a wooden bridge over the slipping area. (Not only did the Wolverton bank slip, it self-combusted. One bright morning the 'sulphuret of iron' mixed in it kindled spontaneously. Earth and sleepers blazed in the sunlight. 'Dang it,' said a rustic, 'they can't make this here railway, arter all, they've set fire of it to cheat the creditors.')

Canals, and some muck dams, were rendered watertight by puddled clay, an idea introduced by Brindley who probably learned how as a mill-wright. Clay and sand are chopped together with a little water to make a sloppy, non-porous mess which you lay in layers. (At first, the chopping was done by hand, but after the 1820s they used mechanical mixers called pug-mills.) On canals the layers were commonly ten inches deep, in dams, half a foot or less. Puddle gangs kneaded the stuff with spades, and trod and heeled it in specially heavy puddle-boots. (Heeled puddle had a rippled or stippled look.)

Navvies were invented because the Industrial Revolution needed them to make canals, railways, and docks. Once invented, they stayed on to swab up some of the mess it made – in particular by damming and piping clear water to sickly towns.

What could be done about sanitation began to be discovered before the problem itself was properly understood or defined. In 1829 James Simpson, in Chelsea, showed you could purify dangerously infested water, by filtering it through sand, a quarter of a century before it was known that cholera and dirty water go together. A year or so later a Nottinghamshire engineer called Thomas Hawksley argued for a 'constant water service' – every pipe from dam to tap should be filled with limpid water like an extension of the lake.

2 When tip-wagons were first used is unclear, though in 1803–6 Telford did have turn-up trucks at work on the Caledonian Canal, probably on the big embankments by the River Ness and the man-made peninsula in which Clachnaharry sea-locks were dug. One kind tipped sideways, but another which tipped backwards *could* have been freewheeled into an arrester barrier.

In 1842 Chadwick published a report describing what it was like to be poor in an island where the sky was half air, half water – it was like living in a drought in a desert: the poor stank from lack of water to wash in. Black rain dropped through the Manchester sky like ink. What was needed, Chadwick argued, was clean water and a clean water supply's observe, sewers.[3]

Sewers, at the time, were cloacal rivers. The rich had Bramah's patent water closets which flushed the bowel movements of the gentry into cess-pits in their own cellars from where night-soil men, once a year and at dead of night, carried them away. What were needed were proper sewers and sewage works and these, for the first time, were made possible by nineteenth century technology, vitrified pipes and Portland cement in particular. From the mid-1850s onwards, Joseph Bazalgette's navvies in London laid out a thousand miles of sewers, some of them as big as rivers.

Clear water came from behind dams in the hills. A dam is big when it's over fifty feet high and in Britain there are about five hundred and thirty of them (nobody seems to have counted the lesser ones, like the Nethermere of Lawrence's *Sons and Lovers*, which in fact is a canal reservoir). As well as an unknown number of the unknown number of lesser dams, navvies built around three hundred of the big ones: fifty of masonry or concrete, the rest of muck.

Muck dam making is an old and probably native English art. Apart from the watermills listed in Doomsday Book, some of which must have had dammed water, the Bishop of Winchester made the Itchen navigable in the 1190s by building a dam at Alresford where it still sits, now so old, its lake shrunk to a pond, people think it's a natural bit of landscape.

For a hundred years most muck dams were copies of the ones made by the canal engineers who either inherited the art or reinvented it when they found they had to keep topping up the permanent way. There was a canal lake, now a weedy pond, in the Frome valley alongside the Thames and Severn. From the 1790s there were: on the Peak Forest, the Todd Brook and Coombs dams; on the Huddersfield, those at Slaithwaite and Marsden; on the Leeds-Liverpool, two dams stacked one above the other at

3 The same Edwin Chadwick who was behind the convening of the 1846 Parliamentary Committee which looked at the navvy and the way he lived. Chadwick was also one of the first of the Poor Law Commissioners under the 1835 Act.

Foulridge, as well as another, three-sided and tank-like, at Barrowford. Until Lake Rudyard was dammed, the Trent and Mersey was watered by pit drainings from the Golden Hill colliery, a mine branching off the canal under Harecastle Hill. Knighton reservoir, on the Liverpool-Birmingham, lay half on leaky rock, half on clay. Telford tried curing its leakiness by scattering clay from boats through the water but in the end he had to drain it and puddle the bottom properly.

The Scots were probably the first people in the British Isles – after the Romans – to drink dammed water on a city-wide scale: Glasgow first of all with the Whinhill scheme (1796), and then Edinburgh which raised the Glencorse dam in the Pentlands in the 1820s. Manchester followed in the '40s, eventually flooding most of the Etherow valley with seven dams, the biggest waterworks scheme of its day.

Under the 1863 Public Works (Manufacturing Districts) Act local authorities could borrow cheap money to buy a way out of the distress caused by the American Civil War. A lot of the half million which was lent went on dams.[4]

Muck dams at first were rendered watertight by a wall of puddle clay let deep into the earth, filling a trench sunk to impervious rock. Later, concrete – rather than clay – was more usual but however it was in-filled the trench was always called the gutter, the core, the gutter trench, or the core trench.[5] Above ground, the puddle is sandwiched upwards between sloping banks of earth: the air-face and the water-face. The lower parts of the water-face, which are dry only in droughts or after heavy draw-offs, were generally covered with broken stones called beaching. Above this, the part of the water-face exposed to the wash of the lake was clad in stone or masonry pitching.

Big earth dams normally have one or more steps, called berms or benches, in the air-face. As on a railway bank, the slope of the dam is called the batter. The berms and batters of the air-face are grassed and nowadays are normally grazed by sheep. Coming up-valley a muck dam often looks disconcertingly like an up-turned meadow.

Masonry dams should be less bulky than muck dams but Liverpool's big, black, Vrynwy is massively overbuilt. It weighs

4 Some canals, as well, were helped by public funds to off-set unemployment after the Napoleonic War. Money from the Exchequer Bill Loan Commissioners went into the Gloucester and Berkeley, the Regent's, and the Portsmouth and Arundel.
5 The Bude canal dam, built across the Tamar in 1805, seems to have a brick core.

half a million tons. Stone for the dam and water for hydraulic power came from adjacent side valleys. The hydraulic pond is choked now but the quarry is still a slate-grey gash in the mountain. The stone is a hard, dark, grey slate, difficult to quarry because the planes of cleavage are perpendicular neither to their bed nor to themselves. It was shattered with gunpowder, detonated electrically, and the exploded rock was then split into manageable boulders with plugs.

For the dam's hearting, irregular rocks – called plums or Cyclopean Rubble – with the sharp end knocked off were bedded in cement-mortar and beaten in with wooden mauls. Smaller rocks were bedded in the spaces between the big ones. What spaces were left were then filled with concrete, rammed in tight with swords. The mortar itself was made from local sand mixed with pulverised rock and Portland cement. It was said its strength would grow with age. It was mixed in mechanical mixers, first dry, then sprayed with water, poured into iron tubs and run down to the dam. Every joint was packed with dry cement-mortar, tamped home until it showed wet.

Where water now stands was once the flat, boggy bed of an old lake below the Berwyn Mountains, looking into England. Vyrnwy was then remote and ghost-ridden. One particularly troublesome ghost was locked in a quill and imprisoned under a rock in the Vyrnwy River. When the time came to dig the gutter trench, the Welsh labourers shied away from the rock and refused to touch it. English and Irish navvies shattered it with gunpowder. Squatting in the smoke and rubble was a toad or frog, rubbing the sleep of ages from its eyes. The ganger shooed it away.[6]

Vyrnwy, in its day a quantum jump, was quickly followed by other very big masonry dams: Thirlmere, Elan, Derwent. In fact there are two masonry dams, Howden and Derwent, in Derwentdale in Derbyshire, and no less than four across the Elan in Radnorshire. In Welsh the Elan dams are Gaban Goch, Gareg-ddu, Pen y Gareg, Craig Goch, which in English mean Red Cabin, Black Stone, Top of the Stone, Red Rock. Gareg-ddu is normally

6 The Victorians were fascinated by stories of toads/frogs entombed in ancient rock: toad-in-the-hole (sausage in batter) is now all that's left of it. Navvies in the Sherburn valley on the London-Birmingham freed a plump brown toad from solid sandstone. It soon blackened and died. Navvies in the Belsize tunnel in London saw toads hopping away from rocks they'd just broken open. On the St Dizier-Nancy railroad a living pterodactyl was blasted from Jurassic limestone. It rattled its oily, leathery wings, croaked, and died. (So it was said.)

drowned – usually all you see is the road stepping across its crest on arches.

Between the dam and the town, water is normally carried in an aqueduct or pipe track. Water is fed into it through a valve shaft or, in older dams, a straining tower, so called because copper gauzes strained out the solids. Straining towers are often turretted and arrow-slitted like Walt Disney castles.

Probably the first tunnel tigers were hard-rock metal miners from Derbyshire and Cornwall. Tunnelling practice itself both altered a lot and didn't change much. At the end as at the beginning some tunnels were still driven by candlelight and gunpowder.

Until the seventeenth century most hard rock mining was done either by the hot or the cold method. Cold mining meant crashing a way through rock with iron and wood: hammers, drills, wedges. Hot mining meant cooking rock to red heat with wood fires and then suddenly chilling it with water to crack it. Whole landscapes were deforested to keep the pit fires burning.

Gunpowder was used in European guns in the early fourteenth century. Around 1430 its quality was improved by caking it with alcohol or urine and grinding it into grains in ball mills. Gunpowder was a mixture of saltpetre, sulphur and charcoal (which darkened it into 'black powder'). It was rare because saltpetre was rare. Saltpetre (potassium nitrate) is found naturally as a product of rotting nitrous matter on which it flowers or effloresces as crystals and from where saltpetremen collected it. 'They dig in dove cotes when the doves are nesting,' a House of Commons man complained of them in 1601, 'cast up malting floors, when the malt be green, in bedchambers, in sick rooms, not even sparing women in childbed, yea even in God's house, the church.' Charles II ordered his loving subjects to save their urine in pots, with the stale of their beasts, for the gunpowder industry.

The artificial nitre bed, built of layers of dead animals and rotting flora steeped in blood and urine, was one way out of the gunpowder shortage. As a result gunpowder, once too precious for all but the military, became common enough for mining. It reached the copper mines of Derbyshire soon after 1670. Over the next century its use became commonplace – in time for tunnelling canals through hills.

At first gunpowder seems to have been poured straight into bare holes in the rock and firmed down with brick dust and chippings. In the Wapping tunnel on the Liverpool-Manchester it was used in tin tubes, like bicycle pumps, but later it was more usually packed in linen bags, often by women in the huts as a sort of cottage industry. (Given the navvy's liking for high-banked fires and heat, it's not surprising accidents were common. *Any number of people were running around on public works with one eye out.*)

Dynamite and gelignite were more explosive, if trickier, and gunpowder itself was sometimes used as a fuse to set them off. The gunpowder fuse was often lit from a burning blob of gelignite, which sputters harmlessly in air. (A rock ganger once absent-mindedly put his blob of gelignite, still alight, into his waistcoat pocket like a box of matches. It blew his shirt off.)

The irony of tunnelling is that what seemed a refinement introduced by the late canals and adopted by the early railways was later abandoned in favour of the method used on the first waterways. Tunnels were bored from both sides of the hill and – simultaneously – from both sides of a series of vertical shafts sunk in a line through the massif the tunnel was piercing. In early canal tunnels the full-sized bore was driven straightaway but from the 1780s tunnels more and more often were made by enlarging a pilot heading which had already been carried clean through the hill.

In the 1780s Pinkerton's Curdworth tunnel on the Birmingham-Fazeley seems to have been made at least in part by enlarging a pilot bore, and the Blisworth tunnel, begun in 1796 on the Grand Junction, was about to be abandoned because it was too wet when the engineer persuaded the company to let him carry on with a through-heading. This heading acted both as a drain and a mini-hole which irised out into the full-scale tunnel.

From the early 1830s to the 1860s all railway tunnels in Britain were driven in this way and, ironically, the change back to the full-bore method began in the Netherton *canal* tunnel in the 1850s.

Short tunnels, tunnels under water, and tunnels under high mountains were driven differently. With them you drove short headings in the conventional way, but every now and then you began "break-ups": burrows slanting up from the heading to the height of the finished tunnel. A second or top heading was then driven and deepened and broadened into the shape and size of a tunnel, supported all the while by a tunnel shape of large logs, called bars, laid lengthwise along the line of the bore. The weight of the hill was carried by the bars which in turn rested on props and wooden floors, called cills, which slotted into the sides of the tunnel and which were lowered bit by bit as the thickness of muck between the top and bottom headings narrowed. In a way the tunnel was draped over a tunnel of logs until it was safely egg-shaped and self-supporting inside its own brick lining.

The Severn tunnel was driven by 'break-ups'; so was the Cowburn tunnel under a spur of the Peak in Derbyshire, and the Totley between the rivers Derwent and Sheaf.

In the Abbot's Cliff tunnel on the London-Dover a simple fan-shape of props standing on central pillars of chalk held up the roof, but more usually the space just emptied of rock/muck was immediately filled in again, almost as solidly, with wood: upright props, dense as young pine plantations; logs, called bars; planks, called wales; struts, cills, ribs, frames, blocks, wedges, jacky pages, brobs, sprag-props, side trees, head trees, slack-blocks, stretchers, sweeps. At the working face the miners excavated a hole for themselves which they left unsupported for as short a time as possible before pulling a roof of logs over their heads.

From 1825 (to 1843) Marc Brunel drove the first successful sub-Thames tunnel, using a tunnelling shield he invented himself (self-invented but inspired by the way the teredo worm chews holes in ships' timbers). With it he bored through ground as fluid as slurry. Often only a thin pie-crust of soft sickly mud separated the top of his tunnel from the bottom of the river. Bits of detritus – old shoe buckles, shovels, shards of china, (even live eels) – oozed through the river bed/tunnel roof and plopped on the tunnel floor. (In January, 1828, the roof blew in. It began as a tumescent lump, a mud blister, which burst like a bomb. Sewage-coloured water exploded through the hole. Air, forced by the water, first made the gaslights flare and then blew them out. Isambard Kingdom Brunel was literally washed out of the shaft, and danger, by a surge-wave.)

Thirty-six miners worked packed side by side in the shield in tiers of three, each in his own cell. Planks were screwed tight against the face. Each miner loosened one plank, scooped our four and a half inches of mud, then screwed the plank home again before loosening the next. The whole shield was screwed forward by jacks. The brickwork followed so closely it always touched the after end of the shield and only those four and half inches of unclad tunnel were ever unsupported at any one time.

The second Thames tunnel, a subway no bigger than a heading, was bored near the Tower in only a few months of 1869 with a new type of shield. Men worked at both ends of a steel cylinder, cutting back the face at one end, feeding cast-iron liners into the tunnel at the other. Greathead, the resident engineer, later mechanised the shield and used compressed air to keep water out of the workings.

When he died in 1895, one of Greathead's shields was driving the sub-Thames road tunnel at Blackwall. By then the shield was so big whole gangs of men could work in it, miners at one end, muck-shifters shovelling spoil down chutes at the other. Compressed air kept the river out of the workings, although twice the air pressure blew holes in the roof at its thinnest part. As the air boiled away the falling pressure in the tunnel let more water in to recompress what atmosphere remained and exploded another blow-hole in the roof. And so on, in sequence, like a row of exploding land mines.

Getting the line of the tunnel straight was the first thing to do. In 1819 the Strood tunnel on the Thames and Medway canal (later turned into a railway) was probably the first to be aligned with a scientific instrument, an astronomer's transit telescope. Shafts were dug and two heavy plumb bobs dropped down them and steadied in tubs of water. The telescope was then lined up on their strings and the exact line of the tunnel calculated.

Earlier, it's likely the engineer walked over the hill stretching a cord behind him and sighting along flagged beacons. In the summer of 1783 this is probably how Robert Whitworth aligned the Thames and Severn tunnel at Sapperton. Probably two plumb bobs were hung down Sapperton's shafts as well, though their strings were then lined up by eye and candle flame. Sea-compasses *were* used on the Liverpool-Manchester but candles were always the commonest way of keeping tunnels straight.

So, in London I was working in a gassoon in the Rotherhithe tunnel when I picked up with Dover Curly who said there was a lot of heading driving at Stoney Stratford, so we went.

We were driving this heading under the river for sewerage pipes. There was Scan Jones and some other mush driving from one side, and Dover Curly and me from the other. When we come to meet in the middle, under the river, Scan was eighteen inches out of centre with us. The gangerfeller comes along. He says: 'Where's your centres?'

He says to us: 'You're all right.'

He went to Scan and dropped the line where Scan said his centre was. 'Where's your other line?' says the ganger.

Scan says: 'What other line? What do you want two lines for?'

Scan got into a hell of a row over that. They had to fill in one side.

You took your centres on two lines on plumb bobs, sighted on to a candle.

Shaft sinking was a navvy job. At Sapperton and probably elsewhere shafts were sunk like wells, walled as the hole was being dug. The bottom-most circle of masonry was built first, on top of a wooden curb, on top of the hill. As the earth was excavated beneath it the whole growing cylinder of masonry sank into the growing hole. The stone lining in fact was lowered ring by ring into the earth. The first-laid circle of masonry ended at the shaft bottom. It was a method called steining.

Man-powered jack-rolls or windlasses were the earliest winding gear over the shafts. Later, horse-driven whim-gins were copied from the coalfields. The horse was yoked to a horizontal drum around which the rope was wound with both ends hanging down the shaft. As the horse trod round and round, one end of the rope was lowered, the other end raised.

At first, as well, water was slopped out of tunnels with archimedean screws or else was spooned out with Brindley's spoons (a flap like a leather non-return valve opened as the spoon dipped into the water and closed as it was levered out. Water poured away through a channel in the handle). But as early as the 1760s, soon after navvying began, a crude home-made steam pump drained Brindley's Harecastle tunnel on the Trent and Mersey, and by the time the railways arrived engineers had steam pumps which could cope with almost anything. When the London-Birmingham was being bored through an undangerous and undistinguished-looking Northamptonshire hillside, at Kilsby, it ran into quicksand. The contractor took to his bed in despair and expired. In the end, thirteen steam pumps sucked away continually for a year and a half before the tunnel was dry enough for work to begin again.

Where things changed, they changed drastically. At Sapperton in the 1780s primitive all-wood railways carried all-wooden tubs with solid wooden wheels with wooden flanges on wooden rails. On day John Byng – Lord Torrington-to-be – took a cold, almost blind, ride into the tunnel straddling a sledge-cart pulled by two horses hitched nose to tail. (Only two cart-loads of muck were brought down with each blasting.) Away from the last of the smokey daylight the tunnel was lit only by Byng's candle and those of the men he passed. He went right to the working face through clinging gunpowder smoke. It was all a bit *too* enclosed even for him, an agoraphobe who avoided straight coach roads if he could, and kept to winding lanes. 'My cart being reladen with stone, I was hoisted thereon, (feeling an inward desire of return), and had a worse journey back, as I could scarcely keep my seat.'

Ninety years later a steam engine pulled an endless wire rope in a mile long loop in the Severn tunnel: hookers-on clipped skips to it as it moved by them. They had electric lights and through-tunnel telephones and pumps big enough to suck up rivers.

In Wales the Severn tunnel opens on to a badly faulted coastal plain drained by a small river system, part River Nedern, part River Troggy. For a time the Nedern near its headwaters is bigger than the Nedern-Troggy on the plain: half way down it sinks into a patch of damp mud and rises again under the Roman walls of Caerwent.

In October, 1879, the miners tapped into a fissure which tapped into the Troggy-Nedern and the whole subterranean water system. Wells and rivers dried up as water cascaded into the tunnel, siphoned up the shafts and lipped over their tops. Steam pumps drained the shafts and a diver in a primitive scuba-suit shut steel doors underground to isolate the flood. When they drained the tunnel they saw the cause, the Great Spring. Damming it took a year.

Next year the sea broke through the roof at a place called the Salmon Pool. Navvies plugged the pool's bottom (the tunnel's roof) with bagged clay. Then the Great Spring broke out again and this time, once the tunnel was drained, they led it into a sump, into which it still flows, and from where it is still pumped out. Then a high tide broke over the coastal meadows, flat as cow pats, on the Gwent shore and swamped the tunnel mouth. Men were floated out in boats.

Mechanisation, of a kind, began early. In 1793 Charles Carne, a Cornishman, had a muck-shifting machine at work on the Hereford and Gloucester canal, where it was putting navvies out of work. (They seem to have resisted. 'The cutting across the Ham,' noted the Committee at a meeting in the New Inn in Hereford, 'not being as yet so expeditiously executed as we expected, and as we are convinced it may arise principally from the ignorance of the men employ'd by Clark, who has contracted for the cutting, and their unwillingness to introduce a new mode of Work upon the Canal, we conceive it to be absolutely necessary that Mr Carne should immediately attend himself, and bring with him Ten or Twelve Men from Cornwall used to work the Machines.')

The Machine – a muck-carrier, not a digger – was, essentially, a spindly gantry and a whim-gin. The whim-gin pulled skips along the gantry and simultaneously lifted them clear of the spoil heap. Navvies filled the skips and the increased productivity came from getting rid of the runners-out. (William Morris was taken on specifically to 'fill the Boxes for the Machines' at one end of the Oxenhall tunnel, and in June the committee sacked 'Dyer and the Men employed under him in cutting for the Machine' for slacking.) In 1794 the Machine was improved with cogs.

In April, 1794, the neighbouring Gloucester and Berkeley began building their own proto-type Machine to the designs of Charles Trye, a committeeman, though it seems never to have worked. Mr Carne, meanwhile, tendered for the Gloucester and Berkeley digging and puddling contract. Did he mean to use his Machine to make a killing?

Southey discovered several bits of steam machinery on the Caledonian Canal when his Scottish tour took him there in 1819. Sea-going ships already reached Fort Augustus where massive iron lock gates, carried from Gainsborough in a single ship, lay on the lochside. A steam dredger deepened the channel between Fort Augustus and Loch Ness, raking black matter through water, funnelling billowing black coal smoke through the air. The black matter was shot from a ladder of buckets into rowing barges fitted with hinged bottoms. When the trap doors dropped open and the spoil fell into Loch Ness the barges bobbed about like corked bottles. Steam pumps cleared water from the gravel in the lock beds.

Farther along, a channel through Loch Oich was being deepened by another dredger, *Glengarry*, built of oak from the woods on the lochside. She was powered by machinery designed by Bryan Donkin, the man who began the canning industry when he invented hermetically sealed cans for the Royal Navy.

In 1803 a beam engine winched railway trucks up an inclined plane from the bottom of the basin to a jetty at the London Dock: the very first use, perhaps, of steam-hauled wagons on public works. In 1801 the Directors of the West India Dock Company asked Rennie to try grinding mortar in a pug-mill using a power-drive from a beam engine. The beam slowly rocked on its pins, paused, the engine slowly hissed steam, but it ground mortar so well it was kept grinding away until the dock was ready. (Unlike the steam-powered pile-driver Rennie proposed but never used.)

By the mid-1820s the Norwich-Lowestoft Navigation Company

had a small array of steam engines clanking away in unison as they strove to turn Norwich into a sea-port by driving a ship-channel through what was then unbroken beach at Lowestoft. After sailing through the beach, ships would cross a specially deepened Lake Lothing into the Waveney, then through a ship canal into the Yare. The ship-channel through Lake Lothing was scooped out by a little steam dredger. At the same time the passage through the beach (which is now Lowestoft harbour) was kept dry by dual-purpose beam engines which ground mortar even as they lifted water. William Cole, clerk of works, wrote a poem about it all:

> Here plies the Dredger with its powerful wheel,
> To scour the Lake and load the ready keel;
> Impelled in motion by the engine's force,
> Whose heavy smoke to leeward takes its course;
> And near, a hardy set their stations take,
> To form a coalition with the lake;
> Revolving screw-pumps with incessant whirl,
> The rising water from these workmen hurl.
>
> With a distinct monotony of sound
> By day and night the Engine keeps its round;
> Alternatively the sinking buckets fill,
> Whilst briskly turns the little mortar mill;
> With nice precision works the ponderous beam,
> Proving at once the mighty power of steam.

But mechanisation proper probably really began in the 1830s in North America where skilled navvy-like labour was scarce. When Brassey's Lancashire and Cheshire men reached the Grand Trunk Railrqad in Canada they couldn't have coped without machines. In Britain Brassey used steam cranes for the first time in the 1850s, in London, lifting muck straight out of the Northern Mid-Level sewer into carts.

'Invention has revolutionised the whole industry within the last fifteen years,' John Ward wrote in 1888. 'It was thought that navvies, like compositors, were outside the magic circle of invention, but time has taught us a rude lesson.'

In 1907, Mrs Garnett looked back nearly thirty years to the Denshaw dam. 'I remember one sunshiny morning, watching at the Junction, from the road above twenty-five piecemen. It was a wonderful sight to see the great muscles on their shoulders and arms rise and fall with the precision of machines, and the way that long bank disappeared! To note their bright, good tempered faces, and as they paused, to hear the ring of their cheerful voices.' (Navvies worked silently, save for a peculiar navvy-grunt at every stroke of shovel or pick.) 'The introduction of machinery, while lessening hand labour, has certainly deteriorated the navvies' physique. We seldom see such magnificent specimens of humanity as were common thirty years ago, now on Public Works.'

The navvy's shrinking physique curiously haunted people throughout the century as though it were a national asset or a source of legitimate imperial pride to own big navvies. In 1873 young Lord Brassey, son of Contractor Brassey, went so far as to blame one named year as the cause of the navvy's downfall: 1846, the peak year of the railway mania, the year of the Lancaster and Carlisle, Caledonian, Trent Valley, North Staffs, and Eastern Union.

Labour was so badly needed lookouts were posted along likely roads to stop men on tramp and bribe them into the nearest beershop where they were induced to work on the lookout's section of track. Work went on round the clock. Men worked over a hundred and twenty hours a week. 'Excessively high wages, excessive work, excessive drink, indifferent lodgings caused great demoralisation and gave the death blow to the good old navvy already in decline. He died out a few years after this period.'

Except he didn't. Thirty years after Brassey mourned his passing, Mrs Garnett gloried in his strength at Lindley Wood and the Junction dam. Ward's worry that steam would put navvies out of work didn't materialise either. Public works grew in scale, needing more and more of them. The only difference was they now shared public works with many more trades, particularly black-gang men (black because they were coal-stained and oil-soaked) who looked after the new machinery.

Chapter 8

Sod Huts and Shants

After work, hut-life offered neither peace nor comfort nor softness. You sat on benches hard as your bones, slept in beds hard as your boots. Even the flat transparent bed-bugs inflated black and hard with blood. Bone-aching beds and furniture you shared, cramped with unwashed men smelling of stale drink and earth. At bottom there was a simple question. How did you house, feed, and nightly liquor up gangs of domestically careless men, remote from settled life? In any of four ways: private lodges, sod huts, shants, properly regulated settlements. Worst were the sod huts. 'I never,' said a clergyman on the South Devon line in the 1840s, 'saw anything to be compared to them.'

From Fontburn I went to Middleton and went to work digging a fishpond for some toff. I made my own lodge there. A turf cabin. A fireplace: wood across the top and sods for the roof: planks to sleep on. Sleep rough and in your clothes. I cooked my own tommy, as well, over an fire in a bucket – rabbit, chicken, swedes, taters (all stolen). I never did see the bottom of that bucket.

If they were made when the earth was dry, they weren't too bad. You could always whitewash the inside walls, they were often rent-free, and in summer they nodded pleasantly with grass and flowers. But if the sods were cut wet, the huts steamed. One sod cabin, twenty-seven feet by twelve, on the Edinburgh-Hawick railway in 1846, housed *twenty* people. Another was built on Saturday and occupied on Monday. Its back wall was a bank, sodden with ground water. Water, soaking through the sod walls, trickled into the beds (*and* the contractor charged a rent).

Twenty years later on the Kettering-Manton some sod huts were three-roomed houses as high as a man. In one, children slept in a meat safe – the Brat Cage – slung from the rafters.

But, however big and posh they were, fungus always grew inside in summer (John Ward said he often lay in bed picking mushrooms) and in winter icicles like pick-blades hung from the sod ceilings.

Canals, as always, belong to the prehistory of navvying: little was written about them and there's not too much to speculate about. We don't *know* how canal navvies lived – possibly in a combination of sod huts and private lodges. (Even engineers sometimes lived badly – the Lancaster's man on the Lune lived in a 'Shade' of waste wood which also covered the saw-pit, carpenter's shop, the stores and the kitchen where the engine man slept.) When diggers were wanted on the Market Weighton canal, in 1772, lodgings were one of the things offered to outside navvies. 'The Works are clear of water,' ran an ad. in the *York Courant*, 'and near good Lodgings, and are now going on with great Spirit.'

Landowners wanted the cut but not the cutters. In the late 1770s landlords were vexed by huts along the Stroudwater in which, it seems, diggers squatted. It was the same twenty years later on the Gloucester and Berkeley where people lived in huts just off canal land until the contractors evicted them when they got unruly.

Against that, a few years earlier, the Thames and Severn built navvy lodging-houses which are still there, still in use as pubs. The Tunnel House, on the Thames side of the Cotswolds, was then the New Inn, the top two floors of which were probably dormitories while the ground floor was the taproom and dining hall. Outside was a bowling alley, sheds, stables and the water cistern. On the other side of the hills in the Frome valley (filled to the brim with trees) is the Daneway Arms – once the Bricklayer's Arms – and still gaunt-looking for the Cotswolds.

The Worcester and Birmingham, as well, built rough brick houses for its diggers. December, 1792: 'Resolved That Barracks be erected on the Land by the side of the Lane at the deep Cutting opposite Edgbaston Hall sufficient for 100 Men to lodge in – with a Building for them to eat in. Messrs Morecroft' – the contractors – 'having agreed to furnish beds and other necessaries.' (The W&B were odd in the care they took. They once sent a hagmaster to the offices of *Aris's Gazette* to correct a news item about a navvy's death the paper had just printed. In return their diggers were sober. At the ceremonial opening of the Selly Oak-Gas Street section in 1784 they held 'aloof from Intoxication and the Smallest instance of quarrel' even though they had plenty of ale and a whole roast ox to feast on.)

Whether the shanty system began on canals we don't know, though since it thrived so strongly on the earliest railways it's a possibility. A shant, essentially, was a free-enterprise doss-house/beer-cellar, put up and run for profit either by a ganger or a professional shanty-keeper who did no other work.

Dandy Dick ran away from his home near Harrow and went navvying on the London-Birmingham in 1835. He worked first as a tipper, then as a bucket-steerer at the Watford tunnel where he joined Bullhead's gang with another lad called Kick Daddy. With them were Canting George, Happy Jack, Long Bob, Dusty Tom, Billy Goat, Frying Pan, and Redhead. Most of the tunnel gangs lived in shants around the tunnel shafts, a gang to a shant.

Each had its own old harridan to mend and cook, wash shirts and make beds. On top of that she was the tapster, keeping the keys to the locked beer barrels on a leather belt around her waist. At night the shants rocked to their flimsy foundations with roaring drunks, a seething mob of them, guzzling ale by the gallon. The old women were often beaten up and were usually both scarred and bandaged.

One rainy May morning Dandy Dick visited a friend who lived in a one-room shant over the tunnel. The shant was a composite affair stuck together like Frankenstein's monster from mouldering bits of matter found lying about the site: part brick, part stone, part tile, part tarpaulin, part mud, part wood. Looking after it was an old Lancashire woman called Peg, as battered as the shant itself, gazing at the world through fist-blackened eyes and a bandage which circled her head, chin to crown. George was out, she said. Dandy waited, sitting on a three-legged stool. The only windows, and the only door, were grouped in the middle of one long wall of the oblong room. Kitchen and beer barrels faced each other from the shorter walls at either end. Bunks, ship-like in tiers, lined the long wall opposite door and windows. Because it was a knock-off Sunday, men sprawled on benches by the door, played cards on the earthen floor, or lay on their bunks, drunk or asleep, their heads on their kit, their dogs alongside them. (Hunting, fighting, and poaching dogs, mainly: bulldogs, lurchers, whippets.)

The kitchen was an open space at the end of the hut consisting of a fireplace (a dozen guns on pegs above it), a copper, a shakey table, a dresser, and a double row of lockers which were the navvies' tommy boxes. Each man bought his own tommy. Peg cooked it. Cooking meant boiling and each man's next dinner – meat, veg, pudding if he had any – was wrapped in linen and steeped in the copper. Notched sticks tied to the bundles hung outside the pot. The nicks and notches were a code telling old Peg who owned what.

'Why, sithee, lad,' she told Dandy, 'this bit o' stick's four nicks on 't, well it's Billy Goat's dinner. He's a-bed yond. Now this is that divil's Redhead's, and this is Happy Jack's. Well, thee knowst he's got a bit o' beef. Redhead's nowt but taters. He's a gradely brute is Redhead. And Billy Goat's got a pun or so o' bacon and a cabbage. Now, thee sees, I've a matter o' twenty dinners or so to bile every day, which I biles in nets, and if I dinna fix 'em i' this road, I sud ha' niver tell where to find 'em, and then there'd be sich as row as niver yet was heard on.'

Red Whipper came in at that moment with a young hare. 'Get it ready and put it in along of the rest,' he growled at old Peg, 'and look sharp or thee's head may be broken.'

Professional shanty-keepers were always with the navvy (*at Lunedale I lodged with Pincher Paine. He didn't work. He had forty lodgers in that old shant. Double beds, too*) though most of them were slowly transposed into near-replicas of themselves by working navvies, generally gangers, who took over as tenant-landlords in contractor-owned huts. The ganger's wife, helped by a skivvy, now did the washing, cooking, and bed-making, as well as the money-making from the sale of booze. At the same time the huts, and the hut-life, got better.

Thirty years after Dandy Dick, Daniel Barrett was chaplain on the Kettering-Manton line. There, some of the huts were still shakey home-made shacks, others were piled turves, but the rest were well-appointed, well-run, timber-built dwellings as good (says Barrett) as an officer's quarters on manoeuvres. Some were black with gas-tar, some were white with whitewash, most had red-brick chimneys. Three rooms were common: a central living room, a dormitory wing for lodgers, a private bedroom for the landlord and his family. Front and back doors were porched. Inside, the walls were papered with clippings from the *Police News*, with funeral cards, with patchworks of swatches from paper-hangers' pattern books, and with cartoons from the *Gospeller* and the *British Workman*. Boots swung from rafters. Brick floors were strewn with silver sand. Men usually washed out of doors, at the back, drying themselves on roller towels. They slept, two to a bed, on straw mattresses with their kit swinging on beams over their heads.

The landlady slept with the landlord in a big iron-bound bed close to her ale kegs in her own private bedroom with her chest of drawers, looking-glass, ewer and earthenware basin. Stuffed birds served as ornaments: live hens and pigs as food. Some owned clocks, sewing machines and violins. Some kept vegetable gardens. Nameplates gave many of the huts their own individuality and dignity: The Terrace, The Hermitage, The West End, Rose Cottage.

At the Basingstoke and Woking widening I lodged with Scotty Jack Caswell, a loco driver, and his missus near Pirbright.

You had to get washed out of doors on a bench, break the ice and get water from a tub. I never knowed no private wash houses on the railways, any road. I didn't like it, either, but being tough you dursen't say anything. They were a rough lot of navvies who followed the railways. You had to be a savage, any how, to put up with the conditions. Many men used to kip out in sod shants they'd built. Horrid life.

There were about ten, twelve of use at Scotty Jack's. The landlady cooked all your tommy but you had to bring your own, though. That's right – I had a lot of bacon and stuff when I got locked up for being drunk. I never heard of her having any board-lodgers, any how.

From Lunedale, I walked to Fontburn and went to work on the reservoir. I was feeding the pug mill there – putting clay into a machine which chopped it with knives and shot it into wagons. First lodge I had there I slept two to a bed with an old navvy who got into bed with his boots on. I soon shifted that lodge. I thought of getting married there to Sarah, a skivvy in the hut.

So I went away to Bellingham and on to Haltwhistle and on to the Castle Carrock reservoir. All I did there was watch the blondin to see it was going all right. Sixpence an hour just seeing the thing kept running. It carried ballast from the quarry to the crusher for the concrete. I never stopped to see the dam. Just the gutter. We lodged forty to a hut, but in single beds.

So I jacked again and went to Whitehouse in Northumberland, and went to work on the reservoir there. Decent place that was. Nice place. I lodged at Old Davy Brown's. You had to sleep two to a bed so I come out and went over to Cumberland Jack's. A hell of a good lodge that was. Good food, too.

Cumberland's place, like Scotty Jack's, was the standard navvy hut, linear descendant of Dandy Dick's shant: even the bungalows of the model villages were only better-class copies.

Model villages began at Lindley Wood where the Mission began and where order was imposed by Leeds Corporation. Lindley Wood, unusually, was a brick-built settlement: brick huts, brick school, brick shant.[1] Only the church on the hill among the trees was of wood, a plain square building, with an open belfry on its gable end, whitewashed inside, heated by a swag-bellied stove. The brick huts, even more unusually, had half a second storey. Half a ceiling gave them half a loft, leaving the rest of the space open to the rafters. In some, lodgers slept in a ground floor dormitory: in others they climbed the ladder at night into the half loft.

Lewis Evans, the Mission's founder, visited a dying girl in one of them. 'The daughter of a navvy, and the wife of a navvy, a girl of about twenty, with a face to which long sickness has brought more beauty than it would have had in strong health – a tender fragile being, seeming altogether out of place amid these rough surroundings. Her sufferings are very great, terribly aggravated by the foul air, coarse food, and rough though kind nursing. Born in a navvy's hut, wandering all her life from place to place with her parents, surrounded always by sights and sounds of evil, what could she know of good? Her mother could teach nothing but the same poor miserable creed she held herself, of which the chief tenet was, that this world was so bad, so hard and rough, so toilsome, that no change could well be for the worse.'

Thomas Walker, rare perhaps unique as a contractor willing to impose some comfort on his navvies, built one of the few navvy settlements which is still lived in – Sudbrook, at the Gwent end of the Severn tunnel.[2] When Walker took over the tunnel, Sudbrook (not then so named) was only a row of cottages, a stump of ruined church, and the earthworks of an old fort. He left a village of houses and semi-detached 'villas'. Even his hospital is now an apartment block called The Walker Flats.

He built temporary but impressive villages on the Manchester Ship Canal, particularly at Eastham where the Mersey forms a broad bight like a bladder filled twice daily with tide and pollution.

1 As well as its original meaning, shant by now also meant a settlement's pub or drinking shop.

2 Maintenance staff still live in the pre-fabricated huts built at Haweswater in the late 1920s. When last heard of, the navvy huts in the Ewden Valley near Sheffield were being demolished because they were fire hazards.

'The cottages or huts adjoining the Eastham Lane,' said the *Ship Canal News*, 'have now very prettily laid out gardens. It was a source of amusement to the residents to hear such remarks as "I had no idea they were so comfortable" from the passers-by, as if navvies were different from the rest of the human family.'

Before it became a motorway interlacing high-rise flats, Birmingham was a forward-looking city which in the 1890s built, unprompted, a model navvy village for people on the Elan Valley dams in Mid-Wales. It stood (its better built successor stands) on the River Elan's south bank, reachable only by a single suspension bridge. At one end the Elan watered the village through its own waterworks: at the other it flushed away human waste through the village's own sewage works. Elan, too, had its own self-manned fire brigade with fire engines and station, and fire hydrants in the streets. Fire buckets hung from every house front.

It was laid in streets of wooden huts, roofed with tarred and sanded felt. Outside they were clad in weatherboarding: inside, with matchboard. There were one-family huts and huts for lodgers where each man had his own cubicle and locker. There were bath and wash houses, a free library, a gym, a public reading room, a school, churches. For a penny a week you could join the Public Recreation Room where there was a snack bar, games, and newspapers.

Needless to say, the canteen – the shant – was closely regulated, too. It opened for four hours a day and even then you could drink only six pints there. They sold Allsopp's single-X beer and bottled Bass, but allowed no women, singing, juggling, reciting, gambling, dicing, card playing, dominoes, marbles, shove penny, or draughts. No food. The idea was copied from Lindley Wood where the shant had been run by, and for, the City of Leeds. (In turn Elan was copied on the Grizedale dam in the Forest of Bowland.)

Immediately across the bridge over the Elan on the flat ground to the right above the river was the accident hospital where Thomas Pugh was carried to die in September, 1898, after accidentally shooting himself with the pistol he was repairing in the blacksmith's shop. The fever hospital was in the trees further along the hill. The Elan's a noisy beck, white-water washing moss-grown rocks. Oaks and larches grow along its banks, like a grey haze in winter.

The village was policed by its own inspector, constable, and bridge janitor whose job it was to keep strange navvies out – trippers and sightseers were free to cross. Only uninspected navvies were barred. On the north bank was an overnight holding hut where incoming navvies were kept for cleaning, checking and disinfecting

So I went away from Lunedale to York with Geordie Woodman. We had a shilling between us and went into a lodging house, a four-penny padding can. Twopence for bacon, a penny for bread, ha'penny for sugar and the rest on 'bacca. We went to Moltby. No work. We went to Bamford and stopped at a navvy hut. Got to Derwent the next day.

There was a navvy settlement at Birchinlee and they wouldn't let navvies in until they'd been perfumigated in case they were carrying lice. I worked in the concrete gang on the lower dam and lodged with Waxie Bean, a Northampton.

That was a good job. Direct labour jobs were always best, not like these private enterprise gangsters. It was a proper little town at Birchinlee. Well, they called it Tin Town, anyhow. Two or three shops. One big grocery shop. A baker's. Barber shop. Baths, as well. You never got that out of private contractors. They were robbers.

The robbers, however, *were* under attack.

As late as 1906 there were no proper overnight huts at all on the Water Orton-Kingsbury line even though it's only a few miles from Birmingham city centre. As it happened, the railway passed close to Hams Hall, stately home of Lord Norton. When he heard what was happening he sent Navvy Smith, the missionary in Birmingham, to see the contractors, offering to share the costs of building proper huts. When they said no, he wrote to John Burns, President of the Local Government Board, who sent Dr Reginald Ferrar to find out what was going on. As a result Navvy Smith found himself one Friday midnight in September escorting Ferrar along the track, peering into tumbledown barns and mud hovels roofed with corrugated iron, flashing a bull's eye lantern on people who had spent the day bent-backed shovelling damp earth and who now lay stiff and chilled on stale dung and old hay.

In Surrey around this time navvies were building the Brooklands motor racing track, an oval concrete bowl with sloping sides like a slightly flattened fairground wall-of-death. The contractors built no huts so many navvies slept untidily rough in the gorse, thus upsetting the well-to-do of Weybridge. The Government asked Dr Ferrar to look into it. Until they were set on fire by the well-to-do of Weybridge, he found, the men had lived in home-made shants of fir boughs called Firwood Avenue and the Hotel Cecil. It was as though all Weybridge wanted of the navvy was his work: extract of navvy, perhaps, a distilled essence, sanitised by being disembodied but, Ariel-like, still capable of heavy labour.

Neither Norton nor Ferrar seemed to get anywhere at the time. Norton was ignored, Ferrar's report was filed. Even John Ward, now an MP, only got fobbed when he spoke about navvies in the House. 'I beg to ask the President of the Board of Trade whether he'll consider the advisability of framing a Standing Order making it compulsory upon the promoters of Bills for Public Works (such as canals, docks, railways) to make provision for suitable and sanitary house accommodation for the workmen and their families.'

'I'm afraid that my Department have no power to alter the Standing Orders,' Lloyd George, for the Board of Trade, blandly fobbed him off.

But, for all the stalling, something was happening and in 1911 the Speaker suddenly asked the House to consent to a new Standing Order. 'It amounts to a great public Act of Parliament,' John Ward, jubilant, exaggerated. In future, Parliamentary Committees examining Public Works Bills had to be satisfied the men would be properly housed. If not, and if the works were more than three miles from a town or village, they could order the contractors to erect proper huts. 'Even if no housing reformers are returned at a future great election,' Ward, still jubilant, went on, 'at least the influence of this Session will be permanent.'

But in 1922 he was still questioning the Minister of Health about the poorness of navvy housing, at the Ashford Common reservoir in Middlesex. 'If my hon. and gallant friend will read my statement he'll find that a great deal's been done,' he was fobbed off.

Chapter 9

Cat-Eating-Scan and Half-Ear Slen

There were ten, twelve of us at Scotty Jack's on the Basingstoke-Woking widening. Wiltshire Jumper, he was there. He could do the cobbler's dance, same as these Russians do, half sitting on the floor. When he'd done the dance, he'd jump up and hit his heels on the table, bang, bang. I think that's how he got his name – not from the jumper drills. He was a railway navvy.

Smallbeer Scan, he was there. Crowbar Nobby. Crowbar used to say if he had no beer his mouth was no good to him and he used to sew it up. He'd ask the landlady for needle and thread and sew his mouth up. It was an easy thing to do to put the needle through once the holes were there – same as earrings. Daft, silly sort of bloke. He had whiskers and all.

Billy Butler, he was there, rope running for Scotty Jack. (A rope runner was the same as a guard, only it was on a muck train.) He had a moustosh, too. We all had moustoshes before the War. Most everybody had a moustosh, little or much. It was for the flu' or something. If you keep shaving your upper lip it sticks out like a scrubbing brush.

Another time, the Horse Guards were camped at Pirbright, and it was a wet day. All the navvies went into this big marquee the soldiers had. Beer was three ha'pence a pint then. We used to buy a gallon at a time. A great big can of the stuff. Well, Jimmy Fingers challenged these here soldiers at tug o' war. Jimmy goes back into the tent. He calls his team out. 'Steamer Ike, Hydraulic Punch, Steam Navvy Nobby.'

'Here,' says this old sergeant, 'we thought we was going to pull men, not a lot of machines.'

The navvies won, and all. He gave Jimmy Fingers a bucket of beer. You could wash your head in it.

Another time at the Llangyfellach tunnel Lincoln Tom put a drill through his foot. He took his boots off and the ganger-feller says to him: 'Why don't you take your socks off, Lincoln?'

'They are off,' he says. 'I never put them on.'

You've never seen such a thing in your life. His feet was so black you couldn't tell if he had his socks on or not. He had toenails on him as long as his fingers. He'd put the drill right through his foot and all, but he was back at work in no time.

When I jacked at Patricroft I went down to Hayfield in Derbyshire. When you started at Hayfield you had to work three shifts and a quarter. Start at six o'clock in the morning, work all day, all night until nine o'clock the next morning. Go home, start work the next morning at six. You were only getting bare time, and all. But where I was working you worked six to six: one week nights, one week days. Double-shifted, we were.

I was filling skips, getting out the foundations of the filter house. Muck dam. It's under the High Peak. I lodged there with old Mother Adams. Proper navvy people they were. They had two relatives on the stage: the Stoke Sisters. Violin players. Funny how a rough family like that married some decent people. She used to drink like mad, swear like a trooper, smoke an old clay gum-bucket pipe. Good hearted, though.

They had two sons. Punch and Jack. Punch got shipwrecked – never was right in his head after that. Then there was Min, a silly, fat bugger. Then there was Edie. She married a decent feller as well. I met them at Ewden after the First War.

For over half a century the Navvy Mission published its *Quarterly Letter* exhorting navvies to behave themselves. Surviving copies are bound in volumes in the church of St Katherine Cree, City of London. Inside the church a quiet coolness is made colder-seeming by the thick-walled silence. The *Letters* themselves have time-crackled edges, crumbling a little, brown and sorrowful. In them we hear the small stifled cries of the dead. Mrs Thomas begs her daughter Mrs C Williams (Pupe) to write her at once. Will Bonny Hooper come or send for his little girl (13) now destitute. Little Darkie, miner (26), black hair and eyes, scar on nose, send at once to your wife, left destitute with three children. Shop Bill please send the week's board you owe Mrs Lecks and also the money she was kind enough to lend you to buy a pair of boots, but which you sloped off with. Beware of Quiet George, a big man, dirty in his habits, who sloped off with his week's rent. Walter Banks is requested to write at once to Mrs Garnett, Ripon, She trusted him and doesn't think he means to cheat her. Where is Hunky Dory who worked at Avonmouth Dock? Will the man, who, after receiving food and shelter, stole a new shirt from the Navvies' Home, Charlton Mackrell, Somerset, kindly return it to Mr Billing, or else apply for a needle and cotton to mend it with.

New Town Jack died alone at the Junction dam. His friends were in Wales though he didn't know where. 'One thing has struck me more than all besides, that the life of a navvy is a very lonely one,' says the recorded voice of one dead man, speaking to us for the sole and only time.

In the cool muffled quietness of the church the voices call, small with time, saying their single sentences and dying into an endless silence like an ache of deafness. If there were more pages, you think, you would hear more. As it is even the voices of the editors, hoarse with unheeded admonition, are brief and snatched. Navvies' voices are quiet and truncated, teased out of the past's fabric. Imagination, like a computer, enhances what was the background clangour of their lives into faint almost unheard noises in the head.

Small worries, small woes, small people. They mattered little then: they matter not at all now. Still, they leave the sadness of people who suffered and whose sufferings are now beyond help. How can you comfort the dead, when the grave is such a chasm?

1884: Mrs Plum, homely as a hearth rug, wrote with all the third-person formality of a Duchess from the mud of the Thornton Moor dam. 'Eliza Johnson, wife of Lincolnshire Bill Johnson, will greatly oblige by sending her recipe for eye-wash to Mrs Plum, Thornton Moor, Bradford.'

Sinker sank his mates' sick club money in booze.

1885: Devil Driving George, a youth and a Salvationist, eloped with his raddled, fat, middle-aged landlady and her husband's clothes. 'This George has never been one of our members,' says the CEU, 'and never will be: we want no such.'

1886: Cranky York, a contrary man, stole money from a sick gathering on the Thirlmere pipe track. Darkie May was sacked at Dunford Bridge for indecent behaviour with his landlady's little daughter in her calf length boots, calf-length frock, and thigh length pinafore.

1887: Ginger Charlie – Black Enoch's mate – stole Peg Legged Devon's kit, slyly, in Birkenhead. Smoker ran away from Silloth docks and left his wife and family to face the workhouse.

1888: One-eyed Conro conned J Gardiner by forging the signature of Three-Fingered Jack, who had a broken leg at Nunhead, south London.

All landladies with young daughters were warned on no account to give Black Lank a lodge.

Mrs Broughton, Rishworth Moor dam, asked John Pitts to give her the money he got when he sold her mangle on the q.t.

Cat-Eating Scan ran away from Bere Alston with Thomas Harris's wife and baby. Mrs Harris rifled the eldest child's piggy bank. Harris didn't want his wife back, just his baby daughter. 'She took against the rest of them, and no doubt but what she'll serve it the same as it gets older. The seven I have got are getting on well, thank God.'

1889: 'Everyone to beware of Thick Lipped Blondin, who lodged with Mrs Herbert, hut keeper, Bere Ferris, and took away her best shawl; she thinks it very hard, as she has six little children, and has to work hard to get a living. (Mrs Herbert sends this.)

All young women and girls were warned: 'Beware of a married man, a make-shift navvy and not fit to walk in a navvy's shoes, known as Curly, late rope runner and engine cleaner at Skipton. He goes as a single chap, and has cruelly wronged a young woman at Skipton.'

1890: Coal, a handy man (he could make anything) abandoned his wife and children in Goole. Coal also liked to preach. He preached a lot in Goole. 'He had better now *act up to it*,' said Mrs Garnett, coldly.

1891: a strong able-bodied ganger ran away with the sick club money from the Saxby and Bourne railway. He was well to be made out, red-faced and splay-legged as he was. *And* he had a good position with a permanent wage. ('Don't go on the Saxby and Bourne Railway, Lincolnshire,' advised the Navvies' Union. 'Wages are low, lodgings are scarce, and the job is generally not up to much yet. There are plenty of "yaller boys" knocking about!')

1892: 'To inform Mrs F Frances, better known as Mrs Johnson, that her husband is dead, who she wanted to put in Preston Workhouse. His son wrote to her from Delph, but the letter came back "not found". She is supposed to be living on the Pipe

Track, with Sand Washing George, if so she can now marry him, and we hope she won't treat him the same if he falls ill, nor bury him with his boots on.'

1893: High Back Dick, otherwise Snotty Nose Dick, sloped his landlady at the Blagdon dam.

1894: Squeezem and Cambridge Tom robbed their landlord's son of his pet rabbit on the Tottenham and Forest Gate. Squeezem repented, later.

1896: Bill Tar Pot sloped his landlady at the Rishworth dam and Mrs Garnett warned everybody (mates *and* landladies) to beware of Half-Ear Slen who enticed a woman from her husband and children on the Great Central. 'For shame on such rubbish, as call themselves men! Mates! cry shame on him if any of you see him, he is well to be picked out, he has a high back, crooked nose and bandy legs.'

1897: Toothless Devon, with a plastic, good for girning face and a rich west country burr, left his family to the care of the Wirral workhouse.

Mrs Pope would pay a pound to anyone who could prove her husband had bigamously married his housekeeper.

1898: Ginger Suffolk, rather short and stout, very fair, rather dark blue eyes, with the word love tattooed on his left arm, and with a speech impediment, left his wife at Christmas. She had a baby to look after and wanted to hear from him.

George Cander sent his little girl Mary to the Home for Waifs and Strays, promising to pay for her keep. But he didn't.

Pincher King wrote home from Melbourne. He was now a sub-inspector of sewers and his head-gaffer was Bob Johnson, late walking ganger[1] on the Long Drag. Pincher had been a nipper at Lindley Wood where he lodged with Mrs Leworthy next to the store with One Thumb Bob, Pretty Dick Draw, Snuffy Charlie and Cockney. He left for Australia with Gloucester Bill and Nobby Jones when the Eccup dam was starting (he was on the Long Drag himself, for a time). He was married, but he kept in touch with the few navvies in Melbourne – Teetotal Devon and

1 Walking ganger – a kind of general foreman, 'walking' because he walked about and did no work.

1. Navvies, the perpetual outsiders

2. Non-navvy drink seller, Manchester Ship Canal, 1880s

3. Navvy woman, 1890s

4. Navvy woman, 1890s

5. Navvies at the Crystal Palace, Sydenham, 1853.
Note the metal tea bottles by their feet and the straw pantry between the knees of the man on the right.

6. Nipper with navvies outside tommy cabin, 1890s

7. Navvies, 1890s

8.

9. On average four men died on public works every day: eight were
badly hurt.
Navvy gang, 1890s.

10. More men became navvies than were born navvies.
Navvy children, 1890s.

11. Nippers on the Great Central, 1890s. The older boy holding the
half-chewed sprag is probably a tipper. The younger boys are probably
the real spraggers.

12. Tipper and younger lad, Great Central, 1890s

13. Wagon-fillers, Manchester Ship Canal, 1880s

14. Barrow-runs, Tring Cutting, London-Birmingham, 1830s

15. Barrow-run, Manchester Ship Canal, 1880s

16. Tipping, London-Birmingham, 1830s

17. Tipping, Great Central, 1890s

18. Intake Bank, Carlisle-Settle, 1870s

19. A whim-gin

20. Islington Tunnel, Regent's Canal

21. Black gang, Manchester Ship Canal, 1880s

22. Navvies, 1890s

23. Blea Moor and the Long Drag, 1870s

24. Navvies re-made old landscapes. Hole on the Great Central, 1890s

Jimmy Dean, among them, though he particularly wanted to hear from Young Steamer Jack. Nobby Jones went to Tasmania when the banks on the New South Wales coalfield went broke.

Joe Leworthy was last heard of in 1906, unloading stores at the Canadian Pacific's Winnipeg workshops. (A crane hurt another Leworthy in 1901 at the Hisehope dam, which now holds back a little lake like a scalene triangle, the dam-side longer than the shore-sides, on the Durham moors.)

1899: Peggy (he had a cork leg), a swarthy man, was asked to remember his landlady was a widow and couldn't afford to lose the money he owed her.

Patsy Bryan, a middle-aged man, eloped with a teenage girl from Dagenham Dock. A disgraceful scamp, said Mrs Garnett. His mates said if they caught him he'd get what he didn't want but did deserve.

1900: White Cockney's wife would forgive him if he gave up his wicked life with another woman. And signed the pledge. And made her a home.

Slop-making Ben, who carried his kit in a sugar bag, was mugged while on tramp near Sheffield. He lost his shirts, coat, and a pair of boots.

1901: Lizzie Mottershead, nearly six foot tall, living with Mad King, would hear something to her advantage if she got in touch with her mother.

1903: H Edgington warned his mates against Slen Jim at the Thornton Heath widening. 'First he stole ten shillings, then the landlady's purse, hid the money under the dog kennel, was bowled out and confessed. A regular thief, mates. Spot him, and beware.'

W Burgoyne warned against a scoundrel called John Evans. 'He got up at 1 a.m. *to rob his bedmate of £5.10s.* that he had worked hard for, and sloped his landlady of twelve shillings lodging money. Is believed to have gone to Cray Waterworks. *Look out for him, lads,* and hunt him off any works.' In Mrs Garnett's opinion he was nothing but a disgusting thief.

Mrs G. was doubtful of a debt incurred by Gentleman Jimmy Drew, repayable at the Tanners' Arms, Grigglestone. Was it a drinking score?

Nottingham Rags sloped his landlady. 'Now, Rags,' advised

Mrs G., 'pay up and be respected.'

1904: Centrifugal hob-nailed away from Mrs Whitfield's cookhouse, a pair of stolen bluchers in his hand. Charles Jones denounced Gravesend Nobby alias Nobby Burton alias Nobby Melton, a ganger on the Dearne Valley railway. 'This rascal has to my knowledge broken up several homes and taken their wives away from their husbands, homes and families, Yours faithfully, Charles Jones.'

'What *fools* the wicked women are who go away and live *in adultery*,' said Mrs Garnett. '*What fools!*'

Comic abandoned his family to the workhouse.

1906: Catherine Charlotte Barnes was a tall, dark-haired, 37-year old woman, tattooed with a hand shaking a hand on her right arm. She was last seen in mourning, with a younger man, shorter than herself, called Lightning, a walking ganger, crane man, or oily waste man, with a fair drooping moustache.

1910: Bill Archer drank a full week's wages at the Chew Valley dam. He mooched more money and vanished.

1911: Bill Heards, at Newport docks, sloped his landlady and several lodgers. 'Landladies, make this black gang man pay before he climbs,' urged Mrs Garnett.

In 1905 Mrs Ottaway was living in Green Street, Derby. 'Having just lost my husband, a thorough old tunnel miner and drainage man, I should like it put in Navvy Letter that some men from Derby Sewerage promised to come to act as bearers, and carry him to his grave, and not one turned up, causing me greater sorrow and expense, and I had no one. I had a carriage for them to pay for.'

Mrs Ottaway spoke for them all. 'I am as I am,' she said, 'and can't be no ammer.'

Chapter 10

Impact

'After every pay the streets were disfigured by loathsome pools of blood,' said the anonymous author of *Life or Death*, a schoolgirl when the London-Birmingham was built. 'More than once we have seen men lying, literally *dead* drunk under the market house, an old-fashioned edifice raised on pillars, with the pigs walking over them, themselves fitter in all respects for a sty than any human habitation. Hapless toads and frogs, even little kittens, were literally torn in pieces.'

'Certainly no men in all the world,' said Mrs Garnett, 'so improve their country as Navvies do England. Their work will last for ages, and if the world remains so long, people will come hundreds of years hence to look at and to wonder at what they have done.'

Navvies it was realised, even at the time, re-made old landscapes and re-shaped old societies. Most people approved (fewer, perhaps, approved of the new landscapes) but hardly anyone approved of the sub-human navvy himself:

> Rattle his bones over the stones
> He's only an old navvy who nobody owns.

He was a kind of un-man with earth in his pores, in muck-caked moleskin, lowering and aloof at the same time, always a by-stander, never belonging to the society he helped alter.

He had a double impact: a purely contemporary one on the terrified people around him and a longer-lasting one, most obvious to anyone who rides a railway train or fills a kettle from a tap. The odd thing was so much fuss was made over, and so many changes were made by, few of them.

Between 1760 and 1830 just over four thousand miles of canal were made, though canal-making itself peaked in the 1790s (1792–3, more exactly) when over sixty waterways were authorised, started, or finished – perhaps a thousand miles in ten years, a hundred miles a twelvemonth, on average.

In the 1790s it was supposed only twenty-five men were needed to dig a mile of canal in a year, although six hundred had laboured in the Harecastle tunnel alone; a hundred dug the approach cutting to the Greywell tunnel in 1788; a hundred and twenty-seven crowded into a single coffer dam at the Lune aqueduct in 1794; and three thousand shifted muck on the Grand Junction in December 1794, the year when the Worcester-Birmingham swore they'd hire no more than four hundred and twenty men on the three mile cut between Gas Street and Selly Oak.

Against that there seems to have been no more than eighty men on the whole of the Chester canal in May, 1773, while on many works only short sections at a time were cut by gangs of between twenty and forty men.

Canals companies even tried to stop their cutters moving on. In 1767 the Staffs and Worcester published lists of runaways in the Birmingham papers. 'Johnathan Melloday of a brown complexion and squints with an eye and is about 5 ft 5 ins. John Catharall was 'Of a dark complexion, Pockmark'd, and has been a drummer 5 ft 7 ins.' Anybody who hired them would be sued. In May 1773 the Chesterfield committee ordered: 'That if any workmen shall run away and shall be brought back by Mr Varley, or any other person employed by him, that the expenses incurred thereby be deducted out of such Workmen's wages.' In July 1794, Philip Russell, Richard Glover and a navvy known only as Old Toby absconded from the Hereford and Gloucester and took work with William Thornbury, tree felling and cutting on the Gloucester and Berkeley. Within a week the Hereford and Gloucester invoked their agreement with the G&B not to hire each other's people and Thornbury was told to sack them. In August, 1796, Gentleman Dick Jones, a contractor in the Netherton tunnel, was told to stop poaching men from the Worcester and Birmingham – it raised wages.

How effective it was is hard to say, but obviously there was no pool of tramp navvies working a few hours and a quarter of a day there as there was at the end of the next century.

If we take the 1790s, accept a hundred miles of canal were dug each year, accept the Worcester and Birmingham's hundred and forty men a mile as being average, accept that the contractor probably needed half as many men again because of drunken absenteeism, add ten per cent for accidents, and accept that most were real navvies and not farm labourers, it is still hard to see how there could have been more than 20,000 to 25,000 professional canal diggers at any one time. By 1830 they may have dwindled to less than 10,000, though probably still more than 5,000 (in July 1827, sixteen hundred men were at work on the northern third of the Birmingham and Liverpool Junction, alone).

Roughly 50,000 men navvied on the first railways in the 1830s. By 1846, 200,000 men were building railways and at least half must have been navv'es or labourers doing navvy-like work. In 1875 the Navvy Mission calculated there were around 40,000 navvymen out of a 60,000 navvy population, though probably those figures were too low: only fourteen years later they were talking of 90,000 navvy people all told. By the early twentieth century the Government itself thought there were between 100,000 and 120,000 navvies in the country. In 1909 the Royal Commission on the Poor Law put it as high as 170,000. (Not all worked at once. The Local Government Board once calculated a contractor needed a hundred navvies on his books to make sure he had fifty at work. The problem was subbing: men worked a couple of days, subbed their pay, got drunk.)

Wherever they went they impacted on unspoilt innocent landscapes like elemental forces, crashing out of a stillness, a hush, caused by expectation of their coming, bursting out like a train from a tunnel, all steam and fire, ferocity and danger. Once the early lines were laid, navvies came spilling in on the railways already built by their own people, cluttering up country railway stations (harassing rustic station masters), choking the highways with bird cages and baggage, prams, clocks, frying pans and bedsteads.

Their impact on a tranquil rural population usually enlivened it, frequently debauched it, and always scandalised the ruling gentry. 'The females were corrupted, many of them,' said a contractor of the mid-Northamptonshire villages in the 1830s, 'and went away with the men, and lived amongst them in habits that civilised language will scarcely allow a description of.'

The 1846 Committee was particularly worried. What if the marauding habits of the navvy lingered on, endemically, and damaged forever the docility of the rustic labourer? The Deputy Clerk of the Peace for Dumfriesshire already despaired for the moral health of the community.

'In what way?' asked the Committee.

'In the drunkenness of the little boys and the going together of men and women to live without marriage.' Abandoned mistresses, he almost implied, littered the parish welfare system. Local lads were debauched by drinking, swearing, fighting, and tobacco: boys, said the Deputy, aghast, of twelve and fourteen. *And* they earned ten shillings a week carrying blunted picks to the blacksmith's shop for sharpening.

And the Queen's peace? 'On pay days,' replied the Deputy, 'I should say the place is quite uninhabitable.'

Poaching bothered landowners just as much. Navvies were good at it (best in the world, they boasted) and since they roamed about in gangs nobody dared catch them.

When he first went to Blisworth on the London-Birmingham, Robert Rawlinson, the contractor, counted fifty hares in a single walk across Sir William Wake's estate. The day the first train ran, Sir William gave him a brace of partridge. 'I'd have brought you a hare,' said the disconsolate Sir William, 'but I don't believe I have one on my estate.'

'There isn't above one,' a navvy later told Rawlinson, 'and we'll have that this week.'

In 1881 Gaffer Brown, a navvy on Swansea Docks, was shot dead while poaching in South Wales. Next year a Mr Magniac was disturbed by the amount of navvy poaching in Bedfordshire. Bands of men with guns and dogs openly poached game, and assaulted the clergy. (He did admit the men lived badly, camped as they were by a swamp of slimy green water.)

At the same time navvies were money to rough country publicans and smarming shopkeepers. A Northamptonshire butcher, on the London-Birmingham, expected to sell the navvies thirty sheep, at twenty shillings a carcase profit, and a couple of bullocks every Saturday. Navvies complained he added bones as make-weights, but the other country butchers were so scared of them he'd cornered the entire navvy meat market.

In the 1870s the Rev Daniel Barrett was on the Kettering and Manton railway when the navvies arrived. Single navvies came on foot, navvies with belongings on every train, swarming into a string of instant shanty towns along the whole line. Some huts were sod. Some brick. Most were of wood. There were settlements opposite Chater viaduct, at Wing crossroads, on Glaston hillside. A settlement called Cyprus was on Seaton Hill. Another was in the Welland valley where the big viaduct crosses into the ironstone hills of Rutland. There were settlements near Gretton, at Penn Green,

Thorny Lane, Harper's Brook and Rushton crossroads.

Behind the navvies came the tradesmen, raising prices as they went, in drays and dog carts, pushing hand barrows: fishmongers, likeness-makers, book hawkers, packmen, cheapjacks, hucksters, milkmen, shoemakers, tailors. In a year the four thousand navvy people who lived there ate three thousand sheep, fifteen hundred pigs and six hundred oxen.

The impact of what the navvies did, the work they left behind, was always more appreciated than the navvy, yet in the bad weather of 1881 a few members of the Hope, near Oldham, Juvenile Christian Temperance Society rode through snowdrifts in a large wagonette to entertain navvies at the Denshaw dam, the way dimly lit by snowlight shining off the moors as they rounded the bend from Denshaw village. Joseph Burgess wrote – and read aloud – a poem:

> They are the Denshaw navvy boys
> and I extol them thus
> Because our town great good enjoys
> Such men have wrought for us.
>
> If you have ever fetched a burn
> from an asthmatic pump
> And waited, starving, for your turn
> till nearly stiff with cramp,
>
> If you with water on your head
> and ice beneath your feet
> In making an incautious tread
> have fallen in the street
>
> If you've been drenched from top to toe –
> a not uncommon plight –
> You'll feel with me how much we owe
> The men we've met tonight.

But it was easy to enthuse about dams: they were small and hidden, scarring only small landscapes, their benefits obvious at the turn of a tap. The railway was harder to like and the Kendal and Windermere, in particular, upset Wordsworth:

> Is there no nook of English ground, he asked, secure
> From rash assault?

'Now, every fool in Buxton can be in Bakewell in half an hour,' said Ruskin, 'and every fool in Bakewell in Buxton.'

But railway speculators and navvies between them ruined things for many a man more humble than Ruskin or innocent than Wordsworth. The Rev Armstrong's family bought a cottage in Southall not long before the Great Western went there, while he was still in frocks. He had his own garden to cultivate, a gate to swing on, a canal to fish in in all innocence. Then came the navvies like corruption.

'The railway spread dissatisfaction and immorality among the poor,' said the Rev Armstrong, 'the place being inundated with worthless and overpaid navigators ("navvies").'

'The rusticity of the village gave place to a London-out-of-town character,' he went on, getting closer to what really upset him. 'Moss-grown cottages retired before new ones with bright red tiles, picturesque hedgerows were succeeded by prim iron railings, and the village inn, once a pretty cottage with a swinging sign, is transmogrified to the "Railway Tavern" with an intimation gaudily set forth that "London porter" and other luxuries hitherto unknown to the aborigines were to be procured within.'

Around the same time, Dickens saw the London-Birmingham's impact on Euston and Camden Town quite differently. The works themselves were like an unnatural disaster area; a primeval place, pre-fern forests, pre-fishes, still hot and steaming; there were mouldering rusty ponds, crazy shored up houses and lifeless heaps of lumpy earth. Only a few speculators nosed about the site. One or two streets had been half-started in the muck and ashes but what buildings there were – a pub, eating house, lodging houses – were there to exploit the navvy. For the rest there were: 'frowsy fields, and cow houses, and dung-hills, and dust heaps, and ditches, and gardens, and summerhouses, and carpet-beating grounds, at the very door of the Railway. Little tumuli of oyster shells in the oyster season, and of lobster shells in the lobster season, and of broken crockery and faded cabbage leaves in all seasons.'

But soon it too was as transmogrified as the Rev Armstrong's Southall, though not into something base and secondhand, but into stuccoed prosperity and fat warehousing. The railway ruled all. Even clocks kept railway time. What had been rotten and decayed was now alive and thriving. Even Members of Parliament dimly understood something important had happened.

For John Masefield, navvies both made and destroyed what he

prized: the Hereford and Gloucester canal. As a child he lived close to where the canal and the Great Western crossed each other oustide Ledbury. Not far from his home near the River Leddon was a canal port, a haven in both senses of the word – a dock and a peaceful place. But it was terror-stained, too: unwanted dogs were drowned where the railway bridged the canal. But, 'Beyond that bridge of drowned dogs for some quarter of a mile or more a lovely reach stretched to Heaven and the sun that shines in childhood. In memory that reach is always sunny, and at one point in it, about halfway along it, some lucky and happy boys were free to swim. The water in that reach seemed always to be clear: fish would rise and moorhens would paddle.' Sometimes he was allowed to take his fishing rod, to catch goldfish. Along the canal, too, was a hillock covered in every season with flowers.

Often the narrow boats were crewed by a man and his wife. She took the helm, her milkmaid's cap a-flapping, while the man – singing or knitting – walked ahead with the horse. It was Life perfected. To his boy's mind the boat people even had their own rollicking Sailor Town in dozing, semi-timbered Ledbury. Bye Street was their Tiger Bay where they caroused and got merry.

In the 1880s another generation of navvies destroyed the canal by building a railway. For years, men mourned the old canal and its quiet places. Now the railway's gone, too.

Into many small communities navvies intruded only briefly. They came, amazed, and went. Behind them they left a slowly blossoming change. Red brick towns grew along the vein of their track.

Until 1869 Winchmore Hill was a small hilltop village ten miles from London, off the main highway on the outskirts of Enfield Chase, overlooking the Lea valley marshes. London was two hours away by a yellow mail coach called Little Wonder which made the journey twice daily, setting off from the Flower Pot Inn in Bishopsgate, through Tottenham village, past the elm trees they called The Seven Sisters.

Years later Henrietta Cresswell, the doctor's daughter, wrote a bazaar book about the village and the coming of the railway to Winchmore Hill. The hill she remembered was as bright and fresh as toddling childhood; a blend of clarity and colour, like a mix of paint and transparency. Even the air seemed brightly painted. It was like a land of long ago. What is now north London was then all rickyards and honeysuckle, wild hops, wild roses, thickset hedges and forget-me-nots. The village pond was padded thick with water lilies and the New River brimmed with fishes, silver bleak and chub, miller's thumb and gudgeon. Noises were clearer and sharper: grunt of hedgehog, bleat of sheep, low soft low of cows. Corncrake. Whirr of cockchafer. Hunting owls, soft as feathers, nightingales in the woods when dusk clung to the eyes like cobwebs.

Memories were fewer, but richer: the summer the hailstones killed cattle in the meadow, flailed trees to death; a Photographic Establishment in a brown van which pitched one summer on the green, taking grey-green positives on glass; the cow-slow evening when a villager rode home on a velicopede with wood wheels; the year of the comet which Miss Cresswell saw in the dusk of another summer's evening, the sky all amber and blue, a grey mist in the willows by the river; straw hives, bistre to ochre, under the eaves; bees swarming in May; drowsily bee-watching, lolling in a wheelbarrow, lulled by the insect-humming garden; following the swarm across meadows in the honey-gold sunshine, tang-tanging a bell to tell the neighbours to shut their windows.

Navvies came to this golden hill in the hot summer of '69, tearing down houses and putting up huts, grubbing up holly hedges and ash trees.

'The excavation was beautiful in colour,' said Miss Cresswell, who clearly saw with a painter's eye, 'the London clay being a bright cobalt blue when first cut through, and changing from exposure to orange. There were strata of black and white flints and yellow gravel. The men's white slops and the red heaps of burnt ballast made vivid effects of light and shade and colour against the cloudless sky of that excessively hot summer. There were also dark wooden planks and shorings to add neutral tints, and when the engine came the glitter of brass and clouds of white steam were added to the landscape. On Sundays and holidays the men were, many of them, resplendent in scarlet and yellow or blue plush waistcoats and knee breeches.'

After the hot summer came the deep snow of January and her house was abandoned to the works. Shrubs in her abandoned but unneglected garden slipped over the edge of the cutting and were retrieved and re-rooted time and time again. Part of the wall was rebuilt but frost got into the mortar and it fell down again. Then navvies began using the garden as a thoroughfare.

'There had been much fear in the village of annoyance from the horde of Yorkshire and Lincolnshire railwaymen brought into the village by Firbank, the contractor, but on the whole their conduct was very orderly, and they can hardly be sufficiently commended for their behaviour. A noticeable figure was "Dandy" ganger, a big north countryman, decorated with many large mother of pearl buttons and a big silver watch chain. He instantly checked all bad language in the neighbourhood of the Doctor's garden. Many of the navvies brought their food or their tea cans to be heated on the great kitchen range, and never once made themselves objectionable.'

The railway should have been ready by 1870, the date on the bridge by Winchmore Hill station, but the wetness of the local clay held it up. The previous year's drought misled the engineers into miscalculating how much water there was in the shallow valley they were crossing on embankments and short viaducts. One of the viaducts cracked when the blue slipper clay sank, and the line sloped up and down ever after. Long after the track was open, the slip slowed the up-line trains.

So the navvies stayed on through 1870 and into the next Spring. Five men died on the five mile track, more were gassed to death by fumes from the heaps of burning ballast where they slept, until the dying on that particular line stopped on April Fool's Day 1871, when it was officially opened to the the crack of fog-signals and the noise of navvies. Soon passenger trains, all hot oil and coal smoke, quickened the village into a London suburb.

The old isolated eccentricity of rural England was soon gone. Today Winchmore Hill is a thoroughly respectable, uneccentric place, trenched in two by the railway and sewn together again by bridges. The embankment is now part of the townscape, thick with mature trees. Of the buildings of Miss Cresswell's day few remain: the Friends' Meeting House, perhaps, and the Old Bakery.

Chapter 11

Moleskin Joe

So I went away again. Gretna Green, Glasgow, Loch Lomond. Tyndrum, the Black Mountain, Glen Coe and down to Kinlochleven and went to work. The contractor for the reservoir was Sir John Jackson and I lodged with the powder monkey. They were just getting the foundations out for the dam then. I stopped there a few months.

They had a blondin across the valley there, as well, and a tally-man used to cross the valley in it to sell things to the navvies. He got stuck out over the valley from one Saturday midday to Monday. I bet he was yelling, too, but nobody heard him.

Moleskin Joe was there. He gave up religion and turned against parsons. There was a woman dead in the road. He went up and knocked on this parson's place. The parson and his dog come out.

Moleskin says: 'There's a woman dead in the road.'

'What's that to me, my man?' says this old parson, only talking grammatical. Moleskin didn't say no more. He picked up the dog and hit the parson with it.

He got a month for that, did Moleskin.

Moleskin Joe tramped to Kinlochleven with Patrick MacGill in 1906. They roasted and ate a stolen rooster by the waterfall at Altnafeadh and, instead of going down Glen Coe, crossed the col to Kinlochleven, boxed in by mountains, heavy-walking through whisky-brown peat water, past the little choked lochan near the top. It's a burnt out wildnerness, deforested by fire.

'I'm an anti-Christ,' Moleskin once told MacGill.

'A what?'

'One of them sort of fellows as throws bombs at kings.'

'You mean an anarchist.'

'Well, whatever they are, I'm one,' said Moleskin. 'What is the good of kings, of fine-feathered ladies, of churches, of anything in the country to men like me and you? One time, 'twas when I started tramping about, I met an old man on the road and we mucked about, the two of us as mates, for months afterwards. One night in the winter time, as we were sleeping under a hedge, the old fellow got sick, and he began to turn over and over on his bedding of frost and his blankets of snow, which was not the best place to put a sick man, as you know yourself. As the night wore on, he got worse and worse. I tried to do the best I could for the old fellow, gave him my muffler and my coat, but the pains in his guts was so much that I couldn't hardly prevent him from rolling along the ground on his stomach. He would do anything just to take his mind away from the pain that he was suffering. At last I got him to rise and walk, and we trudged along till we came to a house by the roadside. 'Twas nearly midnight and there was a light in one of the windows, so I thought I would call at the door and ask for a bit of help. My mate, who bucked up somewhat when we were walking, got suddenly worse again, and fell against the gatepost near beside the road and stuck there as if glued to the thing. I left him by himself and went up to the door and knocked. A man drew the bolts and looked out at me. He had his collar on back to front, so I knew that he was a clergyman.'

'What do you want?' he asked.

'My mate's dying on your gatepost.'

'Then you'd better take him away from here.'

'But he wants help,' said Moleskin. 'He can't go a step further, and if you could give him a drop of brandy . . . .'

The parson whistled up a big, black, snarling brute of a dog. 'Now you get away from here,' said the parson, brutish as his hound.

'My mate's dying,' Moleskin protested.

'Seize him,' the parson, in his deepest pulpit voice, ordered the dog.

'He was only a human being,' said Moleskin of the parson, 'and that's about as bad as a man can be. Anyway he put the dog on me and the animal bounded straight at the thick of my leg. I caught hold of the dog by the throat and twisted its throttle until it snapped like a dry stick. Then I lifted the dead thing up in my arms and threw it right into the face of the man who was standing in the hallway. "Take that and be thankful that the worst dog of the two of you isn't dead," I shouted. My mate was still hanging on the gatepost when I came back, and he was as dead as a maggot. I could do nothing for a dead man, so I went on my own, leaving him hanging there like a dead crow in a turnip field. Next morning a cop lifted me and I was charged with assaulting a minister and killing the dog. I got three months hard, and it was hard to tell whether for hitting the man or killing his dog. Anyway, the fellow got free, although he allowed a man to die at his own doorstep. I never liked clergy before, and I hate them ever since: but I know, as you know, that it's not for the likes of you and me that they work for.'

MacGill and Moleskin arrived above the Kinlochleven dam one daybreak, sitting and smoking awhile on the high ground. All around was rough and tumble country, fierce peaks behind. From their hill you can see the small loch below the dam and the hillock that became Boot Hill for the dead of 1908. Opposite are two peaks like canine teeth with a gap between where the incisors are missing. Early morning light spot-lit Ben Nevis.

Derricks swung over the gutter trench like claws, hauling skips of muck. It was five o'clock on a midsummer morning just before the shifts changed. Below them in the hollow smoke rose from the jumbled shacks, standing floorless, the walls just planks hammered into bare earth among puddles and garbage piles. You could hear the hammers and, in the mountains, the falling torrents of the becks.

Moleskin went down alone and came back with a well-worn pair of boots.

In the settlement, midsummer mud oozed over their boot uppers. In the huts, some windowless, those who had gone to bed were just getting up, standing about naked and scratching. The gamblers, still gambling, hadn't gone to bed at all. Bacon fried, sizzling and spitting, in grubby pans on dirty hot plates. Black tea bubbled in soot-stained cans. Beneath their rags, men's skins were coated with fine clay. Flexed muscles cracked the caked muck into dry scales.

Moleskin found Red Billy, a ganger, whittling a stick by a steam crane.

'Can you snare an old hare this morning?' Moleskin asked him.

'A tanner an hour, overtime seven and a half.' Red Billy had a big red beard[1] 'You can take your coat off now.'

---

1 In 1922 the *Letter* printed a piece about a Red Bill Davis who got pneumonia and religion in mountains sounding not unlike those at Kinlochleven. 'Red Bill Davis, so he was called, loud-voiced, rough of speech, and a bully. He cursed God, the weather, the camp, and each individual therein with a fluency that excited our wonder and roused our indignation.' Shooting and cards were what Red Bill delighted in until one cold winter in the mountains he was taken ill and promised to turn to God if he were spared. He was and he did.

'This mate of mine's looking for work, too.'

'He's light of shoulder and lean as a rake,' Red Billy weighed up, summed up, and dismissed MacGill.

'He knocked out Carroty Dan in Burn's model,' Moleskin defended him.

'If that's so,' said Red Billy, instantly impressed, 'he can take his coat off too.' He added to Moleskin, 'You've to pay me four shillings when you lift your first pay.'

'That be damned.'

'That's the price I charge for a pair of boots like them,' said Red Billy, pointing at the stolen boots on Moleskin's feet.

Red Billy's was a rock blasting gang. MacGill and Moleskin joined a crew of five, working one drill, the drill holder sitting splay-legged holding the point of the steel rod on the rock between his knees while four hammermen struck in turn, the hammers describing four constant rings as they swung in a big circle from hip to drill. The rings circled at a steady rate like a juggler's spinning hoops.

Everybody ignored MacGill for some hours until Red Billy sloped off. 'Do you know that kid there,' Moleskin then said, thumbing at MacGill, 'that mate of mine?'

'A blackleg without the spunk of a sparrow,' said Hell-fire Gahey.

'That kid, that mate of mine, rose, stripped naked from his bed and thrashed Carroty Dan in Burn's model lodging house.'

'*I* knocked Carroty out,' boasted Hell-fire, stabbing at his own chest with fingers like pick blades.

'There's a chance for you,' Moleskin delightedly told MacGill. 'Just pitch into Hell-fire Gahey and show him how you handle your pair of fives.'

Moleskin and MacGill worked till yo-ho, then subbed a florin each and went to the tommy shop where they bought a loaf, a pound of beefsteak, a can of condensed milk and a pennyworth of tea and sugar. Three shillings a week bought a third of a flea-ridden bed and a share of a communal hot-plate in Red Billy's shant. The shant's walls were tarred planks hammered vertically into bare ground and strapped together with wooden couplings and iron bars. It was built around a mountain spring which welled up in the middle of the shack. Floor boards, the only ones in the place, covered the spring. In fine weather they sufficed: in wet, water sluiced all across the earth floor turning it into a private, self-contained mud hole.

Bunks were stacked in tiers of three around the room. No windows broke their money-making line. 'If you go outside the door, you'll get plenty of air,' Red Billy replied to objectors, 'and if you stay out it'll be fresher here.'

Red Bill was an old man, twice married, with a habit of eating his tommy with a tobacco-stained clasp knife. He could regurgitate food like a ruminant, a knack he'd learned as a child when he was so hungry he wanted to re-eat the food he'd already swallowed.

MacGill and Moleskin shared a bed, an upper one, with Hell-Fire Gahey. In the middle of the night a fight broke out over should have the blanket. The fight spilled off the bunk into the blackness of the windowless shack. 'My blessed blankets,' yelled Red Billy in the dark. 'You damned scoundrels! You'll not leave me one in the hut. Fighting in bed just the same as if you were lying in a pig-sty.' In the black-out Red Billy was knocked out and a fight, a proper one, was fixed for that evening in the Ring.

The Ring was a circle of shants. In reality it was a garbage dump littered with sardine tins and bottles. Four men were already fighting: an English wagon filler versus a Glasgow craneman, and a big Irishman versus a small Pole (several Poles were there, oddly enough.) The Pole was winning as well until the big Irishman picked him up and tossed him into the old cans and broken bottles.

Moleskin's strategy and tactics were simple: plod after Hell-fire until he could grapple with him. Hell-fire was nimbler and circled out of reach, striking swiftly and hitting every time until Moleskin hoisted him off the ground and over his head. 'For God's sake don't throw me into the tins,' pleaded Hell-fire.

'I don't want to dirty the tins,' Moleskin reassured him. 'Who was right about the blankets last night?'

Hell-fire wouldn't answer. Moleskin dropped him on the ground and kneed his chest. 'Who was right about the blankets last night?'

'You were,' admitted Hell-fire sulkily.

It was MacGill's turn. For a time he got the worst of it until he, too, got a wrestling hold on Hell-fire and threw him slithering along the ground. Hell-fire got up but another hard blow to the chest stopped him for good.

That night MacGill gambled. And won. Silver heaped at his elbow, threaded with bits of gold. He kept on winning and the cards, the whisky and the fight lifted him higher and higher until he began to falter physically and had to give up. He tossed a fistful of winnings on the floor to appease the losers and went to bed.

After that it was gambling, whisky and work, day in and night out. Hundreds of men, without women, lived up there in a couple of square miles of moutain. Unwashed they were, unshaven, and brutalised. Once, MacGill said, he gambled from seven o'clock one Saturday until six-thirty Monday morning and he only broke off then to put in a long shift on the hammers.

Fights were too common to notice. A man could lie dead drunk in filth for hours on end and be disturbed only by people stealing the clothes off his body. Even the postman was escorted by armed police. Tommy came up the mountain on a blondin-like contraption of wires which sagged under the weight of the beer kegs and bread hampers, dragging the skips close to the tops of the smaller hills where navvies looted them as they passed.

One evening Moleskin, MacGill and English Bill drilled and fired several shot holes. Next morning they went back to shift the muck, English Bill in his new boots. He struck the rock with his pick, hit a misfired charge and shot his own pick blade through his throat. 'He's no good here now,' Moleskin said, sadly. They went for a wheelbarrow to carry him away and somebody stole the corpse's boots. 'We should have taken them before we went,' said MacGill. 'Damn right,' said Moleskin.

The only show of gentleness was towards Sandy MacDonald, an Isle of Skye man, dying of tuberculosis. Sandy was not a proper navvy. Once he was married and settled in Greenock where he worked in a sugar refinery. His wife died. He got TB. His home broke up and he ended at Kinlochleven. 'Life burned in him like a dying candle in a ruined house,' said MacGill. The navvies were kind enough to him. Moleskin made him gruel. MacGill read to him from the *Oban Times*.

'Man! I should like to die there awa' in the Isle of Skye,' said Sandy one day.

'Boys, Sandy MacDonald wants to go home and die in his own place,' Moleskin told Red Billy's gang next pay day. 'He'll kick the bucket soon, for he's the look of the grave in his eyes. So what do you say, boys, to a collection for him, a shilling a man, or whatever you can spare?'

That was Saturday. Sandy meant to leave for Skye on Monday, his fare paid by the gathering. Sunday night he went to bed early and died in the small hours of the morning, his fare to the island in a leather purse around his neck. MacGill said they should spend the money on a cross.

'If the dead man wants a cross he can have one,' Moleskin said, putting the money down as the stake in a card game. Clancy won it and was called Clancy of the Cross ever after.

'But where is heaven if there is such a place?' Moleskin asked MacGill one day.

'I don't know.'

'If you think of it, there's no end to anything. If you could go up above the stars, there's surely a place above them, and another place in turn above that again. You can't think of a place where there's nothing, and as far as I can see there's no end to anything. You can't think of the last day as they talk about, for that would mean the end of time. It's funny to think of a man saying there'll be no time after such and such a time. How can time stop?' Moleskin asked. 'Is there a God in Heaven?'

'English Bill may know more about these things that we do,' MacGill told him.

'How can a dead man know anything?' Moleskin asked, borrowing a shilling to gamble with. That, said MacGill, was Moleskin all over. Philosophy one minute, gambling the next. Perhaps the world's a big gambling table, Moleskin once suggested. God threw everything down like a roll of dice: men, nations, animals and the elements. Then He and His angels watched the struggle and betted with each other on the outcome.

'Of course the angels won't back Kinlochleven very heavily,' Moleskin added.

In October MacGill wrote some articles about Kinlochleven for a London paper. Kinlochleven was amazed. They handed each other the acceptance letter until it was unreadable. Then it was winter and for MacGill all longing and passion calmed away to numbness. Snow fell. Tools froze in men's hands and scarred their skin. Cold stopped men gambling as they huddled by the hotplate at nights, yarning now about hard times and the deaths of navvies. About men who worked so hard in weather so bitter sweat froze to icicles on their eyelashes.

Then one warm evening next summer, the dam nearly done, hundreds of navvies were paid off, straggling down the mountain with the sunset in their faces, high above the River Leven flowing noiselessly in its chasm, all grass and bracken, birch woods like dustings of powder in its depths. A blue jumble of hills blocked out the sea to the west, the peaks like teeth above the lips of the lower mountains. Many men tramped to Rosyth where they built a naval base for the war with Germany.

The waterworks are finished and the boys have jacked the shovel,
See, the concrete board deserted for the barrow squad is gone,
The gambling school is bursted, there is silence in the hovel,
For the lads are sliding townwards and are padding it since dawn.
Pinched and pallid are their faces from their graft in God-shunned places,
Tortured, twisted up their frames are, slow and lumbering their gait,
But unto their hopeful dreaming comes the town with lights a-gleaming,
Where the bar-men add more water, and the shameless women wait.

    Back from Kinlochleven, Songs of a Navvy, Patrick MacGill.

Chapter 12

The Making of Hawick

One Saturday night in 1860 a navvy treated some of the lads of Hawick till they got him drunk enough to rob him of his cash, jacket and waistcoat. That night he slept it off in Mitchie's skinworks. In the morning he borrowed a coat he found hanging there. Next day he took it back.

'An honest thief,' said the *Hawick Advertiser*.

'The damnedest set of keelies I ever met in my life,' said the navvy.

It was all very different from sod-cutting day eleven months before. Then it was like a circus coming to town. Early morning, Wednesday, 7 September 1859, was cloudy and overcast over the Borders. The harvest was not yet in but the nearby dales emptied as folk flocked to Hawick in Sunday best and ribboned bonnets. Hawick's population doubled. Teviotdale had seen nothing like it.

'Success to the Border Union Railway,' ran a sign on an arch outside Mr Milligan's furniture warehouse. 'An open highway for all traffic,' ran the banner over the Liddesdale road by the Tower Hotel. Mr Nichols built a balcony and filled it with children. 'Vive le Hodgson,' said his sign.[1]

Early morning, and the bells rang through the rain. Mid-morning, and the town council greeted incoming dignitaries at the railway station. Noon, and Mrs Hodgson arrived and encarriaged. The foot-goers fell in behind the Cornet (in full Common Riding costume) for the procession through the town: a flute band, a saxhorn band, a masonic lodge, the police, common Hawickians, officials from Carlisle and Edinburgh, the press, the clergy, Members of Parliament, the band of the 16th Lancers. Mid-way came the workmen: navvies with barrow and spade.

1 Hodgson was chairman of the North British Railway whose Edinburgh-Hawick line had opened in 1849 (hence the presence of a railway station in town). This new line continued the railway to Carlisle.

Mrs Hodgson turned the first sod under densely wooded crags just outside town, wheeling the barrow behind her, navvy-fashion. The crowd crowed. They had no idea, said the *Advertiser*, she knew anything about navvying.

A thousand people then banqueted on the banks of the Teviot in a marquee on the Under Common Heugh. They toasted Queen Victoria, her family, her Navy, her Army, a couple of local Dukes, the clergy, and Mrs Hodgson. ('Put the spade of gratitude in your hearts,' urged Sherriff Gordon, 'and wheel up a barrowful of your richest wishes at her feet.') They told each other the price of coal would fall. Bailie Paterson told the town it owed him a debt – thanks to him Hawick was a multi-spindle place. *He* had sent the first piece of woven cloth to London nearly thirty years ago.

They toasted the navvies, between the Press and the Ladies. 'Navvie Cowie replied in a humorous speech,' said the *Advertiser*, the last kind word it had for any of them.

'Liddesdale has not since the time of sturt and strife in the renowned Border days been in such a state of commotion as now,' the paper soon reported. 'Armies of navvies have pitched their camps in quiet valleys, and roaring pay nights, and the accompanying knocks and blows, form a theme of fearful recital to the dwellers in the secluded dells of Liddell.'

Smithies, stables and offices were opened all along the Hawick contract soon after sod cutting day. A gang was soon opening a cutting where Mrs H. did her bit in September. The Hardie's Hill rock blasters shot fractured stone and splintered rock like bullets through the mill and cottages at Lynnwood where the council estate now stands. A mortar machine for the Lynnwood viaduct was in place and clay was already being burned for mortar. The Slitrig Water was getting a new course.

By the end of 1859 shafts had been started at the Whitrope tunnel though more machinery was still needed along with tools and wood for the huts. Already the weather was bad – masons claimed they were lashed to the scaffolding to keep from blowing away as they built a house for Ritson, the Whitrope contractor. The year ended in a storm through which the navvies laboured to save their Christmas pay. It turned into the worst winter for a quarter century: men were laid off, many fell ill. In January, in the bone-hard cold, a drunken navvy in charge of a horse wounded Police Sergeant Guild in the leg. Somebody complained of police brutality.

The weather was still bad in March, but with sleet now rather than snow. Over a hundred huts were up at Whitrope. With the carpenter's shop and the smithy they formed a square with a belfry in the middle. Jamieson's store sold salt butter, blouses and navvy boots but not, it turned disastrously out, fresh vegetables.

A single track dipped and wobbled over the hill over the tunnel. No 4 shaft was flooded and without help from another steam engine the horses couldn't cope with the water. No 3 shaft was only half way down but headings were already being struck off from Nos 5 and 2. People drove from Hawick to wonder at it all, particularly at the wild men in mud-smeared moleskin riding up and down the shafts with one leg in the bucket, the other dangling, gripping the rope with fists like hams – all except a miner called Kingdom, a man with palms like leather pads, who flouted the bucket and slid direct to work down the cable. It was all as casual as walking until one day, finding it slipperyer than he expected, he plummeted down the shaft and shattered his thigh.

The railway left Hawick down the wooded defile of the Slitrig Water into the big open hollow below the hill called Hummelkows and on to Stobs Castle, ancestral home of the Elliots. Castle, river, railway and the enclosing knobbly hills all press tightly together. From Stobs the line climbed the bare brown uplands to the flat space spanned by the big Shankend viaduct before burrowing into the tunnel-like valley of the Lang Burn where the embankment was dumped awkwardly on the hillside and which slipped all the time they built it.

The line breaks into the great sodden hollow at Langburnshiels from where you can see the massif (then bare, now bristly with forest) which the Whitrope tunnel penetrates. Across the divide, the line follows the successively broadening valleys of the Whitrope Burn, Hermitage Water and the Liddel, down to Newcastleton, the Eden and Carlisle.

In March 1860, MacDonald opened the Turf Hotel in the great hollow, filled with damp air and desolation, at Langburnshiels. The Turf was a sod shant with five-star style offering food, drink, and bedded accommodation in several rooms. In July a gang of Irishmen stormed the place, swinging picks, spades and pokers. They battered in windows, battered down doors, battered some quiet Englishmen drinking there. They nearly broke MacDonald's arm but in the darkness (he put out the light) the rest escaped through a skylight and ran into the hills.

The summer of 1860 set in cold and wet along the Borders where things were going irrecoverably sour between navvy and native. The Chief Constable and Sgt Guild tried to arrest a Shankend man a few days after the Turf affray. 'Kick the buggers,' his mates shouted to the navvy. The navvy's wife did kick the buggers while the rest threw stones and menaced the police with pitchforks. The law went home to Hawick.

Every day the Burgh Court was busy with misdemeaning, drunken and felonious navvies. Breaches of the peace, obstructing the pavements, common assault, drunken assault, robbery, drunken indecency came and went commonplacely every day. Even the bare brown hills were unsafe, even for the untamed sheep which watched everybody with the same distrust and disdain, trotting stiffly off, fleeces swaying, whenever anybody got too close. The hill farmers said navvies were raiding the hills for mutton. Probably they were, though the only proof anybody ever found was half an illicit animal under a bed in the Whitrope settlement.

In April Catherine MacDonald (alias Kate Nicholas) was jailed for brawling with Mrs Ellis at Whitrope. Her children were locked away in the Combination Workhouse.

In May's good weather the work-hours were longer, the pays bigger, and men swarmed into Hawick like an infection. The town was swollen with them. Pubs strained their skins like unlanced boils as navvies multiplied bacterially in their warm intoxicating environments. The town's skin swelled to splitting. In places it did split: navvies spilled out of the jail, spewed out of the pubs openly flourishing whisky bottles. But if navvies were the bacteria, the constables were defective white corpuscles quite unable to clean them up. All got drunk together. Superintendents took to patrolling navvy pubs.

Mrs Colonel Vassal of Stobs Castle gave the Cowbyres Mission a library. James Douglas of Cavers gave bi-weekly Grand Soirees in the Subscription Rooms. 'What we want,' he said, 'is love: love between all ages and conditions of men.'

The Subscription Rooms, which will stand classically facaded in Buccleuch Street, were paid for by public subscription in 1821 and built as a place of adult education. By the early '60s the bottom floor was rented as an inn, though the upper storey was still used for theatricals. It was here the soirees were held, their appeal unlessened by the pub downstairs. Upstairs only tea was served with the beef, ham, pies, and fancy bread. Musicians played from the gallery.

Massed, heavily sermonising clergy sat on the platform surrounded by evergreens. 'What dignity is there in navvies' work?' the Rev Parlane asked them. 'A man who is dignified rides in a carriage, has a fine house, and servants to wait upon him: but the poor man is often more really dignified than he who has riches and a high position. The navvy makes himself useful: and the man who does so in the position in which Providence has placed him, whether he be charged with the affairs of a great nation or employed in the cutting and the viaduct, occupies a very honourable position.' (Navvy cheers.)

In October Whitrope blazed when straw in one of the stables caught fire. Horses, cut loose in their mangers, lumbered about iron-shod and dangerous. Huts were broken down to make a fire break. At the end of the year seven men drowned in the Eden near the Carlisle Bone Mill when a travelling crane toppled over.

All along the line the brief drama of navvy *v* citizen was intense. Pre-railway Hawick was not today's handsome town. It was squalid, mean, and warped. Many *houses* were one-roomed and whole families lived in single windowless chambers. Where Drumanlarig Square now stands was a particularly noisome slum centred on three hunched rows: Fore, Mid and Back. The shopkeepers were singularly unsavoury. (There was in any case a widespread navvy contempt for shopkeepers. A belief that selling things you hadn't made was inherently ignoble. It was a base man who donned a long apron and smarmed and hand-rubbed to his betters across a counter.)

One Saturday night in April, 1861, Thomas McGraw from the Whitlaw cutting was stabbed in the loin with a rusty sword by a Back Row grocer and spirit-dealer called Nathaniel Mulvein. Another man who grabbed the sword was badly cut when Mulvein slid the blade through his bleeding fingers. Mulvein pleaded self-defence but he'd slashed some one before and was committed to Jedburgh jail.

June brought fine weather, long work-hours, big pay, and a recrudescence of last's years infection: a contagion of brawling navvies spreading along the road to Hawick. This year it seemed more virulent, with knife fights at Whitrope and brawling all over town. A ganger at the Whitlaw cutting was casually beaten up by passing tramp navvies who thus briefly appear, and permanently vanish.

Through it all the work went on. By the end of summer the arches at the Shankend viaduct were being closed. All the piers were at full height. The Lang Burn kept on slipping but the Whitrope tunnel was almost there. From Scotch Dyke to Carlisle the permanent way was already laid except for a stretch over the Eden. Rails were being spiked at Newcastleton.

Then early in the Spring of 1862 Frederick Kelly's highwaymen began waylaying provision carts near the Turf Hotel. The carts belonged to respectable burghers: James Turnbull, grocer; Mr Mabon, grocer; Mr Young, baker; Mr Tait; William Cairns. The highwaymen stole vegetables and bread, even a jar of butter, but mostly they looked for ale.

Just before St Patrick's Day there was another outbreak of highway robbery, a whole five-day week of unmasked men (secure behind the fear they generated) demanding drink with menaces. One gang who inadvertently stole a jar of treacle took it back to be changed for whisky. The problem was the roads were crowded with drink-carts briskly spanking from one gang to the next. It was one of Hawick's dichotomies: abhorrence of strong drink and greed for the money from selling it.

'One of these lawless ruffians,' Missionary Topping said, 'with a cart of drink, appeared at Shankend: a consultation was held among some of the *navvies*, and one of them stepped out from the rest, to tell him not to "stand and deliver", but to beat an immediate retreat with his bottles, and with this friendly admonition – that if he ever made his appearance with bottles or barrels again, they would smash them before him, and I am not sure but they would also smash something else. The travelling shebeen decamped.' Topping went on: "The men in their sober moments condemn the drink as the source of all their sorrows, sickness, imprisonment, poverty."

Nobody connected with the works – not the Catholic priest, not the contractor, not the engineer – wanted drink to be sold at Whitrope. But still Hawick granted licenses. Local Christians tried to keep the men sober by setting up a chapel, a school, and a reading room with its own library. But Hawick's frock-coated burghers still trooped in massed carts to cash in on the sale of booze.

'Now, sir,' said Topping, 'who are to blame? I know many of the navvies are, but not all. When they are beset on the roads by these carts, and drink of the worst description offered at a cheap rate to them, are not those who dispose of it, and also those who permit such an enormous traffic by unlicensed individuals also culpable?'

'If something is not done,' Topping insisted in the absence of an answer. 'I would say let the blood of these poor men be upon the heads of those who will not try and stop the traffic carried on by these carts.' But nobody listened to J H Topping. Certainly not the navvies. Certainly not the shopkeepers counting the navvies' coin.

In a way Hawick was personified by Dr McLeod. He, too, battened on the navvies by taking money to look after them, then let them decay with scurvy, a curiously self-inflicted illness in a landlocked farming county. Yet, 'The medical practitioner on the railway seems to have gained the esteem and affection of the whole of the navvies from the most delicate to the sturdiest,' an unidentified admirer wrote in the *Advertiser* in March, 1860. He/she had just visited the Whitrope tunnel with McLeod. Near Hardie's Hill cutting where the gunpowder gangs happily blasted the inhabitants with shattered rock they met two navvies steadying an injured man on a horse.

'Doctor, I've got mysel' hurtit, sir.'

'Poor man,' said the doctor with compassion. 'I'm sorry for that: are you badly hurt?'

'I think my knee joint's off, sir,' But joint off or no, and for all his horse-side manner, McLeod merely told him what to do and sent him off home alone.

Next July a wagon on the Whitrope incline ran over the leg of an Irish part-time navvy called McLusky. McLeod wanted to amputate but McLusky's mates advised him to endure the journey to Edinburgh. The *Advertiser* said they were drunk. McLeod took a piece of bone from the leg and they got M'Lusky into a cart. For some reason it took seven hours to reach Hawick, by which time the leg had to come off anyway. McLusky died a few days later, just weeks before he was going home for the potato harvest.

During the St Patrick's Day riots a driver called Cooper fell under a wagon at Fleety. McLeod amputated his arm at the shoulder. A successful operation, said the *Advertiser*: the man died in the Poor House next morning.

In May, 1862, an Edinburgh surgeon called Gairdner wrote to *The Scotsman* about several cases of scurvy he had come across among navvies in Scotland. At the time he was treating a young Irishman who in spite of earning twenty-three shillings a week had lived on bread, broth and oatmeal. On the Border Union, said the surgeon, many men ate nothing but the convenience foods of the day: salt ham, herrings, bread, tea, and whisky. A storekeeper near Hawick had once sold potatoes but found nobody would buy them because they couldn't be bothered boiling them.

McLeod was affronted, not by any hint that he might be culpable of professional malpractice but by the suggestion he was unaware of the pathogenesis of scurvy, a vitamin deficiency disease (not that either McLeod or Gairdner could know that, at the time). 'Dr Gairdner,' McLeod wrote to *The Scotsman*, 'implies that there has been ignorance of the cause and cure of scurvy in this district, but as he has not the honour of being the discoverer of either, they have luckily not remained a secret, and are quite as well known here as in Edinburgh.'

He had never doubted, Gairdner answered him, that McLeod knew all about scurvy. Navvies didn't, though. He had never suggested McLeod could control what went into a navvy's broth-pot but if they were given anti-scorbutic vegetables they would eat them. 'Everybody knows that bodies of men employed at a distance from markets, fed and housed by contract, are to a great extent at the mercy of their employers.'

'The truth is,' came back McLeod, 'the navvies are by no means a class who will submit to eat and drink what may be recommended to them if they do not relish it.' He *had* pointed out watercress beds to them. Besides, the English thrived. 'I think our duties are clear,' McLeod ended. 'His to nurse his protégé, mine still to journey to the wilderness and try to prevent any more specimens of Hibernian scorbutics being sent to increase Dr Gairdner's already onerous duties. In bidding the Doctor farewell in connection with this "scurvy" subject, I hope he may personally keep as clear of the disease as I have done.'

What kind of stupidity was it that broke your work-people's health in the middle of a farming county? Gairdner, exasperated, wanted to know. Undomesticated men needed saving from themselves ('It won't do to send them a-botanising after watercresses.'). If the English thrived it was because they had a peculiarly English instinct for their own bodily comfort.

Then Wild Harry Hudson ran off with Emily Perkins, tally-wife of a hagman called Hall. Wild Harry also took Hall's daughter, his clothes, his bedding and all his cash. Hall was upset. So was Sgt Guild, though not so badly. They caught Wild Harry near Jedburgh and Sgt Guild had to drive his hired gig between Hall and his wife to save her from being beaten. Words however were exchanged. The navvies Wild Harry had hired to carry his loot were fascinated. So were the reapers in the fields. But then Hall spoiled it all by forgiving both Wild Harry and his wife. Sgt Guild was upset.

Then a weekend, St Patrick's Day, and the biggest wages ever paid, neatly coincided and erupted like a split volcano. Hawick fared better than it had any right to expect. The few navvies who got that far were generally too drunk to do anything but fall down.

The Irish raided, over-ran and held the MacDonald's Turf Hotel. English and Scots residents fled. Mrs MacDonald literally took to the bare hills. They smashed windows, furniture and doors. They guzzled the booze and ate the tommy. At Shankend a gang kicked out a man's teeth. At Whitrope they invaded another of MacDonald's chain of sod shants.

At every peaceful bend in all that winding road, crowds of Irishmen brawled, fought, kicked, gouged and mauled. English and Scots fled. The police stayed, but inactively, always on the verge of sending for the Army. Things got worse when an Irishman was killed in a blasting accident at Shankend. Highlanders were blamed and every Scotsman on the job was threatened with death as soon as the dead man was buried. More Scots fled.

Afterwards in the sad, shabby, hung-over ruins of the riot nobody dared testify against the ringleaders. Three highwaymen were taken but Shankend society closed against the police when it came to the rioters. Five were known. Two were jailed. The others resisted. Sgt Guild was there, again, supporting Inspector Porter of the County Constabulary. The fugitives picked up crow-bars. They might be taken dead, they said like true rebels, but never alive. Their sullen, hostile backers scared the police away. The whole affair fizzled out in hang-over and failure.

The job was nearly done. Hawick's natural preoccupations had run on unhindered throughout. The chronic housing shortage. The chronic water shortage. Sheep. The failure of the turnip crop. Who was to pay for the toll gate lamp? Farm sales. Wool.

The tumult and the din subsided. The uproar quietened. In the dales it was like bird song after battle. Hawick never slumbered, exactly. In fact it prospered rather hugely, partly because of its shiny new rails. Stobs Castle even had its own little station where the proud trains stopped, nestling in their own steam. They carried produce and passengers, and young men to war.

Now the track is ripped up. Shepherds in Landrovers now drove sheep along the slipping embankment at Langburnshiels. The aligned spoil heaps over Whitrope have mellowed like old tumuli, and any way are now lost in a new forest. Hill mist blows through the old tunnel, puffing out at the ends like old coal smoke.

Chapter 13

The Long Drag

Long loops of drenching rain drift on the wind across the wet valleys and wild fells. Few birds cry. Underfoot it's soft with trapped water: millions of gallons soaked up, up there, sodden, oozing, squelching at the touch of a foot. The Carlisle-Settle line crosses this hard country at its easiest point, yet it was still the wildest job ever undertaken by bare-handed navvies and the last big job they undertook unhelped by massive steam machinery. The working problems were scale, the weather, geography, bad-luck geology, and the sheer number of ups followed by steep downs in the hills. Navvies called it the Long Drag.

From Settle the line runs up Ribblesdale, under Ingleborough, Whernside and Pen y Gent. It pierces Blea Moor and rounds Dentdale like the 366-metre contour, then crosses the divide at the top of Wensleydale and drops from the wild and desolate to the soft and farmed, down into the Vale of Eden, where the viaducts have Gothic arches and all is rich and fat, to Carlisle.

Bad geology begins just north of Settle, a small stone-built town under its own crags. In Settle itself was a covered ambulance and, more ominously, a bog-cart with a barrel instead of wheels: horses often sank to their bellies in the soft ground, wheeled carts to their axles. Mud once ripped a hoof off a horse. Geologically the clay is a marine deposit, once soft but hardened by its own weight, striated by ice and strewn with glacier-carried boulders. Like dehydrated food it turns sloppy when mixed with water, and here the yearly rainfall can be measured in yards.

At the mountain-end of Ribblesdale, Batty Wife Hole was the capital of No 1 Contract, roaring like a gold camp in a colonial gold rush, brimming with traders and sauntering navvies in billy-cock hats, potters' carts, drapers' carts, milk carts, greengrocers' carts, butchers' and bakers' carts, brewers' drays, and hired traps. There were hawkers, pedlars, vendors of all kinds. There were stables and stores and a hospital (used in the 1871 smallpox epidemic) with a covered walkway for convalescents. There was a post office, public library, the Manchester and Bradford City Missions and the mission school.

'Dispiriting, shiftless, unhomely, ramshackle, makeshift,' was what a *Daily News* man called it. Pigs snouted in the garbage and wallowed in the overflowing gutters. It was a disarrangement of wooden huts, coated with tarred felt, let to married navvies who took in lodgers at thirteen shillings a week for bed, board, and washing. The Welcome Home, one of the two pubs, was a hovel of two bare, cave-like taprooms with a separate building at the back where the landlady shut herself away in times of trouble to let the navvies fight themselves quiet.

But in spite of all that, the place boomed as the entrepôt depot for the wilder parts of the line in the mountains. The victualling contract was held by a Batty Wife man who sent his carts daily into the hills. His beef came from Settle on the hoof and was slaughtered, bellowing, on Batty Green. He also ran a tommy truck on the works' railway, crammed to the eaves with halves of bullocks. Hereabouts navvies ate beef. Mutton was second best, bacon, a filler. Men ate eighteen pounds of beef a week.

Batty Wife Hole also had its own posh suburb, Inkerman, blending into it like a little navvy conurbation. Gentility resided in Inkerman: the surveyor, the contractor's staff, the clergymen, Dr Leveson who was born in Jamaica, schoolmistress Jane Herbert who lodged with Mr Tiplady of the Bradford City Mission, and the colony's police – Archie Cameron and Joseph Goodison, tolerated but despised. The rest of the colony was given over to wild, roistering, rag-tag navvies.

It began when Joe Pollen came up from the Surrey-Sussex Junction in 1869 in a wooden caravan like a peak-roofed cabin on wheels. Snow lay all winter on the hills and in the fleeces of the hill sheep. All winter the little wooden van was filled with Pollen, his wife and two daughters, and ten men from the survey team. Next Spring, when work began in earnest, Joe built himself a tommy shop and started a daily bus service to Ingleton. He was also the undertaker, carrying the dead down to the burying-ground in the trees by the dry bed of the Doe in Chapel-le-Dale.

'What with accidents, low fevers, smallpox, and so on,' he said two years after he came, 'I've toted over a hundred of us down the hill. T'other day I had toted one poor fellow down – he were hale and hearty on Thursday, and on Tuesday he were dead o' erinsipalis: and I says to the clerk as how I thought I had toted well nigh on a hundred down over the beck to Chapel-le-Dale. He goes and has a look at his books, and comes out, and says, says he: "Joe, you've fetched to t'kirkyard exactly a hundred and ten corpse." I knowed I warn't far out.'

One day, late in 1872, the Pollens threw a party for Betsey Smith, a friend from the Surrey-Sussex Junction. It was nearly winter, early in the evening as the shifts changed. Weak, wet light fell on the mud of the camp. Betsey Smith and the Pollen girls sat by the coal-fire in the keeping room, while a lodger cut Joe's hair in the dormitory. Mrs Pollen, a big and burly woman, handed round rashers of bacon and buttered toast until Mr Pollen came back to reminisce about Batty Wife's beginnings.

From the lodgers' room came the muted squeak and scrape of a violin and then a black-eyed young navvy tapped on the dormitory door and came in, blushing. Could they join the company, if they behaved properly and brought a fiddle and a bucket of beer? The company, tired of being polite to each other, said yes, and the lodgers clumped in with a bucket of ale and a whisky bottle. The black-eyed navvy danced and fiddled, double-shuffling and stamping, a kind of clog dance in navvy boots.

After a time Mrs Pollen was called into the tommy shop attached to the hut. While she was gone a strange navvy, calling himself Wellingborough Pincer, knocked at the outside door of the living quarters. Joe, a Wellingborough man himself, welcomed him – until he made for the beer bucket and began emptying it down his throat. Mrs Pollen came back, saw at once what was happening and threw Pincer out: literally and physically, bunching the back of his jacket into a fistful of cloth.

Pincer huddled outside in the chill making himself pitiful, begging to be forgiven. Mrs Pollen relented and let him in. Pincer, unreformed and unrepentant, made straight for the ale can and hit Tom Purgin in the eye. Mrs Pollen, now hard and merciless, dragged him, heels bumping, across the bare floor-boards and dropped him in the mud outside. Pincer banged on the shutters, demanding access to the ale can. Joe, local loyalties all forgotten, then unleashed his bulldog – a massively jawed, strappingly chested, red-eyed brute (also called Joe) – and opened the outside door. In the darkness they heard Joe (the dog) gargling and snarling, then a mud-softened thump.

Pincer sued the Pollens for unlicensed drink selling and setting a dog on him, but the Ingleton magistrate found against him and made him pay the court costs. Pincer disappeared soon after. Gone on tramp, said some: at the bottom a sump-hole in the Blea Moor tunnel, implied others.

The Hole of Batty Wife Hole is supposed to be the source of the Ribble, though it looks more like a sump than a well, swallowing water as it does down its churns. It's an oval in the mud, about twenty feet deep, where Mr Batty dropped his wife's murdered corpse. To the east is a low line of out-cropping rock like a row of rotten teeth. Both are to one side of a vast open bowl filled with little but space, rain, mist, moving air and the Batty Moss viaduct. A million and a half bricks went into the viaduct in spite of a wind that could blow men off the scaffolding.

Several settlements serviced Nos 1 and 2 Contracts: Batty Wife Hole/Inkerman, Sebastopol/Belgravia, Jericho, The Barracks, and Salt Lake City, an isolated encampment on the shoulder of Blea Moor, north west of Batty Wife Hole.

Sebastopol and its posh suburb Belgravia were set square in the swamp beyond the vidaduct. On his way there the *Daily News* man met an old navvy with a whitlowed finger who had been to the doctor's in Inkerman. Together they dropped into a friend's hut in Sebastopol. Outside was squashy bog, inside, a blazing fire. The landlady drew a quart of ale and put the money for it straight into a child's money box.

The gossip was of the up-tunnel goings-on. Black Sam had had his head cut open in a mass brawl to settle the Anglo-Irish question at The Barracks. Johnson's wife got drunk at her own wedding and chucked her bridegroom bodily out of the hut. Then she fell flat in the mud and not even her fancy man would pick her up.

Even a little rain did a lot of harm in that awkward geology and the *Daily News* man walked mid-leg in mud the mile and a bit to the Blea Moor tunnel. A shower of rain, even the jolting of a wagon, turned dry clay into slurry. It settled glue-like on the wagon bed and instead of slipping cleanly out often dragged the wagon over the tiphead. Bulling irons were needed all the time.[1]

'I have known men,' said the chief engineer, 'blast the boulder

---

1 Bulling irons – U-shaped iron bars, one end of which fitted between the spokes of a wheel, the other under the flange of the rail, thus locking the wagon securely to the track, stopping it toppling over.

clay like rock, and within a few hours have to ladle out the same stuff from the same spot like soup in buckets. Or a man strikes a blow with his pick at what he thinks is clay, but there is a great boulder underneath almost as hard as iron, and the man's wrists, arms, and body are so shaken by the shock, that, disgusted, he flings down his tools, asks for his money, and is off.'

Blea (dialect for bleak) Moor is an immensity of barren fell, smooth save for a few beck scratches, and not many of them, though the Little Dale Beck and the Force Gill Beck were nuisances which had to be aqueducted over the railway. (They still are.) Down the mountain, the streams flow together as the Winterscale Beck until it sinks into a swallow-hole near Chapel-le-Dale and wells up again as the River Doe.

The heaviest work and the heaviest men were on the moor near the tunnel, among them the best two gangs in all England, each twenty-five strong. All were English, all were piecemen, they had no gangers, and all they needed was an engineer to check their levels and measure their work once a fortnight. All lived in Jericho – two lines of huts, grubbed about by pigs, with a solitary pub in a rock-roofed, semi-subterranean hole.

The *Daily News* man, along with an engineer, the contractor, and the Manchester City missionary were looked after in Jericho by three full-bodied navvy women. One nursed a child. In the oven was a massive piece of beef. On the fire, a potato pot. The landlady offered whisky, but gave them beer when they asked for it. The engineer said things were looking up in Jericho: there hadn't been a fight for a fortnight, whereas one Sunday in summer he'd counted seven brawls going on all at the same time. A navvy, off work with a bruised foot, said it was the cold weather, but the engineer was certain Jericho was getting respectable.

From Jericho you look across to the bulk of the mountain called Ingleborough. Whernside is hidden by its own huge shoulder. It's spongy, squelchy, sopping country, where the wind snatches the breath from your mouth. Behind, on the Moor, you can still see the spoil heaps from the tunnel and the brick ventilation shafts.

Unrelieved hardness was the trouble in the Blea Moor tunnel. 'Not a spoonful,' said the *Daily News* man, 'comes out without powder.' Most of the rock is limestone, gritstone, or shale, and the idea was to follow the shale as closely as you could. Charge holes were hammered out with drills and about a pint (two tots, to the navvy) of gunpowder, packed around a canvas-covered fuse, was used in each. Dynamite was better and safer but it cost two hundred pounds a ton just to carry it there, five times more than gunpowder. Without its detonator, dynamite burned safely like a wickless candle. Navvies carried it in their trouser pockets to keep it warm. It looked like potted lobster.

Jack rolls, like the windlasses over wishing wells, were the first winding engines at the tunnel, but later they used horse gins and, lastly, steam. The first steam engine was dragged up the mountain over a narrow gauge railway by a series of windlasses called crabs. The boiler came first, then the engine, then the whole thing was rivetted together on the mountain and used to haul up its sister engine.

Most of the miners were from Devon or Cornwall, with some Irish, the only place on Nos 1 and 2 Contracts where they were tolerated. They all lived in The Barracks, which was probably at the tunnel's northern end, overlooking Dentdale.

Eight feet of rain a year falls on these mountains. In July 1870, the cutting at the northern end of the tunnel was still just a hole isolated from the rest of the line. When a wave of rainwater hit it, it filled like a pond. Two men drowned and the rain trapped two others in the tunnel itself. They scrabbled on to a wagon and the men outside could see the taller of them with his face upturned to the roof of the tunnel trying to ward off the water with his hands, paddling it away from his mouth. Rescuers cut a hole to drain the rainwater. The taller man was still alive but the shorter man was dead, his mouth stopped with clay.

'He came from Kingscliffe in Northamptonshire, hard by my own native place,' said Joe Pollen, 'and I got a coffin for the poor chap, and toted him down to Ingleton, and sent him home by the railway.'

From The Barracks you can see the railway arcing around the mountain like the timberline. Above, all is bare and barren, below are broad-leaved trees and farms.

Dendry Mire is a badly drained little hollow on the heights between Wensleydale and Garsdale. At first there was to be an embankment there and for two years they dumped a quarter-million cubic yards of muck, which promptly sank. In places, walls of peat fifteen feet high were pushed up on either side of the vanishing, upside-down embankment. In the end they settled for a viaduct.

Hereabouts, too, a gullet once quietly closed itself like a quick healing wound, engulfing the works railway after a minor fall of evening rain.

Even the Intake embankment at the very top of the Vale of Eden took a year to make. The Eden is only a few yards long here, trickling off the great convoluted slopes of Abbotside, dropping as a waterfall into a pool in a gorge, before turning north past the Intake embankment. For a year they tipped without moving the tiphead a centimetre forward. The muck sludged slowly down over itself like cold unsolidifying lava, an unlovely heap of clay, glistening and wet.

The three northern contracts were in the easy country of the Vale of Eden, but even so the Crow Hill cutting was five and a half years in the making. Some weeks a ton of gunpowder was exploded to blow up the boulder clay and crack open the boulders embedded in it. It's still an unusually narrow gash of a cutting, lined with a welt of conifers.

The irony was that the men who worked the hard country in the south were softer in their behaviour than the men in the easy country to the north. Sports soaked up what energy was left after work in the wild country of Nos 1 and 2 Contracts: cross-fell races over Blea Moor; bare-knuckle fights to pick the Cock of the Camp. In the easy country they rioted – at Armathwaite in the Vale of Eden where cottage smoke idled through the trees in the hollow by the river, the very image of Victorian peacefulness. Armathwaite is still unblemished, an open airy place in a hilly, hedged and wooded country where the Eden flows quick and shallow. Old cottages squat around a cobbled courtyard. Trees hide the castle by the river.

In the 1870s the village had at least four pubs. Two have closed. The New Inn, across the Eden, has gone completely – buildings and all.

Trouble incubated slowly, rather than broke out, one Saturday evening in October, 1870, when an Irish gang robbed a Scotsman outside the Armathwaite tommy shop. At the same time, English and Irish gamblers quarrelled in the New Inn. The Irish stoned the place.

Inside the New Inn a half-drunk Irishman called Cornelius Cox sat by the fire in the front kitchen with William Kaisley, Punch Parker and Portsmouth Joe White. Portsmouth suddenly hit Cox with his clubbed fist and dragged him into the backyard where, in light spilling from the open door, Punch hit him on the head with a dyking spade. Kaisley came out and kicked Cox in the face.

Margaret Graham, servant, mopped up blood in the front kitchen. 'There was very little of it,' she said. 'I don't think above a pint.'

The Englishmen tossed Cox's body over the garden wall into a field where PC Whitfield found him at midnight. Cox had vomited and his hair was glued to his skull with coagulated blood. Whitfield sent him home in a wheelbarrow to die.

Senior police officers from Penrith arrested Punch, Portsmouth and Kaisley on Sunday night. Then, early on Monday morning, Inspector Bertram heard that mobs of English navvies were massing to drive the Irish off the line. At Jamieson's cutting, about half a mile from Armathwaite, he found an Irish gang working peacefully, but on his way back he ran into a mob of English navvies armed with sticks and coppey stools, coming from the deep rock cutting at Low House. He stopped them by holding up his hand like a man on points duty and, to be on the safe side, ordered his own men to draw their cutlasses. The navvies brandished sticks. Bertram and his men rushed them (he told the court), drove them back, and disarmed them.

Back in Armathwaite he heard another crowd was coming from the Baron Wood cutting and tunnel, partly out of sight of the village to the south, cut off by a bend in the Eden and by low crags. The mob marched like soldiers in columns of four. Bertram stopped them in the wooded lane outside the village. They had leaders: Joseph French (29), from Warwickshire; Joseph Draper (28), from Leicestershire and Thomas Jones (29), from Cheshire. Draper took a whip from his smock and cracked it.

'Why the hell are you stopping us here for?' Jones wanted to know. 'You must read the Riot Act.'

'Drive through the bastards,' said French.

Bertram couldn't control them and they broke through to join the disarmed men in Armathwaite. Farmers were too scared to lend him a horse to send for reinforcements, so he went to see if he could borrow a mount from Mr Bell, the works manager, in his office near the New Inn. Through the window they saw the English mob crossing the Eden from Armathwaite.[2] Bell ordered the gates to be shut.

---

2 *Where* it all happened is confused. The railway itself is on the hillside above the village. According to local remembrance, the New Inn was below it, across the Eden. Perhaps the 'works' next to the pub were offices and stores and the men's huts were up the hill closer to the railway.

'Is it going to be an Irish or an English job?' the men shouted, storming the gates, calling for the master. The walking ganger opened the gate for the leaders, who went in to speak to Bell, briefly, before coming out again to tell their mates the company had conceded. The Irish had to go. They led their mob to the Irish huts, kicking down doors and menacing the people inside.

'I never saw such a sight in my life,' said Bertram. 'The Irishmen were frightened, and their wives and children were shouting and crying in great alarm. At that time the two hundred men were flourishing their sticks, and daring the Irish to come out.'

'The buggers aren't coming,' Jones shouted. 'We'll have to go and bring them out by force.'

But it took only half an hour to clear the camp as the Irish made off into the hills and woods smashing what they couldn't carry. By two o'clock only three Irishmen were left: the dead man and his two keepers.

French, Draper, and Jones got twelve months hard labour apiece.

Then at two o'clock in the morning on the last Sunday that October, when autumn was already in the woods along the Eden, a navvy broke the leg of Touchy Harrison, gamekeeper on the Edenhall estate. Earlier Touchy had noticed snares in Baron Wood on the high ground above the looping river and like a fool lay in wait, sitting in the fresh-smelling darkness until the two poachers came back. One, a tunnel tiger called Dale, broke his leg. Dale got two years hard and lost his hare.

It all dimmed a little of the glory of Nos 1 and 2 Contracts, though probably it was no more than the Victorians expected of their navvies: stallion-like strength clothed in flannel and moleskin, and pointless violence. Navvies were always feared for the brutality of their riots.

Chapter 14

Riot

In 1904 I was at Tidworth, building the barracks. You had to be
perfumigated before you could start work there and we lodged in
Brimstone Bottom. A navvy was killed in the summer – shot in the
Ram public house.

('Mates!' cried Mrs Garnett, 'don't cross a threshold red with
blood!')

Tidworth, an Imperial Army town, is in the valley of the Bourne,
a seasonally wet/seasonally dry tributary of the Salisbury Avon.
Every day while the town was being built, the Ram brimmed with
drinking navvies, milling and swillicking ale by the bucket in what
is now the car park bounded by the brook. Then, one humid
morning late that hot summer, work was rained off, and they
packed in even tighter.

All morning there was an undertow of violence. A half-blind
navvy called McHann engaged in brief pointless fights with barmen
and the landlord. The landlord, Arthur Thomas, was uneasy all the
time – he carried a navvy-stopping pistol to bank his takings – and
that afternoon he closed the taps early. He was counting money at
the till when Jukes, a barman, came in dirty from his last fight with
McHann. A pewter pot broke a window. Angry men with blood on
their faces threatened to dynamite the place. Thomas locked the
doors and ran upstairs. 'I've got this for you bastards', he called
from a bedroom window, showing them the navvy-stopper before
firing, twice.

Jukes followed with a double-barrelled shot-gun which he
steadied on the window-sill. Some unknown navvy – possibly
McHann – flung a pewter pot which hit the gun barrel, fired the
gun, and killed a middle-aged Norfolk man called Shaw (or Sharpe,
accounts differ) leaning against a tree, now gone, by the river.

'I'm pleased you've come,' Thomas told the police when they

came. 'You can see how I'm situated.' Outside was a litter of dented pewter and broken glass. 'I thought they'd smash up the bally show.' He was taken, cigarette in mouth and fingers, to Pewsey jail in a brougham.

Thomas and Jukes were freed, their trial stopped half-way through. With them there ended a long, long trail of riot, murder, random bloodshed and mass multi-navvy brawls dating back to the eighteenth century. *All* public works were blood soaked. Blood dripped, spurted, trickled or just steadily flowed, mainly from accidents, but also from knees, knuckles, hobnail boots, spades and pick helves. Violence was everywhere, casually vicious.

Rioting was endemic in eighteenth and early nineteenth century Britain in any case. The upper classes were callous, the lower were riotous. People rioted against new machinery and the price of grain, for Parliamentary democracy, against the price of theatre tickets. In the summer of 1795 canal navvies joined bread rioters, unhappy at the price of corn, near Barrow-on-Soar in the Quorn hunting country. A volley of musket balls stopped them, some of them for good. 'The brown bread was very good,' said the *Gentleman's Magazine* 'but this, it should be recollected, was among that newly created, and so wantonly multiplied set of men, the diggers and conductors of navigations.'

On top of that, navvy rioting was often a kind of revenge by people who felt outside the law and outside society. 'Us behaves to folks according as they behave to us,' a man once told Anna Tregelles. 'Tell the navvy dogs the lock-up's too good for them and us'll rampage for the fun of giving them the trouble of putting us there.'

On top of *that*, navvies were often wild men doing hard jobs, hardened by death and calamity all around them. They were also men who lived by their strength and gloried in it. Fighting was a semi-organised sport with them. (Prize-fighting, in fact, was *the* national sport in the days of the canal men.) In 1805 Ned the Navigator fought and killed Sam Elseworth, butcher, behind the Ben Jonson's Head in Stepney. Men building the Redmires dam near Sheffield in the 1830s fought in a meadow, still called The Fighting Field, behind the Three Merry Lads. Prize fighting was the Sunday pastime on the Long Drag, and spontaneous rings of men formed wherever navvies were idle.

There was even a style of boxing called Toe-the-Line, the rules of which were simple – you faced each other across a line scratched in the dirt and took it in turns to fist-hit each other's head. You couldn't defend yourself: each in turn was an open target.

At the Llangyfellach tunnel there was a bloke what they called Toe-the-Line. He used to work all day, stay in a pub till throwing out time, then go and sleep outside on the grass winter and summer. He was a quiet bloke until somebody hit him. He never knew he could fight afore that.

But even given the tendency to violence, most riots had specific causes. Irishmen to begin with were the common factor in nearly a third of them, either because they undercut wages, because of religion, or because of the resentments between people of different cultures. Drink was a cause of many riots and a factor in most. Tension between navvies and the police caused trouble – not so much full-scale rioting, perhaps, as small-scale affrays in which the police were often badly damaged. A lot of navvies were themselves part-time criminals (if only as poachers and food-thieves) happy to make public works into ready-made hideaways for full-time delinquents.

'Well, you see,' a navvy once told Anna Tregelles, 'it's one of the ways of the line never to suffer a police to pick a chap off the work: and maybe now there's a dozen or more on 'em up there,' he went on, pointing along the unmade railway, 'as wouldn't know but the police was after they; so they'd all set on 'en, and do for 'en pretty quick.'

(Army deserters were sometimes hidden too – not always successfully. A gunner, recaptured on the Beckenham line in the 1850s, was sent back to his regiment with 'D' for Deserter branded on his chest.)

Their Betters were not above using their lawlessness, either, when it suited them. During the 1796 Parliamentary elections, for instance, Lancaster canal cutters were recruited by Lord Stanley's agent to intimidate the opposition. Any heavies would have done and navvies were heavier than most. 'We are going on very ill with the work in their neighbourhood,' grumbled the canal engineer, 'Not a man has been at work since the Canvassing began & I doubt it will be the case as long as the Election continues.'

(A clutch of Peto's men started a riot when he stood for Parliament as a Liberal in Norwich in 1847. They turned up, loyally cheering, outside his committee rooms as the polling booths closed. Somebody from a rival party threw a stone. The riot ran into the market square where a gang of navvies, outnumbered, hid in the Cattle Market Hotel. Windows fragmented, mirrors splintered, a man's scalp was gashed open. Peto won, too.)

Navvying's last thirty years were riot-free, the first thirty were *probably* riotous, but the in-between years were like bomb-bursts, particularly during the manias of the 1790s, 1840s, 1860s.

What seems to be one of the earliest recorded canal riots broke out casually in 1794 on the Hereford and Gloucester. Police were assaulted and a navvy called Dyer was arrested. (Perhaps the same Dyer who'd been fired a few months earlier for the idle way he and his men fed Mr Carne's Machine at the Oxenhall tunnel.) Other cutters were jailed for felony. It was ugly enough to stir the canal committee into paying to have them prosecuted as an example and a terror to the rest. The committee, after all, hoped to live profitably with an unalienated countryside once the navvies had gone.

Next year there was a riotous affray, rather than a riot, on the Dearne and Dove about which we know little except it was quickly put down when the ringleaders were snatched. The cavalry, though called out, was never used.

Some canal riots seem to have been against authority, others came out of a fellow-feeling with the down-trod, like the time in March 1795 when diggers from the Leicester and Northampton Union attacked a column of the Leicester Fencibles as they escorted a couple of deserters back to town. The deserters deserted again while the Volunteer Cavalry coralled the cutters in the Recruiting Sergeant, a pub in Newton Harcourt, where pike-armed navvies stood at bay, blocking the doors, until the horse soldiers winkled them out with sabres. Among the people arrested were Red Jack and Northamptonshire Tom, 'two fellows,' said the *Leicester Journal*, 'notorious for being a terror to every country they have resided in.'

Given a choice of fines or jail, the rioters – like most navvies – went inside. Others were offered jail or the Navy.

Some years later, in 1811, a disagreeable shopkeeper in Sampford Peverel was enough to start a riot on the Grand Western in mid-Devon. It's probably true to say most navvies detested shopkeepers as mean and unmanly creatures and this particular one, called Chave, they found particularly despicable. He had recently bought a shop with a sitting tenant living above it. To scare him away,

Chave hired a 'ghost' to rattle chains and beat drums next door.

At dusk one evening in April, the day of Sampford's yearly cattle market, some navvies who had been idle and drinking for three days spotted Chave on his way home. They followed, jeering all the way, then threw stones at his house. His wife shot a man dead, and hurt another. 'It's impossible,' said the *Taunton Courier*, 'not to feel the deepest abhorrence for the proceedings of a savage ungovernable banditti, whose ferocious behaviour we hope will be visited by the heaviest punishment of the law.'

Next year, navvies who were straightening, deepening and widening the River Witham, rioted because a baker cheated them at a pub called the Plough, below Lincoln. They ousted the Plough's landlord, drank his ale, stole his sign, took the baker's basket and crossed the river to march on Bardney, armed with cutting tools. One man carried another man carrying the inn sign. In Bardney they threw bread (his own) at the baker and hung the inn sign in a tree. They stormed the Bottle and Glass, rolled out the barrels, staved in the ends, and wallowed in ale. They robbed the villagers. The village crusher hid in the village almshouses until more constables came from Horncastle. One was killed. The Riot Act was read and cavalry, jangling, herded the navvies together. Farm carts carried them to jail.

A few years later, in 1829, Joseph Hekekyan Bey, an Armenian engineer, was in the Wirral where navvies were throwing up a sea-wall to protect the end of the peninsula from sea-erosion. Because they belonged nowhere, said Hekekyan Bey, and because there were so many of them, they thought themselves beyond the law. One day they went in a body to Liverpool races where they started beating up the police and public with clubs until a posse of young bloods and merchants' clerks rounded on them. Navvies were being arrested as far away as Congleton late into the evening.

At one time when people were paid once a month in pubs, what the newspapers called 'riots' were routine paroxysms, regular as neap tides, except they were usually nothing more than mass-brawls involving nobody but navvies and not harming them over much. Like the men who spoiled Mrs Garnett's Christmas in 1881 when they 'rioted' in the American Tavern near the Alexandra Dock (which they were building) in Hull. 'Oh! What a happy day for England, and for us it would be,' said Mrs Garnett, 'if this should pass into a proverb, "sober as a navvy".'

Or like the fight that broke out on the Leeds-Thirsk railway in

June 1846. Beer selling in the huts was banned because men spent more time drinking than they did working. They got rid of the drink by drinking it. Drinking it got them drunk. Getting drunk got them fighting, three hundred of them, all mangled together in a meadow of unmown hay on Wescoe Hill in Wharfedale.

One man who was drunk for a week, was stripped by his friends and jumped upon, in fun. 'Pumping upon him,' was how the *Halifax Guardian* put it. After pumping on him a bit, they blacked his naked body with soot and pumped upon him a bit more. They then re-sooted him. By then, though, he was dead.

Long, linear, isolated jobs seemed at least semi-essential to riot, as well. Dams and docks were quieter than railways and it was not by chance that one of the very few reservoir riots happened on a pipe track, the nearest waterworks got to railway conditions. Long, linear and isolated. It also had the classic combination of drink and Irishmen.

In September, 1890, Lupton in Westmorland was the nearest village to two sections of the Thirlmere-Manchester pipe track. One was let to a Liverpool firm, the other to a Dublin company with an all-Irish workforce. Between three and four hundred men worked within drinking distance of the village. Most were single or temporarily womanless.

Both Lupton and Nook, its neighbouring hamlet, overlook Lupton Beck. A mile and a deep green hollow separate them. The Plough is still a pub, free-standing in its own asphalted car park. The Nook Tavern, then a less posh affair (probably an ale-house) is now a private dwelling, a long, low building of local stone.

They drank non-stop all over a weekend and through Monday. That afternoon an Irishman beat an Englishman in a straight fight in the Nook Tavern. Small squabbles then broke out spontaneously, sporadically, until they imploded into an open riot in which the English mounted a full-scale assault on the Plough where the Irish drank in a specially segregated taproom. The landlady tried to lock out the English, now armed with iron bars and staves, but when she failed she bolted the door into her main building, then bolted herself.

It was now eight o'clock in the evening, and dark. Outside it was cool. A breeze rustled the tall black hedges. Inside, before the English came, it was hot and fuggy, loud with Irish brogue and song. Then the English crashed in, and tobacco smoke and navvies swirled and rolled in the oil lamps' glimmer. Men roared like wounded bull calves. The fight spilled out into the yard and the road, except for three men lying in blood, spit, and sawdust on the taproom floor. In the lane a hundred evenly divided men brawled and swayed.

Killings seem to have been incidental to most riots (only one man died at Lupton, after being smacked about the head with a spittoon) and deliberate murder was rare. Hangings were rarer, and at least one of them was a mistake.

I worked alongside Dan Sullivan at Llangyfellach. He was hanged for kicking a woman to death. Later a relative confessed to having killed the woman.

One of the other, few, executions was a double hanging by the side of the Edinburgh-Glasgow railroad track near the place where two Irishmen killed an English ganger in December 1840. John Green, the ganger, had been in charge of the gang only two days. The first day they threw bricks at him, the second they murdered him. Overnight, the newspapers speculated, the gang had drawn lots ribbonman-fashion to pick his killer. Early next morning Green met them in the dark on a bridge near Bishopbriggs just outside Glasgow. He commented on the weather and they hit him with an iron bar, knocking his hat off. 'Oh, God,' called Green, 'are you going to murder me?' One man kept hitting him with the bar. Another kept jumping on him in hobnailed boots.

Police and soldiers of the 58th Foot (later the Northamptonshire Regiment) drove up from Glasgow in omnibuses to arrest the whole gang. Over the next few days they were driven in noddies from the Bridewell to the Sheriff's Chambers in Stockwell Street for questioning. In the end, James Hickie, Dennis Doolan and Patrick Redding were brought to trial. Hickie was transported, the others hanged.

Doolan and Redding shambled to the gallows, as ungainly in their shackles as quadrupeds made to walk upright, until the chains were struck from their ankles at the foot of the gibbet. A bishop prayed for them. Then there was the black hood, then the noose, then the drop that broke their spines with a loud crack in the bright May air. A young soldier, pale as the hanging corpses, blacked out and fell.

The Irish potato crop partly failed in 1845, failed completely in 1846, failed again in 1848. Potatoes were wheat, meat and vegetables to the Irish – many ate nothing else – and when whole crops were blighted (leaves blackened, stalks turned brittle, tubers rotted) they died of hunger. Rats ate the dying and the dead. Graphs of the Great Famine years and the peak years of the railway riots would roughly match and, though the two are never mentioned together in newspaper accounts of the time, bitterness must have moved the Irish.

The Penrith riots began and ended one cold week in January, 1846, in the cutting near Yanwath, south of the town on the wide plain of the Rivers Eden, Eamont, and Petteril, flanked by the blue humped hills of Cumbria on one side, the straight blue hills of the Pennines on the other. Things had been tense for some time, mainly because the English thought the Irish undercut their wages. Both sides were segregated as was usual: the Irish were in the north near Plumpton; the English were in the south near the Pele tower at Yanwath. In between, near Penrith, was a kind of everyman's land where both sides mingled and where trouble began on Monday January 9th.

A drunken English ganger ordered an Irishman to drop his pick and pick up his shovel and the Irishman told him to sod off. Others sided with him and the ganger called on the rest of the English to run the Irish off the works.

Everybody went on strike, huddled in camp. After dark the next day a battalion of aggrieved Irishmen trudged down the half-made track, flattening the frozen mud-peaks, to Yanwath. Uneasy magistrates fluttered behind on horseback, until one galloped ahead to warn the English to retreat. They left in good order, leaving their village to the Irish who, surprisingly, left it unlooted and unrazed.

Next morning English recruits came from Kendal and Shap and between them they looted and gutted the Irish settlement at Plumpton. Wispy smoke rose in the cold daylight. An Irishman was already dead.

The Westmorland Yeomanry now patrolled the Irish quarter of the Townhead, an older part of Penrith, narrow-streeted to shock-absorb raids by Scottish moss-troopers. On Wednesday, after hearing the Irish were mustering outside the town with reinforcements from Carlisle, the Yeomanry redeployed, leaving a gap through which the English infiltrated. Once inside the Townhead they stoned an Irish lodging house kept by a man variously called Mr Levy or McLevy, then dragged a navvy called Dennis Salmon from under a bed and down the long winter-bare garden that backs on the railway. John Hobday, a middle-aged man with a clipped beard, swung a pick helve at him, double-handed.

'I called out for mercy,' Salmon told the jury, 'but the prisoner said: "pitch into the bugger, he's life enough in him yet."'

Tyson Hodgson, farmer and parish constable, pleaded with Hobday, too. 'An Irishman will sulk for an hour before he's killed,' said Hobday, swinging at Salmon.

Next day the horse soldiers on the Carlisle road met the Irish contingent. Faced with armed troops, even irregulars, the Irish hesitated. The Yeomanry loaded their carbines. The Irish fell back. Many took their wages and fell right back to Carlisle where the regular army garrison was already on stand-by. On Monday, a week after it all began, cavalry still patrolled the works, though that afternoon they handed over to the 89th Foot (later, the Royal Irish Fusiliers).

All that remained was Hobday's trial, watched by a gallery-load of his mates. Character witnesses swore what a steady man he was. He had worked for Blisset, the contractor, for fourteen years. Even the railway police found no deep fault in him 'except he got drunk like other navvies'. Others said what a quiet and inoffensive chap he was.

The *Carlisle Patriot*'s court reporter disagreed. 'The prisoner is a remarkable man,' he wrote, 'and may be considered a type of the class to which he belongs. His stature is rather below the common height, but his broad frame gives evidence of immense strength. His countenance is forbidding in the extreme. Every feature indicates habitual crime,

> For evil passions, cherished long,
> Have ploughed them with impressions strong,

while his rough matted hair completed the aspect of the finished ruffian. We understand he has said that for nine years he has never slept in a bed, or worn a hat: that his custom was to put on his boots when new, and never remove them until they fell to pieces, and his clothes were treated very much in the same way, except that his shirt was changed, once a week.'

He was transported, to the dismay of the gallery. Hobday laughed.

A few days later Irish gangs on the Edinburgh-Hawick were paid in a pub in Gorebridge, a grey-stone town above a little ravine. In the pub a packman moved quietly about in the smoke and the noise selling his wares to the navvies. Two of them, pretending to be interested in a watch, took it, looked at it, then refused to hand it back. Railway police bundled them off to the line's own lock-up where they stayed until the small hours of the next morning when a mob of their friends broke them loose. Together, raucous and loud, they trooped off to Fusie Bridge – then a hamlet, now a widening in the road – where they kicked a policeman to death.

The murdered man was a Scot and the rest of the navvies on the line, most of them Scottish, set out to avenge him, mustering an army early next morning at Newbattle paper mills by the crags of the River South Usk, marching south like proud rowdy soldiers, colours flying, voices and arms raised, pipes and bugles sounding calls to bloody war. They captured and sacked the sod settlement at Borthwick Castle. Behind them were the blue Pentland Hills: ahead the Moorfoots were still whitened by snow.

The Irish, unable to cope with this semi-disciplined onslaught, fell back to regroup and finally break at Crichton Moor, a heath where beeches lean like well-used brooms away from the wind. The Scots razed their camps. Next morning the Irish counter-attack was broken by a patrol of heavy cavalry from Edinburgh.

Sheriff Spiers of Edinburgh still wanted two of them for the murder of Richard Pace, the policeman: Pat Reilly, a stout middle-aged man with speckled whiskers, a blue bonnet and big boots; and Peter Clark, a sandy man. Both got away.

Who won usually depended on the head count, victory almost always going to the bigger battalion, both sides being pretty equal in physique.[1] Thus, until regular soldiers were called in, Irish navvies trounced the English on the Chester-Birkenhead in October, 1839.

A hagman called Graham offended the Irish by hiring only Englishmen on this contract, so one Monday the Irish clubbed the exclusive English off the line. Next day the English fell in, army-style, and battled with the Irish near Childer Thornton in the Wirral. But the English were outnumbered and out-armed – sticks against pick handles and shovels – and were trounced. Superintendent Palmer came from Birkenhead.

The Irish had now set up headquarters in an ale-house in Childer Thornton and next morning they sallied out to trounce the English

1 A journalist on the *Dumfries Standard* had another theory. 'When fights occur, the English are generally victors with fists – but the Irish, if cudgels are used.'

again. Palmer sent for the Army: the 96th Foot (later, the Manchester Regiment) and the 14th (Prince of Wales' West Yorkshire). Some of the Irish escaped across the fields, while the rest barricaded themselves in houses in Childer Thornton, until Palmer backed his horse against the doors and let him kick them down like a self-propelled battering ram.

But, if anything, the Irish *were* more ferocious than the rest. 'The most reckless, violent set of people than can be imagined,' Maurice Dowling, police commissioner in Liverpool, said of them in the 1840s. 'They assist each other and attack the authorities whoever they may be; they keep the neighbourhood where they reside' – they were building the North Dock – 'in a constant state of uproar and confusion on Saturday night, Sundays and Mondays, and generally a portion of Tuesday.'

'They are,' he went on, 'very violent towards the police.'

They squatted, rent free, in cellars from where only massive police raids could dislodge them. Several policemen were nearly killed, one of them trying to stop a mass brawl. 'They were in the act of butchering him,' said the commissioner, aghast. 'They were *hacking* at him with their spades.'

The commissioner's troubles didn't end there either. Whole families of Irish counterfeiters traipsed behind the navvies like camp-followers, uttering base coin like a spoor, seducing them into passing dud money whenever they were broke, which was almost all the time.

(Around this time, too, the Irish had a curious punishment for their own people. 'If they are offended with any of their fellow workmen,' Alfred List, an Edinburgh policeman, told the 1846 Committee, 'as a revenge they will go to the hut and eat his provisions, then kick him off the work.'

'With that system of vengeance,' a committee member suggested, 'they are not given to pilfering much, are they?'

'No,' said List, 'only feeding.')

Where there were no Irish, foreigners would do, as in the summer of 1866, when English fought Belgian on the Surrey-Sussex Junction.

There was a navvy settlement at Blackham on common grazing ground, thick with hawthorns and brambles, above the Kent Water, a tributary of the Medway. It is a fat green country, almost over ripe, over rich, over green. Hedges were then as tall as trees. White-capped oast houses stood on wooded slopes threaded with smugglers' lanes. On summer evenings the air was an itch of midges, clamourous with bird song.

One Saturday evening in September two Belgians in Caleb Sherlock's beer shant insisted on showing the English how to box and kick. The English chucked them out. Two other English navvies, hearing the noise, ran down through the brambles and were sandbagged by the Belgians. A general brawl erupted.

It kept re-erupting all night. When Moses Stanbrook, a works inspector, arrived at midnight they were breaking down the huts. Police came with the early morning light, the Sunday bells ringing out over Sussex.

The brawl kept re-erupting all day and long after dusk. PC Nathan Tobutt saw a gang of men leaving Caleb Sherlock's beer shant at ten o'clock. They broke into a Belgian hut and dragged Rosalie Martin from under a bed, her skirts about her head, and beat her.

Moses Stanbrook tried beer bribes. 'For God's sake act like Englishmen,' he said when that failed, 'and leave the foreigners alone.' Somebody hit him on the neck with a stick. More police came.

The magistrates' court was held in the Crown in East Grinstead High Street. All the Belgians who hadn't jumped bail were acquitted but two Englishmen got two months' apiece. 'Any attempt to prevent aliens from honestly gaining their livelihood in this country,' warned the chairman, 'will be severely punished.'

(Firbank's biographer says Belgians were brought to the Oxted tunnel as strike-breakers one undated winter around this time. In the subsequent riot the Belgians fled unclad into the woods (thick with snow) and hid there several days.)

Sometimes the police stopped riots, sometimes they started them, often they were harmed.

In May, 1846, letters were sent to contractors at Kinghorn on the coastal railway between Dunfermline and Kirkcaldy on the Firth of Forth's north shore.

Sir – You must warn all your Irish men to be of the grownd on Monday the 11 of this month at 12 ocloak or els we must put them by forse

for we
are determined
to dow it.

Next week, hand-written placards were nailed about the town:

Notice is given
that all the Irish men on the line of railway in Fife share must be
off the grownd and owt of the countey on Monday the 11th of
this month or els we must by the strenth of our arems and a good
pick shaft put them off Your humbel servants
Schots men.

On Sunday a host of Schots men hobnailed down the narrow street
called Nethergate from the viaduct they were building to the beach,
a fang-shaped bit of sand which doubles up as the harbour.
Inchkeith Island, twin-humped and lighthoused, was hazy in the
morning light. But however wild and threatening they were that
mild May morning the evident readiness of the police to truncheon
them down, calmed them down. Nothing more happened.

In June, 1855, a Division of the Army Works Corps waited at the
Crystal Palace for a ship to take them to the Crimea. The Palace on
the hill winked in the sunlight and Royal Waterman's Square,
brand-new, gave a fair imitation in yellow brick of a Tudor
mansion. One afternoon in Penge some of the AWC men stripped
and began sparring, fists up, elbows down. Some respectable
women were so scandalised they scurried along, as though on
castors, to complain to a police constable. They goaded him and his
mate into truncheon-charging the ring of men watching the boxing.
Both were hurt. More crushers trotted up. Boots pounding and legs
pumping like caricature cops in a flickering movie, a body of peelers
in tall shiny hats then truncheon-charged the entire First Division,
Army Works Corps, five hundred men, all entirely innocent, as
they gathered for afternoon roll-call at the Crystal Palace. One
north countryman was truncheoned between the shoulder blades as
he walked alongside the phaeton where he had put his wife for
safety. Nearly half a century later the son of one of the policeman
told Katie Marsh it was the most dangerous moment of his father's
rustic life. The reality of what they had done occurred to the police
all at the same time, as they stood about to be engulfed through their
own illegal stupidity.

Only Katie Marsh saved them. She drove her carriage between
them and the men, imploring the navvies to stop.

'I shall not go away until you are gone if I stay here till midnight,'
she told them. 'You will not murder these men before my eyes, I
know.'

Seven navvies were jailed. One wrongfully. He was alibied by a tentmaker, whom Miss Marsh traced. But nothing, apart from their wounds, happened to the police who had caused it all. The Bench, in fact, rarely reprimanded the police for mistreating navvies and there are few recorded instances, even, of defence counsel condemning police brutality.

Late one Saturday night in August 1866, PCs Osborne and Moore heard sounds of disturbance in Newhaven High Street. A navvy called Soap leant against a wall, swearing. 'The police,' said the *Sussex Advertiser*, 'very properly interfered; an altercation arose between them.' It didn't last long, the altercation. Soap felled them both, with his *crutch*.

'If these poor men were sometimes treated with a little more leniency,' Soap's defence lawyer submitted, 'if the police would remember that they were the guardians of the public peace, and not the petty tyrants of hard working men, these cases could not occur.'

The judge disagreed. 'It is necessary that police constables and all peace officers should be clothed with more protection than other people.' Soap got eight months', hard.

Not long before, three navvies had been tried for their lives for killing a policeman in Somerset. Would he have died, defence counsel asked, if he had not been acting illegally?

The Red House Tavern (now the Red House Inn) is a free-standing stone box near Yeovil, where the old Roman road to Dorchester is crossed by a lane. Twenty centuries of droving have worn the road into a deep groove. The cross-lane – to East Coker – is sunken, too. Then, it tunnelled through its own border of thick, high hedges ('the deep lane shuttered with branches,' T S Eliot wrote of East Coker nearly a century later). Just after midnight on January 11th, 1862, a group of navvies and a boy called Jeremiah Rowe were horse-playing about outside the pub. George Chant was 29. George Handsford was 24. Charles Rogers was 33. Hubbard, a police constable, walked by. 'Who stole the fowl?' one of the navvies asked.

'The bobby.'

'Damn the bobby.'

Hubbard walked a few more yards until stones were chucked at him. He turned and, in the moonlight, saw Handsford tossing them. Hubbard went on up the hill towards Yeovil, the road lit only by his unbright lamp and the moon. On top of the hill he met PC Penny and together they went back to the Red House, where the navvies still loitered in the cold moonlight. Penny put his hand on Handsford's shoulder. 'What's your name?' Penny asked him.

'What for?' said Handsford.

'I'm taking you into custody for throwing stones at Hubbard.'

But Handsford, though arrested verbally, was unarrested physically. The police wandered off again. By chance on top of Yeovil Hill they met Sgt Keates and all three went back to the pub where the navvies still loitered in the cold moonlight. Handsford still wouldn't come quietly, so they jumped him, wrestling, grappling and scuffing in the dim light, the studs in their boots knocking sparks out of the road, till one of them snapped the jaws of his handcuffs on Handsford's wrist, though all that did was turn one flailing arm into a deadly weapon.

'What? Are you all going to see me taken like this?' Handsford called to his mates.

Chant squared up behind Sgt Keates. Rogers, his white slop faintly gleaming in the moonlight, cracked the two constables on the head with a stick and ran. Handsford's handcuffs struck Penny on the temple. Of the navvies, only Handsford and Chant were now left. Sgt Keates lay stunned in the moonlight. PC Penny lay dying. Keates got up, chased Handsford, knocked him down, and arrested him. PC Penny still lay dying in the moonlight.

Rogers was found a day later hiding under a basket in the back-house of an inn. 'If I hadn't hit him,' he explained to the arresting officer, 'he'd have killed I.'

Mr ffooks, for the defence, began by questioning the legality of the arrest. When an affray – in this case the tossing of stones – was over, a constable had no more powers of arrest than anybody else. He had to get a magistrate's warrant. In this case the affray had been over for an hour before the arrest was made.

He went further. Had there been an affray at all? Those stones had been pitched in fun, not thrown. PC Hubbard admitted they *truckled* at his feet. Didn't the jury think a powerful man like Handsford could have thrown them with force if he'd wanted to hurt the constable? Flipping or tossing pebbles was no felony, merely a misdemeanour, and the police had no powers of arrest for that. The navvies would never have fought the police, had the police not assaulted them. The Jury must teach the police how to behave.

The judge summed up. There were two questions: was the flipping of pebbles an assault? and, if it was, did the lapse of time between the assault and the arrest constitute a continuing pursuit? If the jury said no to the second question, the arrest was illegal and Handsford's resistance was no felony. If they said yes to both questions, then PC Penny was murdered. If they said no, his death might still be manslaughter.

Chant and Rogers were acquitted, but Handsford was found guilty of manslaughter with a recommendation to mercy. He got four years' hard labour.[2]

Workhouse masters and other jacks in office often mugged lone navvies as well. In 1904 Charles Lovett, tramp navvy, was rescued from the masters and porters of Marlborough Workhouse by a policeman called Shaw, though before they came to trial Lovett vanished, and they were freed for lack of evidence. Shaw was threatened with losing his job and Mrs Garnett pleaded with Lovett in the *Letter*. 'Stand up for justice, mates!' But Lovett had gone for good.

Absconding hagmen, if caught, caused riots. Hapton is a bleak four-street town growing uphill from roots in the Liverpool-Leeds canal in the Colne-Blackburn cotton conurbation in the Calder Valley. In 1846 they were building the East Lancashire railway there and in September the police brought two hagmen called Benley and Leech before the magistrates. They had packed their furniture and were about to take off without paying their men when the navvies caught them. There was no money, they told the men. Then there's no food for you, said the navvies, locking the hags in the billiard room of the Angel (now gone). They charged a ha'penny a peek and collected seventeen shillings.

A police raid busted them out of navvy custody into the police cells. Why was there no money, the magistrates asked. It was expended they explained, and since their wives had already fled with their other chattels, there was nothing the law could do. The navvies, however, grabbed Leech and locked him in the billiard room again until the police raided the place and put him back in the cells for his own good. Still, he got his share of the stolen contract money: the men shared what they got from the peep-show.

Only twice, perhaps, did navvies fight for their bosses like cow-hands in a range war.

The first time was in 1845 on the Gravesend-Rochester where the contractor told the company he'd keep their railway unless they

---

2 Medical evidence suggested Penny was killed by the handcuffs on Handsford's wrist.

gave him more money. The company, outraged both by the blackmail and the theft of their line, were even more put out when the contractor sent a ganger to steal the cylinder ends from their locos, leaving them stranded – forlorn, immobilised and cold, their tall smoke-stacks unsmoking – in the old converted canal tunnel at Strood. The ganger made off in a post-chaise, chased by a carriage brimming with the company's men, arms and fists waving through the open windows. The ganger was arrested on the gang-plank of a London-bound river steamer.

By now the company had occupied its own Gravesend terminus, by force. The contractor's men smashed through the doors and turned them out, by force. More navvies with picks and crowbars marched off to capture and occupy the station at Rochester. The police could do nothing and in the end it was the magistrates who persuaded both sides to post token forces in the termini and go to arbitration.

A few miles away, a few years later, the second railway war was fought where the Oxford-Worcester strikes the northern end of the Cotswolds near Mickleton, a village of mixed Gloucestershire stone and the black-and-white of the Warwickshire plain. On the scarp side, the tunnel gapes black and wet over the Vale of Evesham. In the hot summer of 1851 Brunel fired the Mickleton contractor because he was behind with the work and gave the job to Peto and Betts. Marchant, the old contractor, said he wouldn't budge without being paid for the plant he'd bought. Navvies sent to drive him off by force were beaten up.

Then Brunel, backed by navvies, tried to evict him personally one hot Friday in July. Marchant, who knew he was coming, called out the magistrates and faced him from behind their backs, and those of a squad of cutlass-armed police. The magistrates read the Riot Act. Brunel fell back.

A small army of Peto and Bett's men then tried, early on Monday morning, scuffing and trampling as delicately as anybody can in navvy boots towards the mouth of the tunnel. Marchant's men were awake and ready. Skulls cracked. Shoulders dislocated. A man who drew a pistol was felled with a shovel. The magistrates came back with the Gloucester Artillery. It was still early morning, the country rich and fat with cows and ripening fruit. The embankment curved away into the Vale of Evesham and the sunshine.

The day grew hot and uneasy. More men arrived. To break the deadlock the magistrates told Marchant to start work. What happened then was like a 17th century battle in scale and tactics – a ruck of men at push of pike hob-nailing in freshly worked muck: blood soaking into it could ruin respectable folk. Brunel and Marchant stepped aside to talk it over. Behind them a finger was bitten off. Time to back off. Cubitt and Stephenson were asked to arbitrate.

The last two riots on public works, curiously enough, fell within days of each other in the blazing summer of 1904: the killings at the Ram near Tidworth and at Seathwaite Tarn in Cumberland.

Few regular navvies worked at Seathwaite, an isolated little concrete dam in the almost soil-less fells above Dunnerdale, under an immense, silent, grey-green corrie scattered with scree, but nevertheless newspapers began with headlines of *navvy* riots before saying they were sorry for maligning honest men. The rioters were labourers. 'In addition to the genuine navvy,' said the *North Western Daily News*, 'there is always a lot of men who are really hangers on.' Such were Owen Cavanagh, Joseph Foy, and Garrett Kinsella.

The pub where it all happened is now the Newfield Inn. Then it was the New Field Hotel, a little old thick-walled house in an L-shape of buildings in a sharp bend in the road. All around are the woods by the River Doddon. It was a hot summer. People died of the heat. Two navvies died of heat stroke in Colchester. In Seathwaite the hot sunlight burned out the intense rocky greyness of the place.

Owen Cavanagh was a young Millom man, an ex-soldier (he had a bad eye), a labourer – not a navvy – making the road that switchblades up the fell to the dam. He had a drink-damaged liver and peritonitis and the day he was shot he'd started drinking at nine in the morning. By midday he, Foy, and Kinsella were in the New Field. Foy fell asleep and the publican ordered them out. They smashed the deep-set windows and the furniture, a hanging lamp, glasses, beer bottles, a mirror. Everything breakable was broken except the whisky bottles which they opened.

They hurled half a ton of rocks at the vicarage, the church and the schoolhouse in the shade of the trees by the Doddon, before trooping back to stone the New Field. A barman shot Foy in the legs. The publican shot Kinsella. An engineer called Todd shot Cavanagh, who died next day in the tourist luncheon room. The gunmen were acquitted.

It was the end of the warfare on public works, though not the end of the navvy's involvement in war.

Chapter 15

War

'I have had the diarrhoea for a week but I am very well again, thank God for it,' Robert Bagshaw, navvy, wrote home from the Crimea. 'As you wish me to send all the news I can, I must tell you that Sebastopol is taken at last.'

Navvies, as navvies, worked for the Army in four wars: against Napoleon, where they helped dig the Royal Military Canal; the Crimea, where they were a bit of a triumph; the Sudan, where they were a bit of a disaster; the Great War.

Napoleon impinged on them mainly by causing a navvy shortage, though many were pressed or recruited into the armed forces as well. Wages rose. Costs doubled.

'As the soldiers will be disbanded on Saturday, I propose trying if I cannot get about twenty of them to carry up the cut,' said the Lancaster canal's secretary at the start of the Peace of Amiens, 1802. (Privateers also pillaged the canal's cargoes of pozzolana, the hydraulic ingredient in mortar, which came from Italy.)

In the summer of 1803, Hugh MacIntosh, the muck-shifting contractor at Blackwall docks, was troubled by the Press Gang. 'I have within these few days,' he wrote to the East India Company, 'perceiv'd some Alarm amongst the Men employ'd on account of the Danger of being impressed, a Report being circulated of a number of hands being taken from the London Docks, and I beg leave to suggest the necessity, if it is practicable, of obtaining a Protection.' (Protections were certificates telling the Press Gang in unsteady type and quilled ink that the Bearer was exempt from naval service.)

Navvies *were* scarce. In the summer of 1804 Thomas Thatcher poached Kennet and Avon men to work on the Floating Harbour in Bristol. A few weeks later the Royal Military Canal poached the same people for war work. 'There now appears in a Bristol paper an advertisement for two thousand men to be employed in Kent,' Tom

Thatcher wrote in the *Kentish Gazette* in November. 'I hereby inform the workmen that it is my intention to give greater price for work than has or may be offered by any contractor for work of this kind in Kent.' ('And you won't have to walk five miles for your breakfast in Bristol,' he added.)

In the summer of 1802 John Addington, the Prime Minister, laid the foundation stone of the London Dock, downstream of the Tower. The Chancellor of the Exchequer chucked a purse of gold on a stone for the men. A year later the company wrote in its report, 'The uncertain delivery of Materials, an impossibility of obtaining and keeping together a sufficient number of Workmen many of whom have been at times called off to National Works, and other circumstances unforeseen in an undertaking so extensive and unexampled have delayed completion of the Works.'

The National Work, perhaps, was the Royal Military Canal, ringing a cam-shaped bit of Romney Marsh and intended primarily as an anti-invasion ditch, a lot of it built between 1804–9 by the Royal Staff Corps, the Royal Waggon Train, and infantrymen, as well as civilian navvies. Both the Royal Staff Corps, which did the Army's civil engineering, and the Royal Waggon Train, which hauled its freight, were disbanded before the Crimean War – which essentially was the siege of Sebastopol, where engineering and logistics where the Army's big problems.

The French commander, Canrobet, asked Lord Raglan to choose a sea-base. Raglan asked Admiral Lyons. The Admiral chose Balaclava and gave the British Army the eastern end of the siege and two of the war's battles, Inkerman and Balaclava, both fought to stop the Russian field army breaking out of Sebastopol.

The Allies lay in a semi-circle on the heights above Sebastopol, where the British Army was fed, munitioned, and carted (dead and dying) by ox-carts and pack-ponies along a track like a mud-filled ditch which joined the Balaclava naval base to the Woronzov Road, the only metalled highway on the peninsula. What was needed was a good road or a poor railway, but the Royal Staff Corps which might have made them was long disbanded. It was then that the civilian contractors Peto, Brassey and Betts made the country an offer it couldn't refuse: a military railway in the war zone at cost.

Balaclava is hemmed in east and west by limestone hills. The western hills fall straight to the sea but to the east is a narrow coastal plain where Balaclava stands. In town, the harbour lay on both sides of a creek. Kadikoi, in the Balaclava valley, is about a mile inland, its vineyards and poplar groves long denuded by the foraging army. At Kadikoi the valley turns west and runs for about a mile to the Flagstaff at the foot of the plateau on which the armies lay. Horse-drawn trains were to begin on both sides of the harbour, run along the valley to Kadikoi, turn with it to the Flagstaff and then be hauled by stationary steam engines on to the plateau; seven miles, almost, from sea to trenches.

Peto left Parliament to mastermind it, helped by brother-in-law Betts who was in charge of the ships. A recruiting office was opened early in December 1854, in the Waterloo Road and for a day or so three hundred navvies thronged about the place, signing on for five shillings a day, a soldier's rations, and a free passage there and back. Most were English, a few were Irish, and most worked either on the London, Tilbury and Southend Railway, in the Victoria Dock, or on the Houses of Parliament.

They were called, semi-officially, the Railway Construction Corps or the Civil Engineering Corps and were led by James Beatty, a railway engineer from Inniskillen. Apart from navvies there were drivers, carpenters, horsekeepers, well-sinkers, clerks, fitters, sawyers, a draughtsman, a barber, a surveyor and his chain lad, a cashier, timekeeper, storekeeper, and two missionaries, the Rev. Thomas Fayers and the Rev Cyngle, who built a church. For their health they had a set of nurses, possibly Gamp-like, Mrs Fapp, Mrs Prestige, Mrs Williams, and Mrs Duffield.

They went in a fleet of twenty-two ships, steamers and sailers, each so laden her loss at sea wouldn't wreck the entire enterprise. Between them they carried all the rails and sleepers, all the wagons, barrows, tools, forges, cranes and pile drivers.

Hesperus was still building in Mitchell's Walker-on-Tyne yard, next to the ironworks where the railway's rails were forged. They were loaded hot from the furnace into her unfinished hold. Shipwrights worked around the clock getting berths ready. There were little hundred horse steamers like *Propellor*, *Lady Alice Lambton*, *Baron Von Humboldt*, and *Prince of Wales*. Paddlers like *Levant* and sailing ships like *Mohawk* and *Wildfire* which in Balaclava doubled as hospitals.

Wildfire sailed first, dropping down the Mersey early in December. Her navvies mustered at Euston Square Station, filling in allowance papers for wives and relatives, before travelling by train to Liverpool. Stay-at-homes cheered them down the river, emigrants huzzaed them. For the navvies it was a well-paid lark all the way. They stormed the Rock of Gibraltar and in Malta they held boxing matches to finance a randy after they were let ashore without money.

Eight weeks, almost to the day, after the 'no more men wanted' notice was nailed to the recruiting office door in Waterloo, navvies sat and growled, cooped in their ships in Balaclava harbour waiting for the weather to clear. One night there was a pitched fight in the holds. Outside frost and February cold ripped flesh from men's bones.

When they emerged, earthy creatures creeping off the sea, they astonished the Army. Unutterable things, an officer called them, whose nature it was to work upon railways – as though railway-making were encoded in their genes. They strode about, saluting passing soldiers, caped like cabmen, the peaks of their caps hanging over the napes of their necks like coal-heavers, clay-piped and cocky, prideful as became men out to do a job nobody else could do.

Their first job was to make themselves a home and set up a base. For the base they built a new wharf and tore down houses near the old landing place to clear a space for railway lines and sleepers. At the same time, on dry gravelly ground above the town, they erected their own huts, painting names on their sides – Peto Terrace, Victoria, Blackwall, London. Until then, they lived in their ships where every night Fayers preached to them as they darned socks and stitched clothes in the darkened holds.

They landed the engines and tested them, shrieking steam, in the high street. They turned the old Post Office garden – once a bright whitewashed place with grape vines trailing to the sea – into a plank and barrow dump.

Within a few days the weather changed to a false Spring which deceived even native-born birds into nesting and trees into budding prematurely. Sickness incubated in the sudden warmth. Navvy demolition crews battered down the frail houses by the Post Office, tipping the rubbish over the putrefying bodies of the dead. Well-water filtered through corpses rotting and corrupting in the hills.

In Balaclava, William Russell, *The Times*' war correspondent, had a house with a walled courtyard filled with Tartar camel-drivers and poplars. One day he left home as usual and, as was not *un*usual, came back a week later to find navvies had bulldozed his wall and laid the railway through his yard.

Soon they were platelaying out of town (the Royal Navy and the Dorset Regiment had already scraped a rudimentary track to Kadikoi), switching from fearnought slops and thigh boots to flannel shirts and leggings to match the changing weather. (Everybody had a complete wardrobe – from painted suits and cotton shirts to lindsey drawers and mittens. All wore moleskin trousers.) Gales blew, the sun shone, it rained, it sleeted, it snowed, all within minutes of each other. Squalls ripped down tents and sent lumber cartwheeling away. Heat solidified the semi-fluid sludge underfoot, rain re-drenched it.

By mid-February the tracks reached Kadikoi, curving away between the church and the guns. It was a strangely noisy war: gunfire and music, camels crying, people calling in a dozen languages, Eastern and European, then came the unaccustomed rumble of the railway, astonishing the Cossacks beyond the River Tchernaya, rearing their horses and waving their lances at the sight of the lines of little black wagons racketing along on the downslope by Kadikoi.

When they could, they worked double-shifted, day and night. The night shift lay ballast, the day shift lay rails. Refinements like cuttings, embankments, and tunnels were impossible and the line wavered over the landscape. Once, when they had to bridge a stream, a pile-driver was brought up in the night, assembled in the dawn, dismantled at dusk.

The weather changed to and fro between winter and summer, thawing and deep freezing all the buried animal matter. Vultures, flapping blackly, heavy with human meat, worked a kind of shift system: half a week with the Allied dead, half a week with the Russian.

Early March, and it froze again, chilling the shell-cases already being hauled along the railway to a munitions dump near Kadikoi. By mid-March the line topped the col on to the plateau: the stationary steam engines were in place, along with the tripod and the great drum which carried the wires for hauling trains up the slope. On the plain, ponderous dray-horses pulled the wagons between the harbour and the place where they were hitched to the steam engine wires.

Some navvies were already in trouble. One stole a pet bullock belonging to a French General. Another was flogged by the Provost Marshal to the amusement of his mates. He roared like a bull but remarked he had been flogged for the honour of his country.

Nevertheless they worked well in spite of the booths of Vanity Fair and Buffalo Town, civilian camps brimming with whores and gamblers and drink-shops. Their popularity however was soon to collapse.

By Good Friday the railway was streaming with munitions and war material and that evening a train carrying the Highland Light Infantry jumped the track and killed a soldier. The Rev Fayers was there, in the huts on Frenchman's Hill. The regiment, he said, was coming down in the dusk when dew had already oiled the rails. The track steepened around the side of Frenchman's Hill and the brakes couldn't hold the wagons whose rattle roused the navvies. 'Turn the points', shouted one. A man near a turn-out threw the switch and sent the wagons off the rails.

By mid-April the railway was carrying more ammunition than the bearers could handle. 'It is impossible,' General Burgoyne told Peto, 'to over-rate the services rendered by the railway, or its effects in shortening the siege.'

That Spring they built lime kilns, stores, wash houses, and an Admiralty pier. Their well-sinkers sank the Navy a well, as their popularity slowly sank, too. Raglan wrote to the Prime Minister promising to shoot them if they grew more mutinous.

Then one evening in June a thunder storm turned the sky to fire and water and cut the peninsula in two like a brightly lit waterfall. On one side of a straight line water cascaded from the sky: on the other it was dust dry. Rain drowned men in the ravines, washed animals and huts out to sea, washed open the burying grounds of Balaclava, washed the corpses bare, washed bodies from their graves, washing them into a jumbled heap of bones. Rain broke the railway in places.

Beatty was away, surveying the coalfields of Heraclea, and the navvies were uncooperative. 'The only obstructions to be dreaded,' Rusell wrote in *The Times*, 'will arise from the "navvies", some of whom have been behaving very badly lately. They nearly all "struck work" a short time back, on the plea that they were not properly rationed or paid, or that, in other words, they are starved and cheated; the Provost-Marshal brought some of them to a sense of their situation, and, indeed, the office of that active and worthy person and his myrmidon sergeants has been by no means a sinecure between "navvies", Greeks, and scoundrels of all sorts.'

Duty or the cat-o'-nine-tails got them back to work, but in Russell's mind 'navvies' – now insulted with inverted commas –

were forever lumped with Greeks and other scoundrels. By late August they had all gone home. 'The railway corps is gone,' he wrote, 'and out of that stout body of navvies who were ready, while in England, to smash Russians with their pickaxes, but who became most peaceably inclined directly they saw the enemy's works, there now remains only Mr Beatty.'

But a whole new navvy army was already mustered and on its way to the Crimea. The whole idea of navvy non-combatants may well have been Sir Joseph Paxton's – architect of the Crystal Palace – who first mentioned it in an election speech in Coventry in May 1854. In April 1855, Lord Panmure, Secretary of State for War, invited him to recruit a new Corps of Navigators to replace the men coming home from the Crimea.

Paxton mustered his new unit – the Army Works Corps – at the Crystal Palace. It was semi-military and more regularly organised: men signed on for two or three years. They were unarmed, un-uniformed, not part of the regular army, but they *thought* they were bound by the Articles of War and the Mutiny Act. They were mobilised into twenty-five-man gangs commanded by both gangers and uniformed officers. The pay was thirty-five shillings a week for navvies, forty for gangers, and everybody was to get a twelve pound bonus at the end.

At first the AWC was to be a thousand strong but in September 1855, another thousand were recruited and in October Paxton asked Panmure for more. They were behaving too badly in the field for that, Panmure told him, though he did authorise a Commissariat Branch which reached the Crimea in January 1856. At its strongest the AWC seems to have had 2827 men and 77 officers.

Superintendent-General William Thomas Doyne, a railway engineer, was their field commander. Robert Stephenson gave him a reference. Doyne, a gentleman by birth and education, would be able to deal with the officers of the Royal Engineers as an equal it was thought, though it turned out that Beatty was his main problem.

The AWC as a body had more trades than the Civil Engineering Corps. It recruited both navvies *and* general labourers as well as carpenters, smiths, hammermen, plasterers, glaziers, drivers, fitters, storemen, clerks, masons, quarrymen, sawyers, servants, bricklayers, wheelwrights, shoemakers, tentmakers, corporals and sergeants of police, plumbers. In Balaclava harbour a floating workshop, *Chasseur*, housed bellmenders, coppersmiths and moulders.

Katie Marsh cared for them at the Crystal Palace, and saved their allowances in a Friendly Club until the war's end. She gave stamped receipts for their money-orders which once, in a nice gesture of trust, they flung back on the floor of her carriage. She lent them money to pay their drunk and riotous fines. She wrote to them in the Crimea. Mainly they were Lancashire, Durham and Northumberland men. Some were from Kent and Cornwall. Some were Scots, fewer were Irish.

By late June 1855, the First Division had embarked in the London River where the sailing ships *Langdale* and *Simoon* lay off Greenhithe. *Barrackpore* swung to the tide in Blackwall Reach. (When the Marsh sisters visited her, the men manned the rigging sailor-fashion and cheered.) In the Arcade Bazaar at London Bridge the Marshes bought chess sets, draughts, backgammon boards, games of 'railways and coaches', Chinese puzzles and scripture puzzle books to keep them from gambling on board.

With the next intake was No 551 Robert Bagshaw, 17th Gang, 1st Division, Army Works Corps, a lad from Grindlow, a lonely hamlet all alone on a great Derbyshire hillside, backed by a wooded ridge but fronted by a sweeping hollow scored by a labyrinth of stone walls like the foundations of an unbuilt Roman town. It's a little place of stone cottages and walled gardens with a rainy sky and a dry limestone ground. The world outside astonished Robert Bagshaw.

On 21 June, a couple of days before the thunder storm in the Crimea, he wrote home from his lodgings in the Rambler's Rest, Hamlet Road, a street of cottages and stucco villas by the Crystal Palace. He was worried his parents would throw away the letter: it was his authority to the receiving officer to pay them twenty shillings a week while he was away, and alive.

He wrote again, 4 July. 'I now write to let you know that we are got on the vessel on Monday and we live like fighting cocks. At present we are very comfortable and quite hearty. I should like to hear from you but I don't know when we shall set out for our journey. We are going in a sailing vessel and they tell us that it will take us six weeks to go if the weather be favourable. There is two hundred going in the same vessel and we have got tools to take with us of all sorts. And I must assure you that if we had many a poor family we could fill them their baskets with meat we leave, and I hope if ever I return again I shall be able to let you have an account.

If ever you come to London you just take a trip to Greenhithe where we are lying. It is the finest prospect you or I ever saw. You must give my love to my sisters Sarah, Mary, Judy and all inquiring friends. Tell them that I don't repent my journey as far as I have tried. You oblige me with all the news you can when you write to me, and I will send you all the news I can.' He added: 'The vessel we are going in is called Longdale. You must tell the Dusty Pits workmen that I enjoy very good health and plenty of beef and beer three times every day.'

He wrote next from Balaclava, 20 August. He had sailed on 6 July aboard *Barrackpore*, not *Langdale*. 'We have a pleasant voyage, thank God for it. We have had plenty to eat of the very best that could be had. I was sick only two days, passing through the Bay of Biscay.' It was a six week passage, as he had thought, and they had called at Constantinople, at which he marvelled. Greenhithe was quite forgot. He still didn't know where he was going and he still worried they were not getting his allowance. 'Be sure to put three stamps on your letters and address them correctly,' he said. 'Write back soon as possible.'

Russell, like a bearded barrel, still trod the Crimean circuit drinking other men's brandy. On 13 August he reported that 'Superintendent-in-Chief' Doyne had landed in Balaclava from the *Orinoco* after trans-shipping from *Simoon* in Constantinople. The railway staff were so reduced by sickness they were to be disbanded and Mr Beatty and some of his original gangers were to run it. Beatty, as well, was to build more lines to the Sardinian Army camp. Doyne's new navvies were to ballast and re-make the railway and build an all-weather road.

Lord Raglan had died late in June of diarrhoea and cholera aggravated, it was said, by stress. General Sir James Simpson, a long-headed Scot, a veteran of the Peninsula and Sind, now had the Army. The British had gone on strengthening their artillery opposite the Redan while the French sapped towards the Malakov Tower, the real key to the taking of Sebastopol.

The flowers were withered in the sun-browned landscape lined by grey mountains. Close up, the Crimea was black with flies, clustering on every forkful of food, drowning in every cup, sleeping in solid black colonies on ceilings where the merest glimmer of candlelight woke them, buzzing with high-pitched irritation.

A week before the AWC arrived the French and Sardinians fought and won a pitched battle on the River Tchernaya, north of the river's gorges. The dead of three massed Russian divisions, blown apart by gunfire, lay so thick by the river the Allied cavalry wouldn't let their horses drink there. Russell wrote of a three-day cannonade of Sebastopol which had just ended, burning fuses arching through the sky like tracer bullets in later wars. Ice came for the hospitals and *Simoon* and *Barrackpore* berthed, full of AWC men, Robert Bagshaw among them.

By mid-September, Russell reported, sixteen per cent of them were dead. He blamed drink and the things they ate. Mrs Seacole, late of Jamaica, doctored them in her restaurant, a ramshackle of iron stores and sheds close to the railway on the rising ground between Kadikoi and the col. Mrs Seacole, a kindly body (a sort of lesser Florence Nightingale), also tended the wounded in the trenches.

What was more important, was Doyne's immediate problem, the railway or the all-weather road? Beatty and the railway were independent of him and Beatty had the Generals on his side. He controlled the tool-making ship *Chasseur* and was able to raid Doyne's AWC for labour at will. The Land Transport Corps which ran the railway asked for and got AWC brakesmen and pointsmen as well as carpenters to make and fettle wagons and build and run a sawmill at Sinope.

It didn't take Doyne long to decide a road was more important, *and* that his whole command would be ruined if he couldn't control Beatty. Give Beatty the means to tinker with the railway on his own, Doyne told Paxton, or give Beatty and the railway to me. In the meantime he began work on the Grand Central Road, with five thousand soldiers and all the navvies he could wrest from Beatty, two hundred of them. Within a few days exasperation got the better of him and he wrote again to Paxton. 'I am doing everything in my power to make this disjoined system work,' he said, 'but I regret I do not receive from Mr Beatty that disinterested co-operation which I have a right to expect. The utmost I have succeeded in doing is to avoid an open quarrel, which the tone he adopts is calculated to produce.'

Sebastopol had already fallen. 'I saw it all on fire one hour after it was taken,' said Robert Bagshaw, inaccurately, 'and got a gun and a sword from the Russians. We was about four miles from the town when it was taken and the shot and shell shook us in bed for three days before.'

The last barrage began around dawn, Wednesday 5 September: a still morning with light airs from the south-east, too light to ruffle the sea where ships sat reflected upside down, full length, in its sheen. Sebastopol is split in two, east and west, by the harbour into which the River Tchernaya flows. The southern half of the town is similarly split, north and south, by the Dockyard Creek which then ended almost at the British lines and pushed on through them as a ravine. A floating bridge of boats linked north and south Sebastopol, while the harbour itself was closed by a chain of ships: steamers, frigates, old two-deckers.

The final battle began with the firing of buried mines, gushers of flame and earth, reddened by the morning sun. Three miles of artillery fired simultaneously, the heaviest, loudest, most compact massed gunfire of its time. They fired almost without slackening until the last infantry charge at noon on Saturday.

Once taken, Sebastopol became a tourist trap for off-duty troops and navvies. The Russians now shelled the city from their positions in the north. One Sunday in October a shell burst near the Imperial Barracks. An AWC man strolled over to examine the crater, clay-pipe in mouth. After appraising the shell-hole, pipe still sparking tobacco, he strolled off to examine the barracks. The Russians had been messy, and loose powder littered the floor. A tobacco ember snorted from the pipe, lit a trail of gunpowder, phutting and cracking like a firework. It reached the magazine where roof, walls, flame, smoke all blew out together. Nobody said the navvy died.

Work on the central highway began soon after. 'Many a time I have wished myself at home,' Robert Bagshaw wrote to Grindlow. 'But I am settled at present. We have done very little work till this last week and we are making a road from Balaclava to Sebastopol, and our officers tell us that we shall be able to have our dinner at home on Christmas day.'

At first it was proposed to repair the old roads between Kadikoi and the crest of the col and introduce a one-way system – up the old French route in Vinoy Ravine, down the old cart track around Frenchman's Hill. But Doyne thought a new road was needed and, since Beatty had surveyed the railway so well, it was to parallel its tracks most of the way.

A ditch was dug to drain the Balaclava plain. Drains, cross-connected by ditches, were dug in the flat boggy parts near the harbour and the road was macadamised with stone pitching. For a time all the Army's traffic was driven over it, like a non-stop roller, and in the mornings and evenings navvies consolidated it even more.

On the rising ground, the road wound around Frenchman's Hill, terraced into the hillside. From Mrs Seacole's place the old road was widened, drained, raised and metalled. Above her the road was again terraced into the hillside. Wet places were drained by a zig-zag of ditches converging on old water barrels and pork casks under the road.

From the top of the col the highway crossed the plateau and the Woronzov Road into the Light Division camp. A wide strip of top soil, a shallow clay, was scraped away to bed-rock, a kind of oolitic limestone. In places the limestone was left to weather and harden. Elsewhere limestone chippings were carted in. For the winter they planned to hang lanterns from the mileposts to pick out the road through the snow.

At the same time, the railway, which had been hurriedly laid on scraped earth, was properly bedded, drained, ballasted, and doubled into a two-way track. By the end of November two steam locos, *Alliance* and *Victory*, worked the low ground below Kadikoi, supplementing the ponderous horses.

The rest of the Second Division came in October, 1855, some landing from the *Telegraph* and (those who hadn't jumped ship in Malta) the ss *Azoff*.

The Third Division was recruited in November. They had their own chaplain, a muscular christian called Hudson who had already scaled Mont Blanc by the straightest route. Work was scarce in England and 'mechanicals' from the manufacturing towns now volunteered, reaching the Crystal Palace without money and, until they signed on, without wages. Katie Marsh bought them hot penny pies every day from a London pieman and coffee and bread from a nearby coffee shop. Because they needed references she turned her father's Beckenham rectory into an unofficial AWC office from where they could write to their old masters. *Jura* sailed in December, the last of the navvy ships.

In February 1856, a detachment of the AWC came under fire as they took up new quarters in the dockyard where they'd been sent to mend the Woronzov Road between Cathcart's Hill and the Creek Battery. Gunfire had smashed the drains, embedding half a dozen gun carriages in the mud. Russian artillery shelled them as they re-made the road alongside the creek in the harbour. Later they helped the submarine officer dive for brass field guns.

March 1856, was cold and frosty and it snowed. Commissariat Department navvies began building a dam to pipe water to the Castle Pier. Bricklayers and navvies struck work and had a week's pay stopped to induce them to behave. A hut burned down, killing several men. On the 19th, a bright Sunday after a boisterous Saturday, Ganger Marks was reduced to the rank of navvy in his own gang. Cooper's Foreman McPherson was reduced to his trade. Next day fog rolled in from the Black Sea and Marks was made up to ganger again, at a reduced wage, and McPherson was sent to headquarters as a horse thief. On the 28th the water was turned on for Castle Pier.

Disciplined Army and undisciplined AWC now clashed more often. 'The Army Works Corps,' complained General Simpson, 'are by far the worst lot of men yet sent here. It is ruin to our soldiers to be placed in contract with such a set of people, receiving higher pay than themselves.'

Doyne's troubles with Beatty seem to have ended in November 1855, when he and and his staff were transferred to the AWC. But Doyne still had trouble with the Army and his own men. AWC officers *looked* martial – like sharpshooters, said Russell – in their grey, blackbraided uniforms, swaggering about with swords and telescopes, but they seemed unable to keep order.

According to Katie Marsh navvies refused to touch their caps or pull their forelocks to *any* officer and were flogged for it. 'We've come to work,' they said, 'and can't awhile do manners.'

According to Doyne, he scarcely had any authority over his men at all. Those Articles of Agreement everybody signed at the Crystal Palace had no meaning at all in military law. At home, the Judge Advocate General ruled that the AWC was *not* subject to the Articles of War or the Mutiny Act. To the Army they were camp followers, bound by a civil contract – not with the Army – but with Doyne personally. The Army consequently refused to flog or discipline them and all Doyne could do was stop paying and feeding them when they broke their side of the bargain. A letter from Panmure gave him authority to fine them though Doyne doubted its legality.

In April 1856, General Codrington, who had taken over from Simpson, learned the AWC were misbehaving: a hundred men had been idling on the wharf instead of unloading wagons and a homeward bound division were disgracefully drunk on board *Cleopatra* before she put to sea. If they didn't change their ways, he threatened, he would have their gratuities stopped.

Doyne, upset by the ingratitude as much as anything else, wrote to Paxton from Bleak House, the Corps' Crimean HQ. He listed everything the Corps had done: ballasting, draining and reconstructing the now nineteen miles of railway; building extra track to the Sardinian Army lines; helping to run the railway with drivers, brakesmen, pointsmen; making and mending wagons for the railway; building and working a sawmill at Sinope for the Land Transport Corps; building quays in Balaclava harbour and piers elsewhere; working as stevedores and dockers: building the 11th Hussars a stable; building hospitals; sinking wells and building dams. Above all, making the Central Road, and making it as good as any turnpike in England.

The Corps would have done more, he went on, except the Army hindered him. The Army was ninety per cent inefficient and always over-manned – the reason for the men idling on the wharf. On top of that he had a lot of lazy and mischievous fellows whom the Army refused to flog. When less labour was needed he shipped the worst of them home in *Cleopatra* – the drunks who upset the General.

Cleopatra got home to Portsmouth in May 1856. Navvies still in the Crimea were tearing up the tracks which the Government sold to Turkey. Two days after *Cleopatra* berthed, the *Clyde* sailed from Balaclava. Behind them they left the road and a stone tablet set in a rock near Kadikoi: 'This road was made by the British Army, assisted by the Army Works Corps, under the direction of Mr Doyne, CE, 1855.' Near the road they left their graveyard.

Those who came home, came home to a lot of money. In Beckenham they reported in their hundreds to Katie Marsh to collect their savings. Sober, they had to be, and carrying their AWC engagement papers. One West countryman immediately bought a gold watch chain, silver watch, blue pilot jacket, plaid trousers, green velvet waistcoat and blue glengarry. Another (a bricklayer) bought enough bricks, slates and timber to build himself a cottage. More typically Northumberland John blew two hundred pounds of accumulated pay in a single binge in Barnsley.

Robert Bagshaw was still alive, still on the First Division's payroll, still with the 17th Gang, still paying his parents his pound a week allowance, in May 1856. Perhaps he got home.

In 1858 Thomas Fayers met one of *his* Crimea navvies again one bright Sunday morning in January by the Westmorland Lune. Curly Joe was lacing his boots in his hut, his back to the open door, when Fayers called. 'If that ain't our Crimea parson, I'm blowed,' said Curly. He followed Fayers to the meeting ground, boots untied, amazed to see his Crimea parson again. After that Curly often went to his meetings until he was put off by his mates' raffling him.

Forty years later Crankey Oxford, an old Crimea navvy, died at the Barnes reservoir in London.

In 1903 Robert Muras Spowant wrote to the Adjutant-General's office from New Zealand:

> Sir, After such a long lapse of time you may not be able to supply me with a proof of my being one of the Army Working Corps under Sir Joseph Paxton that the Army would be more available for the Field in the Crimean War by this AWC relieving soldiers from the necessary work required. I joined and was sworn in among many at Sydenham Crystal Palace then not in a finished state in 1854 about 500 of us left the Thames London on the *Hansen*, a German paddle Steamer and was landed at Balaclava Crimea.
>
> After Peace was proclaimed some 300 of us returned to London on the screw boat named *Antelope* (the corps I heard numbered 5000). I would be thankful for a Form of Proof of the above if there is a record of my name in said corps – as I am now 78 years of age, born in Spittal, Berwick-on-Tweed, April 1825. They are having a Veteran Home in Auckland, NZ, and the proof I ask may secure me this claim.

He added: 'I may mention that I was a carpenter and worked on the railway works, our camp of V Huts were near on the opposite side of the road; we were a little above the land locked natural harbour of Balaclava on the Black Sea'.

It wasn't long before the Royal Engineers taught themselves to build railways, proficiently, laying up to two-miles of track a day across battlefields, yet oddly enough when the Army needed a line between the Red Sea and the Nile in the Gordon campaign the War Office put the contract out to civilian tender. Lucas and Aird won it, shipping all their material – from locos to electricity generators – from London and Hull, each ship carrying everything needed to lay five miles of track.

They began on Quarantine Island in Suakim harbour in March 1885, but got no farther than Otao, nineteen miles away, even though it was an easy job: easy engineering, easy gradient, easy terrain. Instead of the Army's pacey two miles, less than a mile a day was ever laid.

The Royal Engineers blamed the civilians. Lucas and Aird were too inexperienced in military affairs. They should have built a dock. They should have built a materials' park. They should have run trains to a strict timetable and used the telegraph and line-clear system. They should have used bigger engines to save wasting time getting up steam at every minuscule hill with their piffling little locos. They should have used the metre gauge: it was lighter, needed less ground clearance, and its engines and rolling stock took sharp curves more easily. Above all they should not have used expensive fifteen shilling a day civilians when they could have got local labour for twelve pence.

The line was surveyed by the Royal Engineers. The ground was cleared by Indian civilians and the Madras Sappers. Indians unloaded and loaded the trains. Carts, mules, muleteers, horses and horse drivers were all Government supplied. Rails dropped off at the railhead were dragged into place by horses of the Indian Supply and Transport Corps. Sleepers were carted by Maltese muleteers and laid in place by local labour. All the navvies did was drive the trains, position the rails and spike them.

The navvy force was called the Corps of Volunteer Engineers. Five hundred of them went, beginning in February 1885, when over a hundred sailed in the *Osprey*, all fairly well boozed after a day's wait in the Emigrants' Home in Tilbury. Lucas and Aird sent a telegram wishing God's speed.

In the Sudan they strutted about bowler-hatted, flannel-shirted, beer-swilling, in the heavy sweltering heat that was like a material weight. At noon the rails were untouchably hot. Temperatures were a hundred degrees Fahrenheit and more in the shade of their sideless mess tents.

John Ward was there. In the 1890s he claimed he had led a strike against pay and conditions in the Sudan. It's doubtful that he did. The men were too preoccupied with dying. They died of heat stroke, like Devon Billy Fennymoor; they died of fever, like Lincoln Joe Godfrey. By the late summer they were straggling back home to die in Devonport Military Hospital, like Missionary Moorley who was landed there sick from the *Tiverton*.

Lucas and Aird fared better than their men – they probably made a profit – but it should be said failure like this, by contractors as big as these, was always rare. Big contractors were successes.

Chapter 16

Hagmasters and After

Big contractors – the Lucas and Airds, the Brassey and Petos – were like hominids at the top of an evolutionary tree, slowly risen from more lowly creatures who'd once paddled in mud at the bottom. Contracting began on canals where the hierarchy under which the navvy lived was first fixed: company; consulting engineer; resident engineer; contractor; hagman; walking ganger; ganger; navvy.

The contractor and the hagman were what mattered to the navvy and the contractor was the common story of the small getting big: the story of the small getting big *twice*, in fact. Telford got the contracting system just about right when the railways did an atavistic back-somersault to the messy fragmented ways of the earliest canals. The story of the small contractor getting big began again after the canal/railway break.

Contractors at first were small enough to be navvies. Then they were bigger and *in*efficient. Then big and efficient. Then very big, very efficient, and international.

Early canals were made messily: a bit of direct labour here, the odd biggish contractor there, butty gangs here and there and, everywhere else, hundreds of one-man undertakers or taskers each undertaking a single task like cutting and puddling a short length of canal. The tasker was often a grosser navvy big enough to beat a fractious gang into submission. Sometimes they were called gangmasters or gangers, before the word meant a paid foreman.

A butty-gang was a contracting unit in itself, fit to undertake a task for a fixed sum. How the gang split the money was up to them. The word itself is cognate with buddy – the pal of the kind asked to spare a dime. It was a gang of equals, mates, pals, friends, or buddies. They were probably an importation from the coalfields and lasted, on public works as in the pits, into the twentieth century.

In 1904 when frost stopped the job at Tidworth I went on tramp to Cheltenham. Stayed one night in Devizes, one night in Bath and the next night I slept rough in a barn of hay at Nailsworth. Then I went on to the Honeybourne and Cheltenham railway.

The contractor was Rowland Brothers and we worked the butty system there. Share and share alike. We were putting up a fence at the side of the track. You got half a crown for eleven post holes. That was one chain. There were five men in the gang and you got a shilling a chain for putting the post in and wiring up.

We were in a private lodge there, me and some bloke they called Cockney. Good lodge that was, too. Homely sort of place. Sixpence a night for tea and 'taters. The old landlord was a cowman on a farm. He was only getting twelve shillings a week.

So Christmas come and we got no money. The ganger kept it and did a slope. But the butty system was the best of the lot for navvies, long as some mush didn't make off with the money.

The Navvies' Union disliked butty messes. 'Butty messes are all right where the work is bound to be done piece-work,' they said, 'but whenever it is possible it should be put a stop to. It only means for a miserable additional pittance, gangs do twice the ordinary amount of work.'

At first canals lent taskers the tools they needed. In 1768 the Coventry even had its wheelbarrows made to order ('according to the Model lately sent from Staffordshire'), then had to hire men to watch them ('one man 2 Day watching Barrows – 0-2-0') and others to cart them about. It wasn't long before they realised they needn't bother and as early as 1774 the Chester canal decreed its taskers should find their own planks and barrows which, furthermore, they had to buy from the company as long as the company's stock of them lasted.

Tools meant capital and the lack of it made it harder for the unbusinesslike to be their own masters: harder, but not impossible. The lone tasker lasted to the end.

Well, from Lunedale I went to the Chew Valley dam and after that to Patricroft, driving a heading under a tram road for drains for rain water from Manchester. Sandrock, no timbering. You blasted at the bottom of the tunnel and chopped the overhang off with a hammer and wedge. I was getting twenty shillings a yard, thirty-five under the tram road, and out of that I paid a man six shillings a shift to shift

the muck. He wasn't a navvy, he was a local labourer. I was doing
my own blasting with pills of gelignite.

On the other hand, it did not open public works to the more
farsighted and businesslike and before long professional contractors were cheating navvies and swindling canal companies all over
the country. Most did one job at a time, but some thought they
could take on several simultaneously.

Charles Jones – Mancunian, mason, miner – was a one-job man.
He'd been a tasker in the Norwood tunnel on the Chesterfield in
the 1770s, and later was the tasker who failed to drive the first
Blisworth tunnel on the Grand Junction in the '90s. He was also the
man who at least *half*-bodged the Sapperton tunnel in the '80s.
'Vain, shifty and Artful in all his Dealings,' was what the Thames
and Severn called him when he sued them in the Court of Chancery.

At Sapperton, Jones was jailed three times for debt. Out of jail he
drank and drove a slow and slipshod tunnel, not helped, it seems, by
the Company. When he hit jointy rock they tried to make him
enlarge the bore to make room for brickwork at his own expense. It
may be they got him drunk, in some low-ceilinged inn in the lush
Frome valley, to get him to sign a paper justifying what they'd
done. Then, after engineering it so he could be fired if he missed
work for twenty-eight consecutive days, he was jailed for debt,
getting out only hours before the deadline to find the Company had
sold his belongings, few as they were. His son promised to kill the
clerk of works and was ordered out of the district.

'My Pasehons is Quite wore out,' said Jones.

Part of the arch at the western end where it emerges into the deep,
deeply wooded Frome valley collapsed in the winter of 1784–5. No
two parts of the tunnel joined and the bits that had been bored were
unsafe because the masons couldn't get in to line them. You can still
see the hole made by one roof fall. Next summer Jones was sacked,
and sued the company in the Court of Chancery, but even
Chancery, a slow and slumbrous place, dismissed the case after
waiting some years without hearing from him.

Once Jones had gone, the Thames and Severn hired groups of
taskers, working round the clock. Walking through the woods
overhead was like strolling on a volcano: explosions shook the
ground with small earthquakes.

Canals had no great contractors, no Brasseys, Petos, or Walkers,
iron-stiff with probity. At best they had the Pinkertons, a whole

family of them, all variously incompetent or corrupt.

Near the end of his career John Pinkerton had a joint-contract on the Lancaster Canal with a Glaswegian called Murray, a rogue, like himself, in knee-breches and wig. Their engineer they kept on the brink of despair. 'The clamour is raging you are to have Barrow Beck running into the canal this day – in point blank contradiction to the Act of Parliament,' cried Archibald Millar, that engineer, 'For God's sake do not be so very crazy.'

Pinkerton took Fire too readily and quarrelled with everybody, particularly an elderly Scots contractor called Stevens (who robbed the King's highway of sand and left the public to fall into his unfilled holes). One day he and Pinkerton collided over who could take stone from a quarry. 'Gentlemen,' said Millar, equably for once, 'I very plainly see greed in both sides.'

On top of that, Pinkerton's work was poor and he was away most of the time on quite another contract on the Leeds-Liverpool. It was clear he had to go, and in the fall of 1795 his contract was rescinded. He went to the Barnsley broad boat canal until things went wrong there as well: war-time inflation, to begin with, and unexpectedly bad rock. Pinkerton asked the company for more money and the company asked the same of him. The case, with its sheaves of ribboned, ink-fading paper, was in Chancery and then with York Assizes until 1812, when Pinkerton was told he'd lost. It was his last loss as it turned out: by then he was too old to work.

By 1812, in fact, he'd been in the canal contracting business for the best part of half a century, beginning on the Driffield in 1768 with his brother James. (They were probably born at North Cave in the East Riding.) In 1772 they were joint-contractors on the Market Weighton, a canal which leaves the Humber but never quite reaches the town it's named after. In 1777 they were mucking up the Erewash – the banks and locks leaked and the company threatened to bring in proper workmen to mend them at the Pinkertons' expense.

John then contracted on his own until in 1785 he nearly wrecked the Dudley tunnel by cladding it with bad bricks. He had to pay to get out of that contract, before it ruined him. Then he was in trouble at Greywell on the Basingstoke and his Greywell troubles, whatever they were, kept Winchester Assizes busy almost to the end of the century. Squabbles over the Birmingham-Fazeley lasted fifteen years and the physical faults he left in the canal weren't cleared up for another quarter century after that.

The Birmingham-Fazeley company claimed he bodged the puddling and built the locks of stacks of poor unbonded bricks and brick-ends. Only the bricks facing outward were good. On top of that he drove them a tunnel at Curdworth when they distinctly asked for a cutting.

'He was too moderate,' Pinkerton said of himself in the third person, 'and too gentle to secure his own interest against the falsehood and calumny, with which little, mean, and envious individuals assailed his character, and poisoned the minds of the Company's Committee.'

He claimed his work was blameless, blaming the envy, lies and spite of the company's officials for what happened to him and the canal. The officials the company hired, he said, were of very low quality. Bough, the engineer, was 'at once vicious and needy, too ignorant to penetrate a hypocritical disguise and too low bred not to consider the head clerk a very great man.' (One of the officials was little, mean and envious enough to sue for libel. As a result Pinkerton spent a month brooding on the meanness of mankind and his own misfortunes in the bawling chaos of an early nineteenth century jail.)

Men like Pinkerton, however, rarely got the chance again, on canals. Men like Telford saw to that.

By the 1820s Harecastle tunnel on the Trent and Mersey was in a terrible mess – people could still just about leg through, panting in the bad air, their boats filling the sagging bore like corks in a bottle neck. But Telford's contractors, Pritchard and Hoof, did in three years what Brindley took eleven to do and left Harecastle Hill with two black holes (one small, the other smaller) and a broad, brown, boat-marshalling yard at its foot.

On the Liverpool-Birmingham John Wilson and William Provis contended not only with the boldness of Telford's engineering, but also with the terrain and with landlords. Wilson had to build a wide-curving embankment near Nantwich to keep the canal clear of somebody's property. The bank slipped, dolloping down in great lumps into a public lane. Wilson died before the bank was heavy enough to be stable but his sons carried on.

Provis had the Shelmore Great Bank. It splayed. Its bottom oozed out. Then it sank in the middle, like sad cake. The worry of it is said to have killed Telford. Nothing cured it save, ultimately, Provis's perseverance in dumping muck. (Today it's a fine wooded embankment, laced with water, pierced by narrow road tunnels, a solid bit of landscape.) What was so galling was that the bank was a diversion, a loop, to give Lord Anson's game birds a place in which to live lives of unhindered rusticity preparatory to being shot to death by gentlemen with flintlocks.

Provis also contended with Knighton reservoir, which leaked, and the Knighton branch line, which sank bodily into the Weald Moors. At Cowley they planned a long tunnel but instead got a short one with a long approach cutting because the rock was so rotten.

Regression came with the railways when hagmen, the most reviled creatures on public works, came back into their own grubbing greedily away like maggots, parasiting off better men.

'The Devil has a lot of sub-contractors,' said Thomas Walker, the contractor. 'A bad lot, I tell you.'

John Ward once wrote part of a novel, *Rude Reality*, in which Joe Warren, the young hero, is promoted from fat-boy to turn-out without the pay rise. He asks the hag for his extra money just as a train is derailed. 'To ask a hag for more money is to ask him to part with his life, and a crime never to be forgiven. Though poor Joe was nearly a half-mile way, he was evidently the cause of the accident: in fact the impiety of his ambition for more brass would have thrown any self-respecting engine off ordinary metals.'

'Send that bloody thing about his business,' the hag roars at Stafford George, the ganger.

'What for?' asks Stafford. 'The nipper had nothing to do with it. If he's to be sacked for nothing, I go too.'

But the man was utterly lost to humanity: corrupted by greed, hollowed by avarice. He docked Joe's wages to help pay for repairs to the running road.

'Do you call yourself a man to cheat a lad who is practically an orphan?'

'I cheat no one.'

'No *one*, that's true, but *all* who have any transaction with you.'

But if the early railways brought back the hags, they also brought out a new kind of man who was about to become suddenly rich. Fortunes in those early days were made casually. George Wythes, who died rich, became a railway contractor when railway contracting began. Eighteen thousand pounds was the figure he first thought of for his first tender. Add a couple of thousand, said his wife. Double it, she said before going to bed. Double it again, she said over breakfast. Even then it was the lowest tender and the bedrock of Mr Wythes's fortune.

In the early 1840s people based tenders on guesses – or 'formulae' – about how much muck a gang could shovel in a year, an hour, a day, a month. If your figures were wrong in the right direction fortunes dropped into your palms: otherwise you left gangs of unpaid men behind you.

The fortunes, for those who caught them, could be spectacular. More cash passed through Thomas Brassey's counting houses than through the treasuries of half a dozen European principalities. And Brassey began as a salaried land agent in what has since become urban Birkenhead. He helped Telford survey the Holyhead road, then George Stephenson find stone for the Sankey viaduct on the Liverpool-Manchester. On Stephenson's advice he went into the railway business himself.

Like Napoleon, Brassey had two-o'clock-in-the-morning-courage. 'Never take your troubles to your pillow,' he always said. He was self-contained, self-sufficient, a man who quickly costed work in his head and lived contentedly with the consequences whatever they were. On top of that he was good at choosing people. Once, when he was worried about taking the Great Northern across the Fens (in one place the weight of a man made an acre of ground quiver like a big flat jelly) he met Stephen Ballard, by chance, on Cambridge railway station. Although they were strangers Brassey hired him on the spot. Ballard, ex-nurseryman, ex-manager of the Gloucester and Hereford canal, floated the railway over the bog on a sandwich of faggots and peat sods, which slowly sank, squeezing out the water, leaving behind whatever was solid.

'He remembered even the navvies,' said his biographer, 'and saluted them by their names.' They didn't forget him either – Brassey's benching was a particularly laborious way of filling wagons from below their wheel bases (which meant you were stooped double one moment and were bolt-upright the next flinging muck in an arc over your head. Do that for ten hours at a stretch and muscles harden till they're brittle enough to crack). There was even a song about him:

> I'm a nipper, I'm a tipper,
> I'm a navvy on the line,
> I worked for Thomas Brassey
> And he gave me two and nine.

They gave his son an earldom to match the family income.

Joseph Firbank started work at seven pushing baskets from the coal-face of a Durham pit. At nights he bought himself an education of sorts at sixpence a time before starting out again as a navvy on the Bishop Auckland and Weardale where he saw there was money in contracting. To get his hands on some of it he set up in business as a hagman at the Woodhead tunnel, a dank, bleak hole, slobbering water, legendary among navvies as an easy place to die, a hard place to live – except it was good to Firbank who went on to make a lot of money. Thirty years later he stood to lose a hundred thousand pounds on the Long Drag because of inflation caused by the Franco-Prussian War.

But Firbank was exceptionally lucky, or gifted. By mid-century it was almost too hard for the really poor-born to make money out of railways. Only people like Samuel Morton Peto could do that – men born half-winners to begin with: rich enough to have expectations of success, poor enough to have to try.

Peto (1809–1889) was the son of a farmer and, more importantly, nephew of a London builder who left him half his business when he was still young. (Peto almost lost his first contract because he looked *too* young. He said he would wear spectacles next time to make himself look mature.)

Between 1850 and the mid-'60s money for new railways was scarce: the existing lines paid low dividends, capital outlay was high, fixed interest rates cut profits, you waited years for any dividend at all, and the most obviously profitable routes were already in business. But contractors were now capitalists with money tied up in staff and equipment and it paid them to 'buy' contracts by helping to finance new railways in some way: by taking shares instead of cash, perhaps, or by buying shares themselves, or by paying the deposit while Parliament considered the company's proposals. Sometimes a contractor bought the land, paid the engineer, and guaranteed interest on capital while the line was building – as long as he got the contract.

Contractors even helped finance the building of railways, constructed them, and then ran them. Peto, Brassey and Betts ran the London, Tilbury and Southend after they'd built it.

In this way Peto made Lowestoft into a port and a sea-town out of a fishing village. The navigation company which had dredged the channel through the beach at Lowestoft (to make Norwich into a sea-port) was bankrupt. Peto and Grissel bought the company, built a railway to Reedham, channelled and dredged the cut across the beach, built quays, wharves, a fish market, a town.

All the same the Overend, Gurney banking crash of 1866 hurt Peto and he ended his days on a Cornish mineral railway.

By now there was a certain continuity among the big contractors: Thomas Walker started life with Brassey in Staffordshire and went with him to the Grand Trunk railroad in Canada. Then he worked with Peto and Betts on the London underground before setting up on his own (his first contract was the tube line from Whitechapel to Brunel's old Thames tunnel). He built Barry and Preston Docks, bored the Severn tunnel and dug the Manchester Ship Canal.

Men like Peto and Walker did a lot for the navvy, in their way. Peto spent a thousand pounds a year of his own money hiring preachers, not only to preach, but to teach them to read. Walker likewise gave them schools, hospitals and churches. But at the same time Walker in particular was an autocrat who would brook no discontented workmen – or strikers.

THE NEW VICTORIA DOCK WORKS, PLAISTOW MARSHES.

25. Victoria Dock, London

MESSRS. PETO, BRASSEY, AND BETTS' OFFICE, WATERLOO-ROAD.

26. Recruiting Office, Waterloo Road

The Crimea Navvies

NAVVIES AT THE NORTH-WESTERN RAILWAY TERMINUS, EUSTON-SQUARE.

27. Euston Square Station, London

NAVVIES EMBARKING AT THE BIRKENHEAD DOCKS.

28. Birkenhead

29. Kitting-up on board

30. *Prince of Wales* in Blackwall Reach, London

31. Painted Suits to Lindsey Drawers

32. Railway leaving the harbour

33. The huts above the town

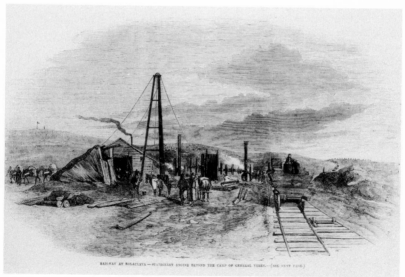

34. The stationary engine which pulled trains up the slope by Kadikoi

The Crimea Navvies

35. Kadikoi

36. Navvies on the Manchester Ship Canal, 1880s

37.

PRICE ONE PENNY

ENGLAND'S SACRIFICE

TO THE

GOD MAMMON.

BY JOHN WARD.

Man's inhumanity to man
Makes countless thousands mourn.

by the POLITICAL COUNCIL OF THE WANDSWORTH BRANCH OF
SOCIAL DEMOCRATIC FEDERATION, and the Trade Supplied by
ROGERS, at the SYDNEY HALL, 36, York Road, Battersea.

FIRST EDITION.

Mr. John Ward.

The new member for the Parliamentary Borough of Stoke, Mr. John Ward, was born at Oatlands Park, Surrey, on November 21st, 1866. As he commenced work when seven years of age, what education he obtained was entirely by his own efforts but by application to study in a few years he became a capital example of self-education. From at early age he cultivated a remarkable grasp of political and public affairs. He became a close student of the questions of the hour, and was soon outstanding for his intimacy with the problems before the country; and this, coupled with a natural shrewdness, won for him great popularity and influence.

At the age of 12, Mr. Ward was employed upon the Andover and Marlborough Railway, and he continued to work as a navvy until 1890, being for some time engaged on the Manchester Ship Canal, &c. "Like all young Britishers," he says, he was seized with patriotic enthusiasm in his youth, and he volunteered for service in the Soudan, in which he served under General Graham, in 1885. For this he received the Khedive's bronze star and the English silver medal for the Soukim-Berber expedition—two

MR. JOHN WARD, M.P.

trophies which he has exhibited during moments of enthusiastic fervour, and with dramatic effect, during the campaign, when replying to the charge that he was a "Lib-

in other parts of the commun—

THE CHAIRMAN

The Chairman, expressing his seeing such a large gathering, took it that their presence the pression of their satisfaction an the splendid message that was the country from Manchester. message mean to them? It m would have no part in the gre the people's food—(applause)— proposed by the Tory party. message in reply to the false had been preached by M lain, who had said that was on the verge of iron, machinery, cotton and ot he had told them were on the br tion, and yet what did we find to-day. That our exports in th had increased enormously. Mr. had said that the milling ind jeopardy. In the last ten years output had been increased by Since 1902 our imports had increa million pounds and our exports pounds. Surely those figures we tion that our industries had not y free trade. He found that Mr. C inaccurate statistics had not been his fiscal propaganda. Only a other night he stated that the W the country contained one million men, a statement which had sin tradicted in the "Times" by Hamilton and Mr. Burns. Inst million, the total number of men, children in the Workhouses only a 220,000. Last Monday evening they entertained by Mr. Percy Glass, of M who had spoken to them for a co time urging the necessity for a tariff with the Colonies. Chamberlain himself, ten years ago that preferential treatment would Empire and excite the hostility of world. (Laughter and applause.) the best answer they could give Glass. In that contest they had two honourable gentlemen, both of were glad to see among them; bu Tory—daughters—one who had su voice and vote the extravagance Government, and their reprograde p ally, especially in dealing with th question. And now he was desiro down that commercial policy that h much for their country in the las He asked them if they were prepa those men in power who would take the dark in dealing with the commu country. He was sure, an Englishb were not prepared to barter away to that way. On the other hand th McLaren, who was prepared to policy of Peace, Retrenchment, an (Applause.) And included in the would be the question of education with which his desire would be to do all parties.

MR. W. McLAREN.

Mr. Walter McLaren said he wa to make the acquaintance of the that part of Staffordshire, a part new to him and to congratulate th magnificent beginning of the Gener They had seen in Friday's and Sat

Elizabeth Garnett

Ripon May 1887

38. Mission Room, Great Central, 1890s

39. Missionary, Great Central, 1890s

40. Navvy Smith, Great Central, 1890s

Dear Mr. Scott,

I had a terrific blow a year and nine months since in the sudden death of my wife. But if anything a still worse calamity has befallen me. Lorne Botha Ward my youngest son (the young medico who just failed to become Ass. Medical Officer for Stoke on Trent a short time ago) has been during the last half year House Surgeon (Resident) to King Edwards Memorial Hospital Ealing.

On Tuesday last 18th I recieved a letter from the Hospital chairman informing me that he was very ill with Influenza. Getting worse, Yesterday I called in Sir J Wilcox who diagnosed Blood poisoning result of matter entering a scratched finger during a post Mortem 14 days ago. and added, the fatal words <u>case hopeless</u>.

I am awaiting the end almost bereft of my reason, that a brilliant young life should be so sacrificed at the dawn of its day.

Hoping against hope I write that my friends may not worry me at the moment.

Will wire you directly the definite and final has arrived

In my awfull sorrow I am yours

John Ward

Dr Ward died Sep. 20th 1925

41.

42.

Chapter 17

Strikes, Trucks, Cash

Walker once broke a strike at the Severn tunnel in less than a week. The Great Western men he inherited with the contract had a grudge against him from the beginning – until he took over they worked leisurely eight-hour shifts: firing a shot, taking a break, shifting the muck, knocking off. Walker wanted a longer day with two tight meal breaks, making for efficient ten-hour shifts. Shots would be fired before snap-time to let the fumes clear while the men did something at least marginally useful to Walker, like feeding themselves.

One Saturday in May 1881, a notice was chalked over the main shaft. 'I hope the bloody bond will break, and kill any man that goes down to work.' The night men wouldn't go down – instead they went to the pub and came back sullen and untalking. Walker left his office.

'Now what do you fellows want?' The men shuffled. 'Now tell me what you want?' Walker said again, 'and don't stop hanging about here.'

One said: 'We wants the eight hour shift.'

'My good men,' said Walker, 'you'll never get that, if you stop here for a hundred years. You'd better get your money as soon as you can, and go.'

They went, though not far. On Tuesday Walker laid off the carpenters and blacksmiths – who straightaway threatened the strikers with a good hiding. Thursday and Friday the strike began to crack: next week it broke apart.

Turn-outs or strikes on canals were usually broken, rather than settled, by locking-out the strikers and hiring new men. More often than not it worked. It was the way Mr Cartwright, assistant engineer on the Lancaster, broke the strike for more pay on the Lune aqueduct in the Spring of 1794. The new men were content enough, or cowed enough, till harvest time, when *they* struck.

'Mr Cartwright,' Archibald Millar, the resident engineer, reported[1], 'endeavoured all that he could to have all the Carpenters & Labourers at work, flattering them with Encouragement of Beer on the one side and threatening those who did not come should have no more Employment at the Aqueduct. The Scots men, Particularly the Carpenters, paid no respect.' He added, 'I hope and expect a little time will correct these combinations. The Harvest will not last always.'

Harvests and navvy-shortages caused by the Napoleonic War sometimes gave the men the upper hand, briefly. (Sir Charles Morgan, in 1793, asked Parliament to compel navvies to harvest his barley at wages *he* fixed. 'I despair of getting in the corn,' he threw up his hands when the Commons threw out his Bill at its First Reading.) Men boating muck to the Lune 'turned out for larger prices' in 1796 and, perhaps because of wartime labour shortages, they may have won – a few weeks later Millar grumbled that wages were now so high the boat emptiers would no longer work full-time.

On railways it was much the same. Strikes were rare, and rarely successful. (The corollary of navvy freedom was that they were solitary men. They were not joiners, or combiners.) Men on the Slamannan and Edinburgh and Glasgow Junction struck for more money early in 1846. Soon, half of them wanted to go back to work, except they were frightened of the half who didn't. Police were brought in from Falkirk and the men who still wanted to strike were fired. Dozens of little flash-strikes in the '40s were like it.

In 1886 the *Manchester Guardian* reported that men on the Thirlmere dam had struck for more pay. 'Large numbers of men are flocking to the district seeking employment,' the story ended. So, presumably, did the strike.

Until the end of the 1850s a navvy would have been quite rich with a lot less than his nominal pay – if the weather had let him earn it, and if truckmasters, sloping gangers, gangers with crooked measuring sticks, and the long gaps between pay-days hadn't robbed him of it.

Truck on public works was probably as old as navvying. 'It has

1 Millar was the man who said, 'Money, money, money is the common cry. We hear nothing of work, work, work.' He thought, too, that the job would get done faster if the company, instead of raising navvies' wages, gave its officers bonuses for the men's good workmanship. The honour of *his* extra pay, he truly believed, would make men work better.

been the custom for the last hundred years,' said Peto a little inaccurately in 1846, 'ever since they commenced making canals.' (Some canals we know *were* sensitive about their officials selling things to navvies. James Hook, a counter (a kind of timekeeper), on the Hereford and Gloucester had his wages raised in 1793 to persuade him not to. He was later fired for asking for more.)

Truck, the word, comes from a Norman-French verb meaning to shop or barter, and as a way of cutting wages – by paying workmen in goods rather than coin – it dates at least from the early 15th century when Colchester Corporation banned it in their town. 'No weaver shall be compelled to take any merchandise or victuals for his wages against his will, but only gold or silver.'

Pre-nineteenth century truckmasters characteristically gave overpriced goods or groceries in place of money. Workmen either ate their wages or sold them at a loss. Either way it was a pay cut. Nineteenth century truckmasters on the other hand more normally gave money wages, as long as most of it came back across their truck-shop counters. The image is irresistably Dickensian: grubbily mittened, multi-caped creatures fingering iron-bound coffers smeared with candle grease.

At first sight, truck as practised on public works seems less grasping than elsewhere: only men drawing subs in the long pay gaps were forced to accept it – if you could last two, four, six, eight weeks without pay, you got full money wages. But if you needed money between pay days – if you had debts, a drink habit, were a gambler, or the pay gap was just too long – you were given a ticket which was worthless anywhere but in the truck-shop.

Truck, as practised on public works, seems to have come from the coalfields, brought in perhaps with the colliers who worked the early canal tunnels. A Royal Commission looking into truck in 1871 took as an example a colliery in South Wales. What they found was very like what happened on public works. Pay day at the pit was the second Saturday in the month. In between were official draw-days when you could pick up – in cash – some of your wages. Between the draw-days were the lie-days when money already earned lay in the company's books. Cash could never be drawn on lie-days. Instead you were given tommy tickets, usable only in the company's overpriced store. (Overpriced, apologists claimed, to finance what amounted to a loan to the miner and to pay for the clerks' extra work.)

The tommy ticket told the counter clerk how much the collier's wife could spend. When she'd ordered what she wanted, the counter clerk chalked the price on the cover of an advance book which she took to the cashier who gave her cash to that amount. Then she went back to the counter clerk, gave him the money and collected her groceries. People who slipped away clutching the cash and abandoning the goods were called slopers, the origin presumably of the word on public works.

On public works, similarly, you could sub only out of your lying time – untouched earnings lying to your credit in the company's books or the ganger's faulty memory. The ganger wrote out a tommy ticket, often on a crudely printed chit like the one from the Edinburgh-Hawick railway shown to the 1846 Committee.

> Work . . . . .   Borthwick . . . .   184 . . .
> Mr Govan,
> At the request of . . . . . . No . . . . . , give him goods to the amount . . . . . , to account, or in advance of wages that may be due to him by Messrs Wilson and Moor, and place the same to their debit.
>
> By appointment.

At the Summit tunnel, where the pay gap was not uncommonly nine weeks, beer-tickets were easier to get than tommy tickets. You could get a tommy ticket only at fixed times: beer tickets were yours for the asking, up to and even beyond your lying time.

Beer tickets were good only in the hagman's own trackside tom-and-jerry or in a pub where he'd done a deal with the landlord. Either way, the barmen kept the score and since the navvy was often illiterate and in any case always drank to get drunk, he had no way of checking he wasn't being cheated. Frequently he was. Tommy tickets, likewise, were good only in the hagman's own store, or in a shop where he'd done a deal with the shopkeeper – generally a ten per cent commission on all captive navvy business. Even if the navvy asked for cash, he was given a cashable ticket out of which a penny in the shilling was docked as commission.

'They give us great wages,' said a navvy at the Summit tunnel in the '40s, 'but they take it all from us again.'

Four theories have been put forward to explain truck. Perhaps the least likely – but most widely believed at the time – saw it as a way of controlling drunkenness. Others saw it as a way of binding the servant to his master through debt. A third theory said it was because of a shortage of small coins and a poorly developed system of personal credit. (Which may have been partly true on canals. Pinkerton paid his men on the Basingstoke in tokens, presumably because of a lack of coin, and before they went on the rampage the Sampford Peverel rioters had trouble changing their tokens for cash.) But perhaps the most reasonable (perhaps even the *real*) reason for truck fits public works most comfortably. Truck, says this theory, needed two things – unmoneyed masters and high-earning workers. Unmoneyed masters, by dictionary definition, couldn't pay money wages, but credit for goods and groceries was easy to come by. This theory, then, predicts that truck would be practised not by the big and rich but by the small and poor: and everywhere this does seem to be true – butties in coal-pits, petty-foggers among nailers, bagmen in the hosiery trade, ganger-hagmen on public works. Until nearly the time of the Crimean War, hags were often only navvies able to supply and subdue a gang of men. Truck's culprits *and* victims were navvies.

And hags often *were* victims. Head-contractors defrauded them. One ganger on the Trent Valley line in the 1840s nearly starved to death when his contractor refused to pay him, denying they had ever agreed a contract to alter the bed of a stream. Corrupted witnesses called to corroborate the contractor's testimony refused to perjure themselves when they reached the witness box. But, 'You have no jurisdiction,' the contractor told the court, walking away free.

John Deacon told the 1846 Committee he had kept tommy-shops on several sub-contracts. He was under-capitalised, the head contractor paid *him* once a fortnight and he needed some way of paying his footloose navvies. Tickets were a sort of paper money: men about to leave sold them at a loss to people with money who were staying. 'Though you got', Deacon admitted, 'better men for cash wages.'

Sometimes bad luck forced good contractors into truck. Anna Tregelles knew one in South Wales in 1847. At first he did all right and paid cash wages. Then he took on a second contract which turned out to be all wet muck and contrary rock. Blasting shot fountains of top soil in the air but left the rock uncleft. In summer it wasn't too bad. He switched men from good to bad contracts and everybody made money. In winter, the good high-earners wouldn't work the bad ground. The contractor got poorer. He opened a tommy shop to get his money back. At first he paid half in cash, half in truck. Money got scarcer, his food poorer. Meat was discontinued. Thin strips of poor bacon took its place. Soon his tickets were worth only half their face value when it came to things like boots. Good navvies left. Make-shift men, previously unemployable, were taken on.

Altogether Parliament brought out twenty-eight pieces of anti-truck legislation though *the* Truck Act is generally thought of as the one Edward Littleton introduced in 1831. Littleton was MP for Staffordshire where truck was most rampant, particularly among nail-making petty-foggers, iron-masters and coal-owners of the smaller sort. Littleton was an owner of the bigger sort, out to ruin his little truck-mastering competitors. The Bill itself was largely drafted by William Huskisson, a man better known as the first railway accident statistic, killed as he was by a loco the day the Liverpool-Manchester opened.

The Act in fact was pretty ineffective, seeing that all prosecutions were private and not many folk wanted to litigate themselves on to a bosses' blacklist. Besides, bad as truck was, it was better than no wages.

This Act as well missed out navvies. 'At the time my Bill was passed,' Littleton said, 'several Railways and Canals were being constructed, where it was necessary for the Contractors to have shops. I could not resist the Appeal made to except their cases. Perhaps the same reasons do not exist now.'

They probably didn't exist in 1831 either. Shopkeepers would wait in a wildnerness if there was money at the end of it, Peto implied to the 1846 Committee. He told them, 'At one place I saw several butchers' carts, loaded with meat, and the butchers' men crying out 'Who wants a fine leg of mutton?' At Ely you'd see thirty or forty bakers' carts, all piled up with bread, going into the Fens on Saturday, to supply my men.'

But even though the 1831 Act didn't apply to public works there were at least three prosecutions under it.

A hag called Riley took a sub-contract under a man called Warden on the Oxford, Worcester and Wolverhampton. Warden paid in tommy tickets: Riley sued under the Truck Act; the case was tried at Gloucester Summer Assizes, 1847. The Judge began by ruling the case *could* be heard because, although the contract was to make a railway cutting, clay from it was used to make bricks and brickmakers came under the Truck Act. The jury ruled that Riley was an employer, not a labourer: the fact that he navvied alongside his men was immaterial – he still expected to make a profit from their work. The Judge gave him leave to appeal to the Court of Exchequer to get his debt settled in coin as well as groceries, but the Exchequer Court judges also ruled he was an employer, that employers were excluded from the Act, and that he could therefore be paid in goods.

The other case was tried a year or so later in Grimsby, where the tommy shop on the dock was the contractor's afterthought: cash wages had been paid long enough, in 1850, to give local shopkeepers a taste of navvy money. So when Hutchings, the contractor, set up his own tommy shop, Grimsby's tradesmen set up a Reform Association to challenge it. William Parker, shopkeeper, took a ticket from a dock navvy in payment of an account and asked Hutchings to cash it. All Parker had to do in court was prove that Hutchings refused to do so.

Hutchings claimed the case was not covered by the Act and brought in witnesses, timekeepers, hags, and other time-servers, to speak in favour of the tommy system. All twelve hundred men at the dock were happy with it, they claimed. 'If this were correct,' said the *Wolverhampton Chronicle*, 'why were not some of these men brought to prove the fact? The poor fellows are paid monthly in cash, if they can wait so long. If not, they must either take tommy or starve.'

Judge Smith found against Hutchings. 'I never gave a decision with greater pleasure and satisfaction to my own mind,' he said, 'and this I do fearlessly, feeling satisfied that I have tangible grounds for the validity and legality of the verdict.'

Some magistrates, too, inclined to common justice whatever the law said. In the 1850s William Palk, a gentleman of no fixed employment, advised navvies who couldn't get cash, even as change in a truck transaction, to sue their contractor in the Exeter Guildhall. More than that, he found a lawyer to plead their case. The magistrates found for the men and made the contractor give them their money, which he did just before firing them, and just after parading an unruly bunch of drunks through the streets waving banners proclaiming how good his truck shop really was. Stafford Prince, who lost his job, gave Palk a pair of singing canaries.

Legally, navvies didn't come under the Truck Acts until 1887 by which time truckmasters were in any case long gone from public works, put out of business by the new big contractors. Right from the beginning, in fact, the truckmaster's end was in the hands of engineers like Brunel who had anti-truck clauses written into his contracts ('if you can trust a man for a shilling's worth of provisions you can trust him for a shilling') and contractors like Peto.[2]

Peto only sub-contracted to moneyed hagmen, each of whom had to deposit a tenth of his contract price (some were worth £3000) in token of keeping the rules. The rules were strict: no truck to begin with, and weekly pay. Timekeepers told the office on Friday afternoons what the week's wages were going to be and coin in sealed bags was ready for the gangers by noon next day.

'You are not aware,' Peto asked a witness called before the Select Committee examining the 1854 Payment of Wages Bill, 'that on 17/20ths of public works, the truck system is abolished by the contractors themselves?' In spite of the curiously precise arithmetic he was probably right. Truck certainly didn't bother the union when it was formed, any more than did the sloping gangers and the long pay-gap which so exercised the 1846 Committee. In all cases the cause was the same: the penniless hag.

Penniless hags, as well, made it unlikely a navvy was ever paid what he earned. The long pay-gap, itself, was a device for confusing the unlettered man about what he was owed and some people ended the month owing money to the truck-ganger. Men were paid, half-drunk, in small coins picked out of a basin in the middle of a taproom, then hustled away to count it in a corner. If a man was short-paid it was his word against the ganger's and his henchmen. And if all else failed, the ganger could just refuse to pay anything and, since the contracts they made between themselves were not covered by law, the navvy had to put up with being robbed. It all made what a navvy was supposed to be paid slightly academic.

Proto-navvies on the Bridgewater are said to have got tenpence a day – five shillings a six-day week. In November, 1774, the Chester committee ordered: 'That the Daywage Men on the Canal be paid only 16d per Day for the best Hands and Others hired as Low as they can.' The strike on the Lune in 1794 was for fourteen shillings a week and a ten-hour shift, which may mean they already earned ten or twelve shillings.

The wages of contemporary farm labourers varied with distance

2 Brunel's anti-truck clauses don't seem to have worked too well. The same flaxen haired navvy Mayhew met in Cripplegate told him: 'After I left the Brummagem line, I went on to the Great Western. I went to work at Maidenhead. There it was the same system, and on the same rules – the poor man being fleeced and made drunk by his master.'

from London. In the 1790s a Berkshire farm hand could expect to earn seven shillings a week for most of the year, ten shillings at harvest time. In Kent he could expect nine to ten shillings throughout the year. But in remoter Westmorland a man, his wife and three children *between* them could expect only eleven or twelve shillings a week. On his own, the man's wages were probably five or six shillings.

The Napoleonic War doubled *prices* from threepence to sixpence for muck shifting, but navvies' wages went up only locally. Men on war-work on the Royal Military Canal still only earned thirteen and sixpence a week in 1807. On the Caledonian some got only eighteen pence a day – nine shillings a six-day week. But when Thomas Thatcher advertised for diggers at the Floating Harbour in Bristol in 1804 he promised at least five shillings a *day*. If not, 'I will advance the price of work so that every good workman I may employ shall get such wages.'

'You cannot get a good Navigator under three shillings a day,' George Stephenson said in 1835.

Henry Palmer, an engineer who employed Navigators on the London Dock in 1832, said, 'Eighteen shillings was the lowest I paid, (even for Irish labourers.)'.

Between 1847 and 1877 beef prices rose nearly forty per cent. Mutton went up fifty per cent, potatoes, a hundred per cent. Rents doubled. Mechanics wages rose by fifty per cent. Labourers' – not navvies' – by sixty-four per cent.

Comparable weekly wages:

	1843	1846	1849	1851	1855	1857	1860	1865	1866	1869
Getters (pickmen)	16/6	24/-	18/-	15/-	19/-	18/-	17/-	19/-	20/-	18/-
Fitters (muck shifters)	15/-	22/6	16/6	14/-	17/-	17/-	16/-	17/-	18/-	17/-
Masons	21/-	33/-	24/-	21/-	25/6	24/-	22/6	24/-	27/-	27/-

Common labourers between 1851 and 1869 earned from ten-and-six to twelve-and-six a week. Coal-getters got between fifteen and twenty shillings.

Translating old money into modern equivalents is difficult, but perhaps twenty 1845 shillings roughly approximated to twenty-five

1980 pounds. At the top of their tide, therefore, the nineteenth century navvy only earned around £30 a week at 1980 rates and even then he needed to work at least fifty per cent longer. Adjusting for hours worked, the navvy's best wages were perhaps as little as £20 a week at today's rates. Not a lot when you consider how it was earned: lifting over two hundred tons of matter over your head every week, sledge-hammering drills by candle-light, straining up a barrow-run with the weight of muck stretching your shoulder muscles till you thought they'd never pull back into shape again.

1846 and 1866 were *the* peak years for navvies. Never again in peacetime did they do so well either relative to the cost of living, or to what the rest of the country earned. Men at Thirlmere and on the Manchester Ship Canal in the late 1880s and early 1890s still only got fourpence-ha'penny an hour – twenty shillings a sixty-hour week. In the depression of the early 1880s, in fact, John Ward claimed there'd been an actual reduction in wages which in the south western counties were down to between half-a-crown and three-and-sixpence a day. He had himself worked on the Swindon and Marlborough for half-a-crown, sixpence less than the men of fifty years ago.

Between 1902 and 1909 the cost of living rose by four or five per cent: between 1909 and 1913 by nine per cent. Wages by now were not uncommonly fivepence or sixpence an hour, even sevenpence in London. Men at the Alwen dam in North Wales were offered sixpence-ha'penny an hour in 1913, the year the Union persuaded firms in Birmingham to pay sevenpence for the first time (thirty-five shillings, that is, for a sixty-hour week).

These of course are fixed hourly rates. Navvies themselves preferred either the butty system or payment by the piece of work done. Contractors preferred paying by the yard. 'The reason is quite plain,' said John Ward. 'The hole gets all shapes, and the navvy is unable to measure it; the contractor's agent measures it, however, with the result that if you count the waggons this week, and get so much money, next week you may send out more waggons and get less wages.' But, unswindled, piecemen earned the most. Piecemen working in Chat Moss on the Liverpool and Manchester earned up to the three-and-sixpence a day as early as 1827.

The Great War raised wages more than did the one against Napoleon. In 1917 men on new canal works at Rood End Lane, in Birmingham, were offered tenpence-ha'penny an hour with bonuses for good timekeeping.

After the War things were never the same again. Wages now were fixed by a Civil Engineering Construction and Conciliation Board who graded jobs in classes from V to I, with a special London rate above that, according to how urbanised an area was. The Union, now the Public Works and Constructional Operatives', along with other societies representing public works men (such as the Transport and General Workers') had to get jobs reclassified to get more pay. In the winter of 1920 the PW&CO won an increase for men at the Hurstwood dam near Burnley by convincing the Industrial Court the dam was in a congested area. Wages went up to two-and-a-penny an hour. In 1923 the TGWU took credit for getting Harwich reclassified as a Grade III (small industrial) town with a farthing an hour increase in wages.

Wages were index-linked and when in 1930 the cost of living dropped four points, wages, according to the Working Rule Agreement, had to drop an ha'penny an hour. The Trade Union side put in for a penny all round increase which was accepted by the Employers' Federation and eventually the Conciliation Board, on which both sides had representatives.

Comparable yearly earnings:

	1906	1924
Coal-getter	£112	£180
Carpenter	98	191
NAVVY	78	150
Farm labourer	48	82

These, though, are best-case wages. In reality few men earned that much consistently. Bad weather halted all earnings for nearly half of 1871 on Firbank's Lichfield and Croxall contract. Twenty-four days were worked in May, the best month; only twelve in February, the worst.

The Irish as well, often worked for less – one of the reasons they were segregated into all-Irish gangs and perhaps the main reason for many of the riots of the '30s and '40s. The riot in which Stephenson was swept up on the North Midland line in 1838 was caused, said the *Leeds Mercury*, by the Irish working for 'less rate of wages.' (A troop of artillery with a field gun was sent for, as well as the local Yeomanry.)

In the early days, what the pay was supposed to be, even what you had earned, was sometimes immaterial: you got paid when the company had money to spare. In January 1795 a meeting of the Stratford canal was attended not only by the committee but by a great number of navvies as well. 'Very Clamerous for the Money due to them,' say the minutes of the meeting, 'and also being in great distress for the want of the same. In order to preserve peace and quietness the Committee promised them that Money should shortly be remitted to pay them.'

The Huddersfield Narrow was an expensive waterway: only twenty miles long but crammed with locks, aqueducts, reservoirs and tunnels – and one of *them*, the Standedge, was the highest and longest in Britain. Floods damaged the canal's banks in August 1799 and by the following March there was no money for wages. In December the committee decided to pay in full those workmen who were owed up to thirty pounds: men owed more than that got five shillings in the pound.

Then, hagmen ran away. Richard Hudson abandoned his contract on the Basingstoke canal in December 1788 and left his men, country people, not navvies, unpaid. John Pinkerton promised the local labourers he would re-let the work as soon as the frosts broke: they would be able to elect their own gangers and they would all be paid fortnightly. Simon Hamor quit the Leeds and Liverpool in a hurry in July 1791, leaving *his* debts behind him.

Navvies had *no* redress, nor were they the stuff trade unionists are made of.

Chapter 18

The Navvies' Union

It was at Chew Valley I joined the Navvies' Union, at a public in Greenfield called the Red Sign. Colonel John Ward, he started it and I see him once outside the Lamplighters in Avonmouth shouting to join him, but I spoke to his second in command at Chew – a little old feller called Gardener. 'If you don't join the Union you're nothing but cowards and curs to your very hearts.'

Later they joined the All-together Union and went bust.

1889 was bright and hot and in the heat and sunlight of that summer the semi-skilled in London had two great victories. In July the Beckton gasworkers won a reduction in their working day almost for the asking. Then a small society of tea warehousemen led by Ben Tillett put in a claim for sixpence an hour – the 'Docker's Tanner' – and a guaranteed minimum four-hour day. Tillett organised bands of music, marches, and daily mass meetings in the bright sunlight on Tower Hill. Money came from as far away as Australia. In five weeks Tillett won.

Until then unions had mainly been for artisans or workers like pitmen and cotton-spinners. In the 18th century they began as combinations of craftsmen exposed to the world by the decline of their guilds and by the removal of State regulations on labour and wages. All combinations, of masters *and* men, were suppressed from 1799–1800 because of Parliament's fear of Jacobinism.

The Combination Laws were repealed in 1824 without having noticeably suppressed anything. The word 'Union' became more common, particularly in shipping and ship-building, but unions were still mainly self-help societies for artisans, offering short-stay lodgings to fellow-members tramping for work, for example. They were exclusive (they worried a lot about the numbers of apprentices in their trades) and they were very concerned with sickness and old age benefits.

179

In the early 1840s a new kind of unionism began among miners, engineers and cotton-spinners, trades created or strengthened by the Industrial Revolution. In the 1850s the engineers organised the first national union with a London headquarters while a meeting of trade unions and trades councils in 1868 is generally held to be the beginning of the Trades Union Congress.

Some trades working alongside navvies had combined, off and on, several times since 1824. The Operatives' Builders' Union (it had a Grand Lodge and a Builder's Parliament) was a reaction to the way contractors were coming between employers and craftsmen, itself a development perhaps from canal practice.

1834 was the year the Grand National Consolidated Trade Union organised the first protest march – over the Tolpuddle Martyrs. It was also the year Cubitt, the building contractor, locked out his workers for boycotting beer from a non-union brewery. Employers demanded their workmen sign 'the document', a pledge not to join a union at all.

A Builders' Labourers' Union was formed for a time during a dispute in 1859. In 1872, Patrick Kenney founded a General Amalgamated Union by its name potentially open to navvies – but it too declined and Kenney was later jailed for pinching spoons from the Holborn Restaurant at a TUC dinner.

But the Beckton gasworkers and Tillett's dockers began something quite new. As the hot summer of 1889 cooled and, in London, Hansom cabs like upright coffins-for-two briskly clopped in the gaslit fog of autumn and winter, ardent young men, mostly socialists, began organising everybody in sight: waitresses and shop assistants, Post Office Letter Sorters, labourers of all kinds.

For navvies there was the Navvies', Bricklayers' Labourers' and General Labourers' Union, founded in the autumn of 1889, possibly in London, possibly on the Manchester Ship Canal, possibly in both places simultaneously. 'The Class War,' said the new union, 'leaves no room for invidious distinctions, craft jealousies, or unorganised forces. The workers of each and every occupation must combine or starve, and the trade unions of all must federate or die. Just as the coal-dust of the miner is as honorable as the type-dust of the printer, so the hod-carrier and the navvy, with their few paltry pence per hour, are *at least* as important social and industrial factors as the grasping and over-paid contractor or employer.'

'The struggle of the future is between riches and poverty,

between labor and idleness, between justice and legalised plunder.'

'Our motto is "Union – no dogs or blacklegs need apply"; our programme is "Less work, more money, and better securities of life, limb, and labor"; and our ultimate object is not one-third or two-thirds, but that full three-thirds of the rightful dues of all Labor, of which Labor has so long been deprived by Monopoly, and which can only be attained by the realisation of that Social Commonwealth to which we look forward with confidence and with hope – where all will share fairly in both the work and the pleasure of life.'

'To this end – ORGANISE, AGITATE, ACT!'
They listed the reasons for joining. Among them:

Union equals strength. Disunion equals weakness equals insult, insecurity, ignorance, injustice, joylessness.

If you want to be free, free yourself.

Why are rent-thieves, profit-grinders, money-mongers so rich? They stick together. Imitate the enemy.

Everybody's doing it – even washerwomen and sandwich-boardmen.

The union, when it takes control, will deny non-unionists work.

It's cheap, now. Later, it will be dear.

Unions are going to take over Parliament and re-create the world.

('If all this does not seem to *your* mind sufficient reason why *you* – yes, YOU! – should join the Union or give it (whether openly or secretly we don't care) your support at once – why, then, you are either a capitalist, a fool, an enemy, a blind mole, an old fossil, or a BLACKLEG!')

John Ward, General Secretary right into the 1930s, always said he began it all, but then, in 1891, so did Arthur Humphreys. Doubtless it was both of them, along with a few others. Humphreys, the first General Secretary, was not born a navvy. He became one on the Ely Railway in the Fens. For a time he worked for Walker at the Millwall Dock and the Whitechapel Underground. At Whitechapel, Walker wanted to lower wages but Humphreys (said Humphreys) led a strike against him and won.

Leonard Hall, the Union's first District Organising Secretary and editor of its short-running newspaper, the *Navvy's Guide*, was a middle-class boy, a doctor's son from Cumbria, forced by family troubles into working as a nipper on the Lancashire-Yorkshire line when he was thirteen. Then he sailed steerage into a succession of penny-dreadful adventures and wheezes: successively he was a sailor, soldier, cowboy, student. Twice he was shipwrecked. Once he was knifed in a duel. Twice he was shot: once for speaking his mind in a Slave-State election, once for starting a mutiny in a Virginia oyster dredger. He was still only twenty-one when he worked his passage home in a cattle boat and began a fifth or sixth career as a journalist with a brightly coloured line in autobiography, then a sixth or seventh as a union official.

Tom Cusack, National Organiser, was a very reluctant union man at first. For a time he worked alongside Ward on the Manchester Ship Canal where they flung muck into the same wagon. They met again outside the Totley tunnel on the Dore and Chinley, Ward now a union official, Cusack a tunnel tiger. 'No amount of persuasion,' said Ward, 'could convince him to drop the pick and shovel to become a trade union organiser.' But when they met again early this century at Derby sewage works Cusack was at last persuaded to join.

January 1891, was the month the union brought out its own newspaper, *The Navvy's Guide*.[1] It was edited by Leonard Hall, it was printed in Eccles, it cost a penny, it promised advertisers a ten thousand circulation, and it seems to have run for only six months. Its motto was the question John Ball asked in the Peasants' Revolt, 'When Adam delved and Eve span who was then the gentleman?'

It opened, 'To our Friends, If there is one class more than another at this moment which requires every possible means of airing its grievances and improving its position, it is the class which comes under the wide description of "navvies and general laborers". Although numbering in this country some hundreds of thousands strong, yet no body of men have hitherto submitted so patiently to a heavy and galling yoke, year after year, as they.'

'Until recent years,' the first edition went on, 'the newspaper and the printing press were the close monopoly of the "classes", of the well-to-do and the powers-that-be – weapons for the aggrandise-

---

1 Its first, full title was: *The Navvy's Guide and General Laborer's Own Paper*. In February, March and April it called itself: *The Navvy's and Laborer's Guide*. In May and June: *The Navvy's and General Laborer's Guide*.

ment of the privileged, and for the further enrichment of the rich, by the deeper impoverishment of the poor; whilst the rights and wrongs of the "masses", the claims and sufferings of Labor, were consistently misrepresented, belittled, and too often stifled, by the blatant twaddle or the sinister treachery of that army of intellectual prostitutes who are hired and paid by the strong and the cute to cajole, mislead, and bully the weak and ignorant. Within half-a-dozen years, however, we have changed all that. A compulsory Education Act, cheap literature, free libraries, and increased rapidity of communication in every department of life, have resulted in the raising of an opposition band of writers and thinkers – men "of the people, for the people", capable of putting into intelligent and forcible English the feelings and wants of their own class, and personally devoted by heart and conviction to its interests and its cause.'

'The work on the Ship Canal,' Ward wrote in the first issue, 'has never been a "healthy" job, as is evidenced by the number of inquests which weekly take place on killed outright or fatally injured laborers, in which the ordinary verdict – mostly a dead fraud and falsehood – arrived at by the juries of tailors and grocers who "sit on" bodies (with a vengeance!) is "accidental death". In nine cases out of ten we have no hesitation in saying – and we speak from personal, local and practical observation – that the verdict should be that of manslaughter against the contractors or Company.' (Walker's executors threatened to sue for criminal libel. The printer apologised: Ward didn't.)

Around this time Missionary Cox criticised navvies for grumbling about low wages at the Thirlmere dam. More money, he wrote in the *Letter*, means more drink-caused stoppages. Less drink, more money, was his equation: stop drinking, and contractors will pay you more. Poor Cox, he nearly lost his job. The Mission printed a notice disclaiming they favoured a low-wage policy. Mrs Garnett hoped landladies would give Mr Cox a cup of tea when he called.

'A Mr Cox,' began a grateful *Guide*, 'writing in that would-be mesmeriser of the British laborer, *The Navvy's Letter* or the *Christian Navvies' Organ*, is kind enough to admit that "it is not a good thing for a working man to be paid too low, but," (we know these "buts") "the reason of the low wages paid on many works is the fault of the men." To a certain extent we agree with this last, yet when Mr Cox proceeds to twaddle about drink being the cause of low wages, we must vigorously join issue. Don't let us be misunderstood. We are no champions of Bung, and the Gin and Swipes interest has nothing to expect from *The Navvy's Guide*. But it is an economic cause – the law of supply and demand – and not the quantity of drink consumed, that regulates wages and the hours of toil. That pernicious tarradiddle circulated so presistently by the Pharisees and the Shylocks, that individual thrift is the cause of individual wealth, is a lie. It is monopoly, not self-denial, that gives riches.'

'What snivelling Judas was it,' asked the *Guide*, 'who wrote in the *Labor News*, before the recent strike of the Gasworkers' Union at Darwen, Lancashire, had scarcely begun, that "the strike was a fiasco", a failure? If the *Labor News* had not proved itself long ago to be a slimy reptile and a dirty betrayer, there would have been no necessity for starting *The Navvy's Guide and General Laborer's Own Paper.*'

The *Ship Canal News* was, 'a snivelling, huckstering, cheap self-advertising sheet, prepared and issued by the Ship Canal fuglemen. A fraudulent specimen of spoiled butter wrapper. A miserable monthly liar. A chronicle of "crammers". A prevaricator's primer. A catchpenny calumniator. A pandering pedler. A villainous vilifier. A magazine of mischief. A monetary misleader. A sneering story-teller. A reckless reporter of "riots".'

('It is,' said the *Sporting Chronicle* of the *Guide*, 'about the wickedest little wildcat of a paper that I remember to have seen. It is all teeth and claws. There never was such a journalistic little tearer.' Needless to say, newsagents refused to sell the second issue.)

Membership for the union was drummed up by muscling in on disputes (mainly in the building trades), by accosting navvies leaving work, through hand-bills and by holding meetings – mass or otherwise. A procession carrying a banner reading 'Courage, Perseverance and Combination' left Patricroft for the Ship Canal offices on the first day of March, 1891. Ward, Hall, and Humphreys spoke from the back of a lorry.

Humphreys told the crowd if they didn't join the Union he wouldn't let them work when the Union controlled them. Foreign blacklegs would be forced to join, too.

Hall said the Royal Commission on Labour was chloroform to the working class. Look who'd be on it: Aird, the contractor who underpaid his navvies; Joseph "Screws Judas Iscariot" Chamberlain; The Prince of Wales, a snitch who betrayed his card-sharping friends when they stole money from each other; Lord Randolph

Churchill, still trying to grow a moustache; Lord Derby who gave himself four thousand pounds a week and his labourers thirteen shillings; Lord Londonderry who had devastated County Durham rather than let his colliers join a union.

A resolution – that union was the workingman's only hope – was carried, with a few dissensions. 'Bummers', Humphreys shouted at the dissenters from the back of the lorry.

Ealing branch held a meeting, simultaneously, on waste ground in London. George Haley, branch delegate, spoke from the back of a wagon. He'd been a kipper-monger, and a navvy in the Severn tunnel. Recently, he told the crowd, he'd tried to organise washerwomen, only they were too scared to attend his meetings. All the same it was wrong that women had to work like that. Children died of neglect and men were driven to drink. (He was a teetotaller, himself.) Last winter was a good one for agitation, but he would refuse any gifts offered him for his part in it. Nor would he be bribed into keeping quite. If he stopped speaking in public, it had been hinted, he'd get a better job. But he could always go back to fish-mongering.

Early in 1891 the union had thirty branches: twenty-one in London (their headquarters were in Benledi Street near the East India Docks), and nine along the ship canal. Over half the London branches met in Coffee Houses or Cocoa Rooms.

In February 1891, Eccles branch had three hundred and fifty members, two hundred of whom had joined in the last three months – the earlier crop having been dispersed by floods, bad weather, and the navvy's roaming habits. The shifting public works man was always a big problem and it seems likely the Union was always stronger among settled town labourers and building workers than among genuine navvies. (The *Guide*'s 'Where the Work Is' column listed twice as much work for builders' labourers and road-menders as for genuine navvies – although, of course, that may only mean there *was* twice as much non-navvy work about.)[2]

Throughout 1890 the Union claimed it handled a strike a week, on average: short-lasting, single-site, micro-strikes by the sound of them (the biggest, lasting a fortnight, involved only seven hundred

2 'I have never seen but one, and an early number, of the General Labourers' Union paper,' said Mrs G., who couldn't bring herself to call it the 'Navvies'' Union, 'and I counted sixteen mistakes in its list of public works in progress and pitied any of our men who had taken its information as their navvy guide. Many a cold, long tramp they would have had for nothing.'

men). Raises of a ha'penny, three-farthings, and a penny were won.

Yet in their biggest dispute, on the Ship Canal, the Union argued people *back* to work. It was in February 1891, and there are two versions of what happened, the *Manchester Guardian*'s and the *Guide*'s. According to the *Guardian* the strikers were violent and riotous: men at Mode Wheel who wanted to work were stoned, the works railway was damaged, a train was almost toppled over an embankment. 'It was a lock-out, not a strike,' said Hall. 'The men behaved throughout, even when molested by the police, with the utmost good humour.'

It began over a farthing – a fourth of a penny – pay-rise which was given to everybody except men already earning fivepence an hour. The fivepenny men accosted the walking ganger who said, in language so foul it shocked them, they'd get no more. What began as an affront over a farthing, ended in anger over the walking ganger's behaviour.

A meeting was held in the light of a street lamp at Eccles Cross. Leonard Hall, the chief speaker, showed them a telegram from Benledi Street – the union gave him leave to do what he thought best but in London they deprecated the strike. In Hall's opinion, too, it was ill-advised. The Company was desperate for money and had just gone to the Corporation for help. Not to have to pay wages for a few weeks was just what they wanted. Recruitment to the Union, he lied, was nearly complete and he planned to shut down the Ship Canal very soon. Join him. Join the Union.

On the other hand, he went on, they *had* been insulted and should have some redress for that. He suggested the meeting should elect three delegates to go with him to Salford to ask for an apology.

Next morning they all met again on waste ground near the canal offices. Ashmore the company's agent, didn't believe the men had been insulted – they used fouler language themselves, habitually. Ashmore then drivelled on, said Hall, about the men's ingratitude for the soup kitchens the company had provided in the late frosts. (Howls of derision at *that*.) The men had not been sacked, Ashmore finally said, and they could get back to work, or not, as they pleased. Hall left that to the meeting though he reminded them they were poor, uneducated men whose only hope was unity. Join the union, don't strike, and when they did all turn out it would be for sixpence an hour, not a paltry farthing. Soon every man would be controlled by the union.

The meeting voted to strike. It made no difference. Men were

186

plentiful and the union never did control them.[3]

Because of the Union's catch-all title, its potential membership was probably somewhere around two million. The mark of its failure was that it was always so small, even at a time of tiny unions, that its right to exist was sometimes questioned. In 1906, for example, a writer in the *Labour Leader* listed its outgoings:

Unemployed, travelling & emigration benefits	£25
Sick and Accident benefits	£361
Funeral benefits	£58
Payment to Federation	£72
Working Expenses	£642
Funds in hand	£265

'I do not suppose Mr John Ward would relish the absorption of his paper union by some organisation better able to help the men,' the *Labour Leader* went on, 'but if the few members of the Union were wise, they would insist upon such a transfer, and not keep a useless society together simply to enable Mr John Ward to draw his salary and pose as a Trade Union leader.' The Navvies' Union was 'simply a benevolent society. And the financial position shows that as a friendly society it is hopelessly insolvent.'

That year, 1906, it had a thousand members, a fifth of what it had in 1891, and it bounced about around this figure until 1913 when membership in most unions climbed (mainly because you could get the dole more easily by belonging to one) and it went into the Great War with around five thousand. How many were navvies is hard to say: probably not a lot.

All the same it was probably right to call it Ward's Union, like a 17th century regiment named after its colonel. He was the common factor through its whole history. Hall left, probably in 1891, to work for the Lancashire Labour Amalgamation and Humphrey's name disappears two or three years later.

Throughout the '90s there was talk of federating trade unions into a new society rich enough to help them, individually, during strikes, and big enough to induce some friendliness between them at other times. It might even be the workers' end of an axis, the other

3 Next year, when a wage rise was refused, two men tried to burn down Latchford railway station. The fire raisers were seen by a navvy called Abraham Thomas. They beat him up. Wagons were dropped into the empty canal. A watchman was killed. Even the nippers struck and marched along the banks with home-made clubs, recruiting other lads by force.

end of which was Parliament itself. The TUC put the idea to a committee. Ward, a big and loud man, was on the founding committee until the 1897 TUC sacked him because it was overloaded with labourers.

Nevertheless his union joined the new society, the General Federation of Trade Unions (GFTU), late in 1899 and he was himself elected to its Management Committee in 1901. He was balloted back year after year until 1913–14, when he was given the Treasuryship which he held until 1929.

Small as his union was it gave Ward a footing in the GFTU, and the GFTU gave him a footing in Labour politics.

Chapter 19

John Ward

John Ward, a brigand-like figure with a bandit's moustache and sombrero, was born in 1866 at Oatlands Park, near Weybridge and the River Thames. His father, a plasterer, died when he was three and his mother took him home to her birthplace, Appleshaw, where Hampshire rises into Salisbury Plain.

At one end of the long village road workmen were just finishing the Methodist chapel: at the other, the ancient squat/square-towered church had already being standing for centuries at the edge of Chute Forest. The village itself is in a dene, dry with underlying chalk. A flood relief ditch brimming with cow parsley runs like a dry brook from end to end. Otherwise it's all russet red tile and thatch. Where the lane forks to Ragged Appleshaw is a playing field which Ward, years later, gave to the village as a memorial to his family.

He ran away from the plough to the Navy, though too young to enlist, and then began navvy-work as a twelve-year old nipper on the Swindon-Marlborough, fatting wagons and looking after the turn-outs. In winter it was often so cold his hands froze to the couplings, ripping his skin away to the flesh. He carried the scars to his grave.

Stories differ about when he learned to read. One says he was already a full-grown navvy in lodgings at Weyhill, near Appleshaw, where he joined his landlord's son in lessons given by a neighbour. Another says his grandfather taught him when he was ten, though he then helped himself by spelling out the names on farmers' carts and mouth-and-finger-moving through Robinson Crusoe, copies of which were given away with packets of tea.

He was born with a love of adventure, but adventure in the sense of wanting to do something original, rather than craving danger. He was discontented with his life and did something about it, enlisting to begin with in what he called the Corps of Railway Constructors, building the Suakim-Berber Railway in the Sudan, where he won the Queen's Silver Medal and the Khedive's Bronze Star and Clasp. The Sudan made him anti-war but not anti-revolution, and back in England in 1885 he joined the Battersea Branch of the Social Democratic Federation, the main far-left party of his day.

Next year the SDF tried to tag a mini-cavalcade of the poor on to the tail of the Lord Mayor's Show, to protest at the flaunting of wealth and to ask the Government to help the unemployed. When the City police stopped them marching and the Metropolitan Police banned a meeting in Trafalgar Square, the SDF decided to test the legality of all by making sure somebody was arrested and tried. Ward was the chosen arrestee.

The day of the Show was drizzling, damp, yellow-murky. Rain and booted feet smeared the pavement with a thin paste-like slime of mud. At 2.55 the head of the Lord Mayor's Show reached Charing Cross and curled around one corner of Trafalgar Square and down Northumberland Avenue, led by Mounted Police, the Royal Artillery, the Scots Guards, drums and fifes and banners and arms of the famous and, more importantly, the important. There was a model of a steam launch with her propeller turning and the band of the Royal Naval School, Greenwich. There was the Civil Service-donated Walmer lifeboat. There was the noise of shouts and cheers, faintly clashing bands, rumbling iron-tyred wheels, uneven chatter of hooves and the slight ring of horses' shoes. More banners, standards, more arms, bands. Beadles with staves rode in carriages. More banners. Floats representing Australasia (with gold diggers at work), the West Indies, Cape Colony, the Montreal Ice Palace. There were cars symbolic of India and the British Isles. Under-Sheriffs rode in state chariots. The Mounted Sappers Tower Hamlets Engineer Volunteers jogged past (noisy with brass, drums, fifes, fully laden FS wagons) followed by a jumble of aldermen, trumpeters, the Royal Fusiliers and the Lord Mayor (waving tricorn hat) with his chaplain, mace bearer, sword bearer and the 10th Hussars. Police closed around the tail of the cavalcade as it was drawn down Northumberland Avenue and sealed it off from the hissing and groaning crowd in the Square.

The SDF told everybody they would speak from the balustrade at the St Martin's end of Trafalgar Square, thus duping the police into parading, double-ranked, in front of the National Gallery. The Lord Mayor's Show throbbed on down Northumberland Avenue but only Ward clambered on to the balustrade – to divert the police who were already in the wrong place like revolution-ready dummies. The rest of the SDF bulldozed their way to Nelson's Column and held the meeting on the plinth.

Ward yo-yoed on and off the balustrade, policemen limpeting to him. 'I must speak,' the police said he said, 'I'm paid for it. I must speak or be shot.'

The crowd egged him on, shaking umbrellas and walking canes. Some said he was kicked. Inspector Attwood and Sgt Tooth, of V Division, said he wasn't. In the end, smeared with pavement slime, he was taken to King Street Police Station. William Marcus Thompson, a radical Ulster journalist, barrister, and Ward's counsel, tried to turn the case into a trial of the police's right to ban meetings. Mr Vaughan, the Bow Street Magistrate, said it was about obstructing the police and fined Ward ten shillings.

A few days later the police let them have their meeting; in fact they held five simultaneously, one of which Ward chaired in his navvy rig and Sudan medals at the exact spot where he'd been arrested. Red flags and red handkerchiefs dotted the sombre crowd like clots of blood. John Burns was on the platform with him. Above them drooped a banner, 'We must have work or bread.'

Ward was still a navvy: at one time he worked in the tunnel below Belsize Park in London, at another in the Salford basin on the Ship Canal. But he was also still a youth who saw the world brightly in red and black – lurid as blood, black as the grave, bleeding human flesh and black landscapes; children in their rags: gaunt, lame beggars. All kindliness killed by capitalism.

His philosophy began by claiming for all human life the absolute right to live, and then the right to belong. If you belong you have, navvy-like, the right to the navvy's shilling. Capitalism, it seemed to him, denied that. It was pitiless. It lived by competition; and competition, at the lowest level, is about who kills to live and who dies. Capitalism in its own dying had no claim on our pity. Capitalists were unconvicted killers. They enslaved the poor, invoking the liberty of the individual as their right to do so. But where was the liberty for the slaves? Where was the liberty in endless labour?

Empires, he believed, fall when too few people own too much. Britain was so falling and to Ward, in his twenties, the late '80s were times of high revolutionary excitement. The world was in transit. Capitalism had killed Christianity, which had failed anyway. Now Capitalism was being killed by a new humanity.

What was to happen then, he saw more dimly. Everything would be nationalised. Art, literature and science would be freed. Equality would make people kinder to each other. Lesser minds would spend their time listening to greater ones talking about physics and philosophy.

'The long and dreary struggle between darkness and light is nigh ended – good is triumphing over evil – right over wrong – freedom over despotism. Soon will the light of the opening day breathe a new life into the soul of man, and shed the balm of true happiness over his life – and give back to him that "contentment" and "peace" for which myriads of the noblest have striven.'

For his part, he was going to help bring it about by running for public office and he began by standing as an SDF candidate in West Lambeth in the 1888 London School Board elections. 'I have suffered from the mismanagement of our present system,' he told electors. 'Plump for the workmen's candidate, and ensure "National intelligence" in preference to "National ignorance".' He convinced nearly eight and a half thousand of them, but lost.

Next, in 1890, he put himself up for election to the Wandsworth Vestry, going along one day in May straight from work, collarless, with a muck-streaked face, to register as a candidate at the Town Hall. He stood as 'Citizen' John Ward with two other socialists.[1]

The whole parish was placarded with posters, mostly the flaring red of the Tories and the buff of the Wandsworth Ratepayers' Association. Voting took place next day in the Town Hall – now replaced – in the hollow of the Wandle valley. It was a hot day and a hot evening. Crowds shoved and crowded outside the Town Hall. Van loads of electors drove straight from work: Sandwichboarded men – shouting 'vote early' and 'no plumpers' – pushed through the police-herded crowds.

After the polls closed, the candidates slipped away for a tripe supper at the Spread Eagle, between the Town Hall and the brewery. The new yellow brickwork of the Brewery Tap was just blackening in the smokey air. The whole place smelled of poverty, sweat, horses, horse dung and the sharp clear tang of ale from the big brewery by the Wandle.

Thirty-one new Vestrymen were elected that day, making eighty-four all told. Sixty-four were Tories. Two were socialists:

---

1 A Vestry was an elected council which ran a parish's public utilities – sweeping streets, keeping street lamps lit, looking after sewers and footpaths.

Citizen Ward (485 votes, sixth from bottom) and a Mr Brown.

Early in June the Vestry met for the first time to elect people to the Board of Works. Ward asked Mr Freeman, manager of the gas works, whether – if he were elected – he would discriminate against the Board's workmen whose politics were not his own. (A voice, 'Get down, Ward.' 'We don't deal in politics here.' Chairman, 'Order! Order!') Freeman said he didn't care if a man belonged to a union or not, so long as he did his work.

At the end of the meeting Ward asked for a list of the Board's workmen, their hours, and their wages. The Vestry had no powers in these matters, said Mr Gilkes. But the Vestry elected the Board, objected Ward, fobbed off for the first time in a long, long history of political fobbings off that lasted well into the next century. Ward and Brown asked for the list again and again until the Board finally flatly voted not to tell them. Why should the parish know how much of its money the board spent?

Ward also insisted that Vestry workmen get sixpence an hour minimum. But the Vestry, the Vestry objected, was swamped with applications as it was. Elderly men were glad to take any wages offered. 'Are we to trade on their circumstances?' asked Ward. If we paid trade union rates, objected the Vestry, we would have to take on young men, *and* see they worked hard. *That* would be cruel to the elderly.

More bizarrely he busied himself with the crimes of landowners who stole commons, ponds, and ancient public charities. He and another Vestryman signing himself EGROEG REHSIF (George Fisher when he wasn't hiding from his foes), even wrote a pamphlet about it, most of it a reprint of a report written in 1848 and suppressed at the time by the Vestry, particularly by Vestryman Thomas Phillips, one of the thieves it named.

The problem was not just historical, either. Ward was particularly outraged by a man who had recently stolen a publicly owned pond called The Black Sea (long since drained and jerry-built over) on Wandsworth Common. One day Ward and his friends went to walk around it and were ordered off by a Mr Wilson who had fenced it in and called it his own. Wilson even asked the magistrates to protect his property from the Wandsworth Rabble.

Ward was re-elected to the Vestry in 1891 but seems not to have stood again.

The first ever London County Council elections had been held in 1889 when it had been agreed (tacitly) that candidates would not stand under Parliamentary party names. There were, therefore, two new parties – the Progressives (Liberal-backed) and the Moderates (disguised Tories). The Progressives won and immediately politicised the Council on national party lines. They wanted to control the police, reform the City, abolish coal dues, and to tax ground rents. The next Council elections, in March 1892, were more overtly political. Ward stood as a Labour-Progressive in Wandsworth.

The night before election day, bill posters were up and about all over town posting bright and bilious placards. Polling day itself was bright and sharp with a frost that stopped racing at out of town tracks. The Progressives increased their majority. Wandsworth, against the trend, turned out its sitting Progressive and returned a Moderate: an Oxford man who devoted half his life to science, half to philanthropy. Ward came fourth. 1892, as well, was the year he married Luian Elizabeth Gibbs.

By now Ward had been a union official for nearly three years – Secretary of the Gas and Navvies' Association the *Wandsworth Observer* incorrectly called him. (In 1889 he was chairman of the Battersea branch of the Gasworkers' Union for a time. That year, too, he found the National Federation of Labour Union which, though it seemed to start hopefully, quickly faded in the early '90s.) At the same time, he spoke regularly at the Trades Union Congresses.

He was against the Boer War and told the 1900 Congress 'that practically £100 million of the taxpayers' money had been spent trying to secure the goldfields of South Africa for cosmopolitan Jews, most of whom had no patriotism and no country.'

At the 1902 Congress he spoke against 'wars of foreign aggression, which only tend to enrich the sinister figure of cosmopolitan finance.'

At the 1904 Congress, in Leeds, he spoke against conscription. 'Many of the resolutions you have dealt with at this congress are useless, because you and your fellow workmen have been under the influence of Jingoism and spread-eagle Imperialism, and have squandered your resources in war. For years we had a succession of revenue surpluses, which made old age pensions within the range of practical politics without increasing the taxation of the community. Wild reckless Imperialism has swallowed all and left nothing to the old and helpless. War destroys trade, and the proposal to take the manhood of our nation from the pursuits of industry for two of the best years of their lives is the maddest proposal that ever emanated from Bedlam.'

Once or twice since the repeal of the Combination Acts, trade unions had come up against the common law which assumed you were responsible for what you did, if what you did harmed others. Gladstone gave trade unions the right to strike without having their funds sequestered to pay for damages. Disraeli legalised picketing. But in July 1901, everything seemed to back-somersault. A court granted injunctions against the railwaymen's union whose members were on strike on the Taff Vale line in South Wales. Unions could – again – be sued as corporate entities for the harm they did by striking. Their money could be sequestered to pay damages.

To the unions it seemed the judiciary made up the rules as they went along. To fix things their way once and for all they made up their minds to get enough of their own people elected to Parliament to ensure that future laws would be made to their liking. How to go about it was no problem: a mechanism was already there – the TUC's Labour Representation Committee, recently set up to choose Parliamentary candidates and plot their campaigns.

By this time Ward was a rapidly moderating, centre-moving man, a member of the National Democratic League, set up in 1900 as an alliance of the not-*too*-left. Clearing the plutocrats out of Parliament by paying MPs a salary was one of its aims: the armed overthrow of Parliament was not.

In 1903 the Labour Representation Committee met in Newcastle. Ward, now chairman of the NDL, moved that the LRC's rules be altered to allow his League to affiliate. He was voted down and a counter-proposal – the Newcastle Resolution – forbidding LRC members to have anything to do with either the Tories or the Liberals was carried. Ward would not sign – he was already negotiating with the Liberals in Stoke-on-Trent – and his name was taken off the LRC's lists. At the next General Election he would stand for Stoke-on-Trent as an independent Liberal-Labour candidate.

The next General Election came in 1906. After it those LRC men who were sent to Parliament became the Labour Party. Ward, excluded at first by the Newcastle Resolution, never did belong to it. Why, he was asked during the election, couldn't he support the LRC? Because, he said, of its cast-iron rules. He could not relinquish his right to be his own man in whatever cause he thought proper. (But, 'I have absolutely declared, times without number, that I'm going to Parliament, if Stoke returns me, to make one of the Labour group in the British House of Commons.')

The election campaign began early in January. Ward was now forty, still un-grey but with receding springy hair with a natural wave in the forelock. Now he sported not so much a brigand's moustachio as the long-pointed handlebars of the kind later favoured by the RAF. He had fierce blue eyes and slightly flaring nostrils. He began his campaign still weak from scarlet fever picked up on a visit to Hanley sewage works. His wife Luian (Lilian, according to some accounts) stood on the platform at all his meetings. Douglas Coghill, Tory, defended a small majority. Chinese labour in South Africa and Tariff Reform were the big questions.

Before leaving office the Tory administration had issued licenses allowing yet more indentured Chinese into the Rand. They were needed in the goldfields, said the Tories. Lies, said Ward: they were to keep down wages.

Mine owners were afraid white labour would take their trade unions with them and ask for proper wages and the vote. That apart, the Potteries had expected crockery-buying white families would settle the Rand. More importantly, the Chinese were *slaves*. Mine managers could flog them.

'Is moral and decent for a democracy of Britishers to vote for slavery conditions terrible to relate? It was supposed the old flag floated over absolute freedom. And don't forget I myself have fought under the old flag.' Here, he ripped open his coat to show his Sudan medals. 'Whenever I risked my life under it I always understood it to be the emblem of human liberty. So long as I'm a Britisher I'll protest against slavery being introduced as part of British national policy.'

The Attorney-General in South Africa said it was too late to stop the latest batch of Chinese. 'I'll be hanged if I wouldn't stop them,' Ward told his meetings, 'I'd give orders to our admiral under our Anti-Slavery Act law to collar them as prizes if they shipped them there. The idea of these gold-bugs thinking, after they'd bamboozled the officials in South Africa, they can bullnose us. I'll be hanged if I'd allow them to do anything of the kind. I'd put Jack on their track.'

Coghill on the other hand (said Ward) favoured slavery. And he favoured employers being allowed to rifle union benevolent funds. Did the electors agree with that? 'No,' they shouted.

Ward was for Free Trade, against Tariff Reform. In the Potteries, the Tories spoke only of tariff barriers protecting the potting industry. In the countryside they spoke only of tariff reform protecting farming. But Tariff Reform meant general import controls with the world putting up trade barriers against us. It meant a two shilling tax on every quarter of imported wheat. Did the electors want that?

He supported women's suffrage. ('Give women the vote,' shouted one woman, 'then John Ward would be *carried* in.') He made no great thing of being a navvy, mentioning it only once. 'It's been hurled against me by the Delilahs of the Primrose League that I've been a navvy. I'd say that's more creditable to me than otherwise.' He spoke to packed meetings, usually in chalky school classrooms, his audience overspilling on to window-sills and the edge of his platform. Most were on his side, handling the hecklers for him. 'Tha goo and sell mussels.' 'Go and mind the baby.'

The night before polling day his supporters marched through the rain-slicked streets, by the bloated black bottle kilns, carrying two loaves of bread: a big one tied with a blue ribbon (representing Ward) and a little 'Protection' cob wrapped in Coghill's colours. They marched by the regimented houses, by the trams clanking in their grooves, hissing under their electric wires, by the naphtha lamps flaring outside the open greengrocers. As they marched they sang their election song:

> Rouse then, workers; rally round, the voters,
> Ready, steady, everyone must vote:
> Liberals and Labour, we are both united,
> We have confidence in Ward for Stoke.

His majority was 3372. He was sent to one of the greatest of the reforming Parliaments. It, or the next, voted for old age pensions, unemployment and health insurance, free medical inspection for school children, Labour Exchanges, workmen's compensation. It taxed the rich, it denied power to the House of Lords. It gave the trade unions the Trades Dispute Act.

Ward spoke a few days after taking his seat. Was the Board of Trade aware of the trouble caused by paying local education authorities yearly instead of quarterly? Well, yes, said the BOT, but it was all terribly technical. For Ward it was the beginning of another two decades of being fobbed off.

He spoke for the Labour Group in the debate on the King's

Speech. An Opposition amendment regretted that a Government minister had brought the country into contempt by calling Chinese labour in South Africa 'slavery' when it was obvious the Government was doing nothing about it. It *was* slavery, said Ward. The companies wanted the Chinese not because blacks or whites couldn't do the work but to cut their pay-rolls. More labour, less pay, was how it worked. 'Do you imagine for one moment that the mothers of England, when they saw their sons off to the war in those dark years of 1899 and 1900, thought they were sending them to leave their bones in that country in order to support and maintain and introduce a policy such as they were defending today?'

Over the years he asked about the flogging of Africans in Natal and the shooting of strikers in British Guiana; the cost of human food in London Zoo; the pay of charwomen in the Public Record Office; how many places had Distress Committees; why there was no school for navvy children at Ladybower; what percentage of workmen on Aird's Asswan dam were British? (Five – mainly gangers and tradesmen. What European labour there was, was mainly Italian.) Did the House know a penny a day for tools and medicine was stopped from navvies' wages at the Ambergate dam? Had the Labour Exchanges recruited scabs to break a navvy strike on the new docks in Liverpool?

So he sat below the gangway on the Government side, a cross between a brigand and a navvy in a large sombrero. He voted the right way, but he never dazzled, and because he never belonged to one of the big parties he never climbed. He was, curiously navvy-like, like a by-stander.

Before the Great War he spoke more often about Rosyth Naval Base (the union had a branch there), than about anything else. After 1909 all Government contracts had a Fair Wages Clause written into them, an idea copied from the London County Council where John Burns had introduced them in 1892.[2] The contracts for Rosyth were signed in March 1909, and next year men and employers were arguing about what a 'fair wage' was. They asked the Admiralty. Two *years* later the Admiralty replied. What the contractors were paying *was* a fair wage.

'You know very well that we submitted the case to the

2 The fairness of Fair Wages impressed workmen less than it did politicians. At the Blackwall tunnel, in 1892, the men asked the London County Council to change 'fair wages' to 'trade union rates' in its contracts. 'Fair Wages,' said William Crooks, Poplar's LCC representative, 'meant anything a contractor could obtain men for.'

Admiralty,' contractors told Ward ever after, 'and that they declared fivepence an hour was the proper rate. Why should we pay more?'

Too few men would go there for so little and the Labour Exchanges had to advertise all over the country. Just before a strike in the autumn of 1912, Mr Gemmell, manager of the Rosyth Labour Exchange, went to Dublin to recruit more men. When he heard about it Ward forced an Adjournment Debate in the House. Had the contractors sent Gemmell to recruit scabs?

Any Labour Exchange manager who behaved like that, said the BOT, would be fired on the spot. Gemmell had gone to Dublin at least a week before the strike was heard of. The strike itself, said the BOT, was caused by the Rosyth navvies mistakenly thinking the Irish were to be paid more than them. Shortly afterwards, Ward opposed a routine little Bill authorising the Navy to build a wooden fuelling jetty at North Killingholme, near Grimsby. He moved an amendment. He was sorry to keep the House out of bed, it was almost midnight, but something had to be done for navvies on Government contracts. He didn't trust the Admiralty. (They told him the House of Commons was the over-seer of their contracts. If that were true, the House was housing people at Rosyth like pigs.) All he asked the House to do was kill the North Killingholme Bill unless clauses in it insisted on decent housing, medical care, and a minimum wage for navvies working there.

Dr McNamarra, for the Admiralty, conceded the housing side of the argument immediately. He made the Public Bill into a Private one – men at North Killingholme would be treated according to the House's own rules on housing navvies.

A statutory minimum wage was different. He couldn't concede the principle that Parliamentary policy – in this case the Fair Wages Clause, but it could be something more important – could be over-turned surreptitiously under cover of insignificant little Bills.

The trouble with the honourable member for Stoke, he said, was he couldn't accept reality.

Chapter 20

Churching the Ungodly

'Navvies,' Ward once said, 'are not, like Hodge, priest-ridden, for religion is a thing they know little of.'

Navvies, said every Christian, are godless pagans heading headlong for damnation. Christendom's counter-attack came in two phases: pre-Navvy Mission Society missions, and the Navvy Mission Society itself.

The problem with the pre-Society missions was they were unconnected and haphazard: even the heaviest dose of religion was no good if the navvy never saw a Christian again. For this reason they were pretty ineffective, in spite of the fact there were plenty of them. In the late '60s, *four* separate missions competed for navvies on the short Kettering-Manton line, where Daniel Barrett was the Bishop of Peterborough's appointee. He had a seven mile parish and three chapels with wooden belfries hung with bells which chimed, not tolled, and flagstaffs for flying the cross of St George on Sundays. He opened his mission to a congregation of forty-two – of whom only the odd two were navvies, and one of them was so drunk he had to be led away, protesting he'd heard it all before – in jail.

What the Society offered when it came was a continuity of effort, aim, and house-style. Like booking into an international hotel you always knew what to expect on an NMS job. The trouble, then, was navvies liked the amenities that were offered more than the religion that was preached.

I never heard any one say anything against the Navvy Mission. It was a blooming good thing. They were always preaching at you at dinner time, that was all. I didn't want no bugger preaching at me while I was eating my bit of snap.

Nor did they always like what was preached at them – a

Christianity stripped to its Jewish and Iranian origins, full of eastern demonology and the promise of pain to come. It was this threat of never-ending violence against the person that most offended navvies: violence against people who never asked to be created – to be set up and knocked down like coconuts in a cock-shy – and then be tortured with inhuman cruelty for trivial offences in a pitifully short life in which they were chiefly preoccupied with staying alive. It was a kind of terrorism: people were terrorised into being Christian. Except many weren't, and wouldn't be.

'Do you mean to say,' a navvy asked the Rev. Fayers, on the Lune valley line in the '50s, 'that arter working on these railways, enough to pull a feller's heart out, we'll be hard worked in the next world?'

'Yes,' said Fayers – and repeated it to Old Alice, a middle-aged woman (prematurely old) bright in lindsey petticoats. Old Alice didn't believe him, either.

'Why I goes about the country for the good of old England,' she argued, 'I puts up with all they put upon me, and when navvies slope me, I bears it all, and shan't go to a bad place.'

'Jesus says no one can get to heaven but by him,' Fayers argued back, 'and the reason you hope to get there does away with Him altogether.'

'Nowt o' sort,' snorted Old Alice, pretty sure hardship now ensured and easy hereafter.

Apart from anything else it grated against a sense of fair-play. Unfairness was bad enough on earth, in heaven it was intolerable. 'They certainly wonder', said one lay preacher, 'that God should have made some rich and some so dreadfully poor.' Yet some Christians like Katie Marsh seem to have had no concept of equality at all, not even in death. Miss Marsh lived in constant terror she was less holy than her mother who, in consequence, would be graded so much higher than her in heaven's hierarchy they'd never meet again in all eternity.

Most navvies, as well, disliked parsons. How could leaning on a pulpit twice a week pay better than shifting two hundred and fifty tons of muck? 'Many of them regard a clergyman as their natural foe,' said the Rev. Munby, vicar of Turvey, in the early '70s. 'Once, I heard a party of them say: "Look, here comes the parson. Let's heave a truck at him."'

In return many parsons disliked *them*. 'Too bad to go among,' said a Baptist minister. 'Not an atom's worth of honesty among them,' said the Rev Thompson, missionary on the South Devon line, 1840s. 'Vile and immoral characters,' intoned the Rev Sargent, missionary on the Carlisle-Lancaster, also in the '40s.

Navvies, on the other hand, were much more open to parsons' wives and daughters, untouchable in muck-long frocks, not unlike pedestals. In return, by accepting them, those wives and daughters made navvies more acceptable to society by changing people's perceptions of them. And a sense of acceptance by society must have made the navvy more receptive to society's religion.

Pre-NMS, there was Anna Tregelles (whose book, *Ways of the Line*, inspired the nameless authoress of *Life or Death*) and, above all, Katie Marsh. Contemporary with the Mission there was Elizabeth Garnett and the dozens of women who did the Society's donkey-work – from not-quite-gentlewomen like Katherine Sleight to bluebloods like the Countess of Harewood. Supreme among them, the navvy's arch-friends, were Katie Marsh and Elizabeth Garnett.

Miss Marsh never married and though Mrs Garnett obviously did, her husband died on their honeymoon soon after her wedding. Both were daughters of Anglican clergymen.

Katie Marsh, born in 1818 in Colchester, was always unintimidated by the great, accustomed as she was to the illustrious of the land through her father's connections, by marriage, with the nobility. She had, she said, no politics (just anti-Gordon-ics and anti-Bradlaugh-ics) though that didn't stop her telling Mr Gladstone to defy the electorate of Northampton and throw Bradlaugh out of Parliament. 'Save our country from the Apostle of Atheism,' she told him.

At first she seemed an ordinary spinster-daughter of the parsonage and it was the shock of being thirty that turned her into one of the foremost evangelists of her day, influential both in Britain and the USA. Navvies were only a brief bit of her life: she knew them only when they came to re-erect the Crystal Palace near her father's parish of Beckenham and later when the Army Works Corps was drafted from there to the Crimea. By then she was in her late thirties, plump and plain, not unlike the later Victoria, with ballooning frocks and ballooning face.

Beckenham Rectory, a small mansion set in lawns dotted with disc-like flower beds, overlooked the rural hills of Norwood. Beckenham itself, still a village, housed some of the Crystal Palace navvies. Miss Marsh first met them one Sunday evening in March 1853, on the pretext of seeing a sick parishioner.

'Harry ain't here now,' said the navvy who opened the door. Could she wait?

'Well, you can if you like,' said the man, 'but we're a lot of rough uns.'

'I don't mind that,' said Miss Marsh.

Nobody, least of all ladies tea-cosied in crinolines, spoke to navvies like that. Navvies were brutish half-men looming on the edges of mankind. The prognathous jaw that bit. The impact of her book about them, *English Hearts and English Hands*, was the greater because of her refinement and femininity (the impact of a book by a professional Christian, a clergyman in a stove-pipe hat, would have been that much weaker). From her book it was clear navvies were *not* Neandertals without the body hair: they were kind and manly, shy and simple (too ill-educated to be politicised like artisans), guileless but beguiling. Her book was a major navvy turning point.[1]

Elizabeth Hart, later Mrs Garnett, was born at Otley in Yorkshire in 1839. Mr Hart, like Mr Marsh, was a vicar but more poorly connected. Where Miss Marsh spoke to most of the English-speaking world, Elizabeth Hart spoke mainly to navvies; where Miss Marsh scolded Prime Ministers, Mrs Garnett scorned the socialists of the Navvies' Union.

Elizabeth Hart (Mrs Garnett) was a natural-born organiser, unasked, of other people's lives. If her husband, a clergyman, hadn't died on their honeymoon she would without a doubt have terrorised some hapless parish into Christianity through unbending good example and unending chiding. A small, strong-jawed, strong-willed woman; irrefragable; strong with the robustness of simplicity: the world's complexities always puzzled her.

Laws, she thought, were quite literally based on the laws of Christ yet it was awful to see, every day, his laws superseded by men's. 'Look at the newspapers', she would say, 'and they are full of disagreements and strikes, and quarrelling, everyone trying to get all for themselves. Men think everything can be done by law, and so they make laws until they law away all an Englishman's self-responsibility and freedom.'

Strife distressed her. Why must people argue when Christ instructed them to be friends? 'Dear Friends,' she pleaded, 'do let us

1 A turning point for others, too. Aggie Weston, foundress of the Sailors' Homes, admitted the book inspired her to begin her work for the Royal Navy.

navvies stick together, and be pleasant to one another. Give your contractors a civil bow. It's a very heavy burden to plan how to get you work to pay your wages. You know how hard many of these men's lives are,' she went on, turning to the contractors. 'Think for them. See there's plenty of skilly, and a dry cabin with a good tea-can stove for wet weather, and spin out the work in winter.'

But if she was disingenuous she was also open-hearted with a deep abiding affection for these big and wayward men. She was genuinely appalled at their sightlessness in endangering their souls. How could men care so little for eternity, they wouldn't lace their boots to walk half a mile to be saved? So she hectored, scolded, nagged and bullied them. At times she sounded like a schoolmistress in charge of an unaccountably drunken hockey team; but she never looked down on them and her loyalty to them never slackened.

'We trust that you will feel when you receive this,' she told them in the first issue of the *Letter*, 'there are those in the world who love you still. Hitherto, as a class, the Navvies have not been duly cared for. That day is past.'

She was often – she was *usually* – indignant at their conduct and *always* shocked at any lack of pride in a navvy's calling. She called them 'mates'. She called herself a 'navvy'.

They were her entire life. 'I was for many years,' she said in 1898, 'the *unpaid* clerk, Librarian, Editor, Drawing Room Speaker, etc, besides being one of the Committee and Managers of the Society. I have *never* been paid *one penny*,' she went on, 'and if ever I get so poor that I have to be paid, it will be "good-bye" and you will not see me again. *No*, I will work for the love of Christ, and for the love of you, or *not at all*.' To many she *was* the Mission: the one person they really knew (apart from the missionaries) because for nearly forty years she nagged them endlessly in the *Letter*, the Society's official magazine, which she edited all that time.

Until 1893 it was, more properly, the *Quarterly Letter to Navvies from the Navvy Mission Society*. That year *Men on Public Works* was substituted for *Navvies* in accordance with the new reality. Navvies now shared public works with black-gang men and other trades, all in need of saving. It was a small green-backed pamphlet only ever called the *Letter*, *Navvies' Letter*, *Quarterly Letter* or the *Green 'Un*. Its colophon was a diamond shape made of a round-nosed shovel, a pick, an axe, a saw, and a pan, with an open Bible in the middle. At first its bold lettering – of which there was a *lot*: it was an *emphatic publication* – was in a heavy square-serif Wild West typeface which gradually thinned down as the magazine matured.

Mrs Garnett always suspected people read it, like the Chinese, from back to front. At the back were the endless lists of dead and injured and the scandal sheet: who'd eloped with whom, who'd sloped who, who'd gone missing, whose children were in the workhouse. At the front was the epistle-like 'letter' itself, often from Mrs Garnett, often from a guest writer. It was always uplifting.

Drink was its big theme ('How many bundles of meat have the Bobbies walked off with this summer?' Mrs Garnett wondered in 1881, deploring another year of drunkenness) and it frequently carried moral tales, dreadful warnings, true-life confessions and recipes for cooling drinks for alcoholics wanting to dry out.

In its summer 1903, edition it told the tale of a drunkard who cut his throat. He lay on his back, a look of dumb craving in his eyes, as his friends and relatives crowded round his death bed. "Do you want a minister?" asked the doctor. The man shook his head.'

'"Would you like a prayer said?" He moved his lips but no sound came. He was dying fast, and they could not make out his dying wish. The doctor stooped and put his ear down to the man's mouth, but he could not hear what he said. At last the man took his fingers and fairly pinched the wound close, and feebly said, "Doctor, for Christ's sake, *give me another glass*."'

Then there was W-P-, a drunkard who died of drink. The autopsy showed his heart weighed only two ounces instead of eight. 'It was dried up with that stuff called whiskey. I thank my God He has kept me from the cursed cup.'

The *Letter* also printed what must be history's least sung anti-booze ballad, so appalling it could only damage sobriety's reputation. (To make it worse it was written by a Scot but attributed in the chorus to an Englishman.) It went to the tune *The Days We Went A-Gipsying*:

Chorus:
Yes, I am an English navvy, but, oh, not an English sot,
I have run my pick through alcohol, in bottle, glass, or pot,
And with the spade of abstinence, and all the power I can,
I am spreading out a better road for every working man.

Sometimes they printed useful hints, like how to stop bleeding. On the covers were the job lists that were, in fact, the navvy's best source of information about new jobs, old jobs, and where to tramp to next. These alone would have meant the *Letter* was widely read and its print runs were always high – 155,000 copies of one issue in 1904, its highest ever. Even at the outbreak of the Great War editions ran to a hundred thousand.

Mrs Garnett's involvement with the Mission was an accident of time and place which brought her, free and uncommitted, to the Lindley Wood dam where and when it began. She first saw the place one Saturday evening after dark in the fall of '71, when it was already cold with the coming winter. The gutter trench was being sunk, lit by the glare of the pumping engine fires. Feeble lights shone from the huts a mile or so away. The shingled church with its high pitched roof stood in a clearing in the woods above them. She thought she might be in Canada. It was a place she could never forget: the red huts in the sun, she remembered, and the wood itself blue with harebells.

The Mission was not yet founded though its founder, the Rev Lewis Moules Evans, was already at work at Lindley, already ill with tuberculosis, and the idea for it had already been given him by a navvy he met in a third class railway carriage somewhere in the north of England. 'Outlaws, sir,' the navvy told him, 'that's what we are. Wanderers on the face of the earth, and outcasts from society. Decent people, them as lives in towns and villages and has homes of their own and no occasion to tramp, they gets a notion into their heads as we belongs to a different breed from what they do. They reckons us a sort of big strong beasts, very useful in our way, but terrible dangerous and not of much account except for strength.'

'Why, it was only t'other day as I heard a woman telling about a railway accident, and she said as there was three men killed and a *navvy*.[2] We ain't *men* at all, we ain't got no feelings nor no souls, nor nothing but just strong backs and arms and a big swallow for beer.'

He was middle-aged, middle-height, a man who'd been a navvy since he ran away from home as a boy. For years he'd been as roving, drunk and dissolute as the rest. Then one Christmas a year

---

2 A common story. A twentieth century version is set in a pub in Wales:
'Who's that coming down the mountain, landlord?'
'Two men and a navvy.'

or so ago he was dropping down through woods off the Yorkshire moors, on tramp and lost. Ahead of him through the trees he saw yellow candlelight spilling on the snow and he heard singing. A ramshackle chapel filled with navvies. He went in, glad to rest in its warmth, drowsy and half-listening until the clergyman said something that transformed his life. 'What he said sounded so strange and new to me,' said the navvy, years later in the third class railway carriage. 'He told us about the Saviour who came at Christmas time, all out of love for us: and he made it plain he meant us. I felt as if I'd found some one who cared for me.'

The feeling transformed his life. He learned to read – he pulled a Bible and prayer book from his pocket – though still at times he was afraid. Places like that chapel were rare. 'What we want is more work like that,' he said. 'Regular work. We're most of us very ignorant, and it isn't likely as we can teach ourselves and we want some one to come to us and teach us.'

Around this time Evans was given the living of Leathley, a hamlet in the Washbourn valley where the Lindley Wood dam was being built for Leeds Corporation. Evans used to walk alongside the stream to the dam through the birches, oaks, foxgloves and bracken of Lindley Wood. He called himself a navvy – 'I work on public works.'

'I've come three miles to tell you something that will do you good,' he once told a navvy. 'Won't you come a few yards to hear it?'

'You see, sir, I've not got a hat,' said the man. 'It's not respectable to go to a place of worship bareheaded: now if I'd a tile . . . '

'Then here's mine.'

'Nay, put your hat on, sir. I'll come as I am.'

'I want *you*,' Evans told them, 'Not your jackets. Come just as you are.' Though he added, 'You need only leave your pipes behind.'

The Christian Excavators' Union, which predated the Mission, was also founded around this time at Lindley Wood. It was open only to working navvies, who wrote the rules.

'I desire by God's help,' aspirants testified, 'to serve the Lord Jesus Christ, and to lead others to do so.'

'To this end.'

'I promise to abstain from drink, swearing and ungodly living.'

'I promise never to neglect praying each morning and night.'

'I promise to keep the Lord's Day Holy and when possible to

attend a place of public worship.'

Each man had three months to clear his debts, prove himself, and make himself ready before he was accepted. Each carried a card and, after 1883, a badge (two hands clasped over a Bible) proclaiming his intentions. With it went the blue ribbon of temperance and the white ribbon of purity. Mrs Garnett always said they were the salt for Christ on public works. The *Navvy's Guide* said they were spies.

The CEU began with thirty-seven members, rose to about three hundred in the early '80s and peaked at nearly seven hundred in 1913. By 1916 they were down to just over eighty. The War took a lot of them, old age the rest.

Evans must have had the Mission in mind for some time though he did nothing about it until the dam was nearly finished. Then he began with a market survey, in 1875. Questionnaires were sent to most of the public works he knew about. How many worked there? How many churches? How many clergymen visited them? How many Sunday schools? How many day schools?

Less than half the engineers answered but from those who did Evans calculated there were about forty thousand navvies in England. With women and children that probably meant a total of between fifty and sixty thousand people. Only three jobs had a child's day school, three had a night school, only one had a Sunday school.

Evans, already dying of tuberculosis, sheltered in Italy in the winter of 1874–5, before writing an article – *Navvies and Their Needs* – for the religious weekly, *The Quiver*, asking for help in setting up a Mission. This he followed with a leaflet, also called *Navvies and Their Needs*. 'Navvies,' it began, 'form a class by themselves, isolated: *First*, by the nature of their work, which is often carried on in places remote from towns or even villages. *Secondly* by their roving habits: and *Thirdly* by the belief, which commonly prevails among them, that they are looked upon as outcasts.'

These were the key insights on which he built the working philosophy of the Mission. More important (initially) than being taught religion, navvies had to be taught they belonged. The roaring and the uproar had to stop. They had to quieten down to listen. For that they had to have more in their lives than drink and work. Evans proposed giving them drink-free mission rooms and night schools where they could learn to read and write, then libraries for when they could. (And not just religious books either. Geology, unsurprisingly, was popular. Once the Mission was running properly Mrs Garnett sent whole 250-volume libraries, complete and catalogued, to most public works which had a missionary.)

It was to be a kind of nursing, a kind of therapy. But since the navvy moved too fast to give it time to work, the therapy had to be waiting for him wherever he went. What was wanted were mobile missions and nimble missionaries to meet the fleeing heathen wherever he ran.

Towards the end of 1877, Evans followed *Navvies and Their Needs* (article and leaflet) with a flurry of hand-written and printed appeals and within a few weeks – probably in November – he was able to set up his new Society formally, with himself as its first Secretary and the Bishop of Ripon on its first committee.

By the summer of 1878 Evans, no longer coughing up dark blood, was fit enough to travel to the dams at Cheltenham, Denshaw, Fewston, and Barden Moor, fixing the society physically on the ground. Early that autumn he was even fit enough to make the sea-crossing to the Isle of Man Railway where, in spite of the sea, in spite of mountain air, soft dark gouts of blood began welling up into his mouth again, leaving him pallid and enfeebled, too weak to speak at that year's Church Congress in Sheffield. The Dean of Ripon spoke for him.

'Navvies are looked upon with suspicion,' the Dean told Congress, 'and are treated as if they were the wildest and the worst of beings – the poachers, the drunkards, the Sabbath-breakers, the brawlers and blasphemers, the adulterers, and heathen of the district. Thus a bad name is given to them, which they reciprocate, and keep themselves to themselves.'

Evans told everybody else – whatever he told himself – his lungs were sound and getting better. All he had to do was keep clear of damp. In November, which was both cold and clammy, he insisted on travelling to a CEU meeting in Ripon and on the way home he had to wait in the cold on Otley railway station, pacing about in the oil-lit darkness, breathing wet Yorkshire air. As soon as he could he saw a doctor, afterwards telling his friends he was still on the mend. He died suddenly early in December and they buried him in his own graveyard, followed by mourning navvies. He was thirty-two.

But his society was safely founded in spite of the contractors, engineers and city corporations who wished it wasn't. 'Of an evening the men should be in bed,' said one engineer. 'They are better without reading.'

'*Again* and *again*,' Mrs Garnett recalled, years later, 'we were refused even a bare old building for a day school (even though a friend was responsible for all expense) and we showed them the School Board Schools (just started) and the Parochial Schools both refused to admit our children on account of the room limit. *It was hard to bear.* Insults are not pleasant to the flesh, wrong motives were imputed and on all sides suspicion, and derision our portion, but if a work be God's, it will go on.'

And go on it did. Within a year or so the Mission had its own house-style that lasted to the end. You always knew what to expect on a Mission job: a lay missionary (preferably ex-navvy) and a mission room, a library, a room to smoke and read in; schools for children; bible readings, concerts, tea parties and meat teas. The missionary, as well, was ready-made to run Sick Clubs, savings schemes, first aid and even violin classes.

Everything centred on the Mission Rooms: wooden huts furnished with wooden pews and harmoniums, heated in winter by iron stoves with long thin flues. In place of altars there were wooden pulpits draped with cloths embroidered with the NMS's entwined initials. On the walls were posters: 'Dedicating the Temple', 'Christ at the Feast', 'The Gracious Call'. Gothic-lettered texts read: 'By grace are ye saved', 'Learn from me for I am meek and lowly in heart', 'Seek ye first the Kingdom of God and His righteousness'.[3]

To the Victorians the Mission was eminently worthy. It listed the Primate among its patrons, as well as the Archbishop of York, most of the English bench of bishops and sundry Lords and gentry. No navvy, however, sat on its committee and only one woman ever did: Mrs Garnett. Yet in spite of the male upper classes on top, at the bottom it was run by women and working men.

The Society, essentially, was a loose collection of local Navvy Mission Associations coordinated from a central office. For many years this was wherever the Secretary lived – Ripon sometimes, Leeds and Warrington at others – until the Society took permanent desk space in the cellar of Church House, in the quad next to Westminster Abbey, in 1893. The central office, mobile or fixed, paid only a third of any mission's costs, and a third of every

---

3 At least one mission hut survived, at least until 1980, at Hutton Roof on the Thirlmere pipe track of the north Lancashire fells. Until 1980, it was the Village Hall.

missionary's eighty pounds a year wages: the rest was found locally by the local NMA – by cajoling contractors and city corporations, through public subscriptions and drawing room fund raisings. It was here middle class women were pre-eminent.

Katherine Sleight, at first, was typical: a widow of private means attracted to the Mission when the Hull-Barnsley railway came near her home in Newint. She busied herself on the new Hull dock and railway, handling the Distress Fund in the hard times. She became a-typical when the loss of her private income made her take a salaried job as the Society's Association Secretary in London. She did well – doubling the number of bodies associated with the Mission, opening a fund to pay the wages of a nurse on the Thirlmere dam – but in time she got very fat and her feet became agonisingly tender (often she had to stop in the street and change her outdoor boots for carpet slippers.)

On Christmas Eve 1897, she took to her bed clearly dying of dropsy and heart and liver disease. Beef tea, milk and oysters were all she could swallow and the swelling of her limbs grew grotesque. Finally her mind gave way and she thought she was back in Hull talking to her dead mother. She died in 1898, aged forty-six.

Missionaries were black-suited, white-shirted, dark-tied working men who in summer wore straw boaters with a dove of peace badge pinned to the hat band. The whole Society, naturally in Victorian England, was very class-biased and once the navvy swapped his moleskin for semi-broadcloth he crossed into another lonely life. The navvies he left distrusted him as one of the others: the others refused to accept him as one of them. Ordination – self-betterment by class-hopping – was discouraged. David Smith was typical.

As a missionary he was nicknamed Navvy Smith and later – to his evident disgruntlement – Daddy Smith. He was born in 1866 in Newhaven, Sussex, where his father, a smith by trade as well as name, sub-contracted the iron-work in the new harbour. From Newhaven the family moved to Bristol where docks were building at Portishead, Shirehampton, and Avonmouth. Navvy Smith started work there, carrying bricks at the bottle works, and then carrying mason's tools to and from the blacksmith's shop on the New Dock.

Navvy Smith, born in the '60s, became a Christian in the '70s, a smith in the '80s, a missionary in the '90s. In 1888 he was smithing on the Ship Canal when he met the Rev Robert Grimston, the

Canal's chaplain (later the Mission's Secretary), and the man who did more to alter his life than anybody else save William Perry, a squire's gardener near Bristol, who first converted him to Christianity. At the time he met Grimston, Smith was pushing an injured man home in a wheelbarrow. Grimston offered an unusually ineffectual hand before going off, more usefully, to commandeer a locomotive. Later, Navvy Smith became one of his missionaries on the Great Central, running the Good Samaritan Home for tramp navvies at Bulwell, north of Nottingham.

After that Navvy Smith ran missions at the Catcleugh dam in Northumberland, the Privett tunnel in Hampshire, at Sodbury tunnel, at Shirehampton docks and finally in 1906 and for the next twenty years in Birmingham. For four years until the War closed it in 1916 he was joint-editor of the *Public Works Magazine* (a missionary-level version of the *Letter*, as far as we can tell).

Tom Cleverley (sometimes spelled – and presumably pro-nounced – Cleaverley) was born a navvy at Penarth docks in 1855. For ten years or so he wandered about the country working first as a nipper then a full-blown navvy on railways, docks and dams until finally, all unknowingly, he wandered into the Lindley Wood settlement and a different way of living.

'In those days,' said Mrs Garnett, 'Sunday was called Hair-cutting and Dog-washing Day – hair cutting in the morning, dog washing in the afternoon, and a free fight in the evening.' One Sunday she met Tom Cleverley, at Lindley Wood, taking *his* dog for a walk. 'Now, Tom,' said she to him, 'will you come to the Bible class?'

'No,' said Tom, 'I'm going for a walk with my little dog.'

'I believe you care more for that dog than for your own soul,' Mrs Garnett told him.

For Tom Cleverley *that* was the turning point of his life. He went to the Bible class, became a Christian, then a missionary. As a missionary he worked at the Cheltenham dam, on the Oxted-Groomsbridge, on the Ship Canal, and on the Great Central.

Within a couple of years of its founding the Society had twenty-one full-time missionaries, a figure which went up to fifty-four by the century's end. Numbers then steadied at fifty-three before dropping to forty in 1913.

The Society was always tremulous for success and counted wins and losses in a curiously actuarial way – totting up lists of statistics about the number of people going to Bible classes, prayer meetings, confirmations, and Sunday services. But if simple arithmetic tells us little, how effective was the Mission?

To begin with the police always vouched for Mission jobs. Crime dropped when missionaries turned up. The Mayor of Ludlow even put a figure on it: police court cases were cut by two-thirds when the Mission opened on the Elan pipe track. Christianity didn't break out spectacularly – it didn't throughout the country – but most people on public works were Christian, in a confused non-sectarian way, in the end. Navvies were christianised, if not churched.

'Looking back over fifty years what changes one can see,' said Navvy Smith, in 1923. 'The navvy is a far more sober man today; he is better dressed, better educated, takes a keener interest in his social well-being and enjoys a status in human society which he never thought of years ago. Who will deny that this is the outcome of Christianity *and Labour* marching hand in hand?'

Chapter 21

The Great War

I was driving a heading at Rosyth Naval Base when war broke out and I enlisted. Six months later I was in the Royal Artillery fighting like a mad fool in France.

In 1915 Patrick MacGill was with the London Irish in the 47th Division, 4th Army Corps. In September his battalion led the attack on Loos, walking in lightly falling rain over ground soggy as a sponge, walking in a line which wavered only where a few of them kicked a football across No-man's land.

MacGill stepped out between the poles of a stretcher which tensed and pulled in his hands until the back end dropped and trailed, bumping. Ahead reared the black crucifix in Loos graveyard. Bits of men littered the mud. A naked man, his clothes blown away, ran laughing in a circle until he was shot in the head. The dead lay heaped by the enemy wires, the football punctured and crumpled. Eventually they ringed all Loos in a new front line: broken church, broken streets, and the twisted ironwork of the pithead winding gear which they called the Twin Towers. They ate well off rations looted from the dead.

One night MacGill left the dug-out to get a bottle of iodine from the RAMC post in Loos: a black night, the blacker outline of the broken buildings silhouetted against a black sky. On the way he met two soldiers burying corpses. A dog had been scavenging off human meat.

'He's Old Nick in disguise,' said one. 'He feeds off the dead, the dirty swine.'

A starshell suddenly lit the graveyard where gunfire had blown out and scattered the villagers' white bones. The dog, stark in the sudden light, skulked away into the dark.

He drank rum with Mac, the Scottish orderly. 'Not bad, a wee drappie,' said Mac. 'It's health to the navel and marrow to the bones.'

Outside, high-explosive shells burst about the Twin Towers. Long-nosed bullets snapped about what was left of the houses. A bullet stung MacGill's wrist. It hurt. Blood dripped black from his fingers but it took him back to Blighty, for a while. It was an army, he said, that would be remembered for its soldiers. Talk of Waterloo and Englishmen would always think of Wellington. Talk of Loos and they'd remember a million men in puttees.

Navvies joined in droves. Whole jobs were abandoned because of a navvy shortage. Snowy, Big Ned, Slasher, Scan, Young Clipper and Yorkie joined the Sportsman's Battalion of the Royal Fusiliers in a body from the Derwent valley dams. Harley Wright joined the Dorset Regiment with his pet cat which was expected to become the battalion mascot. Navvy Smashing Bristol joined the Transport Lorry Department from the Cardiff dams. William Lyons (Cambridge Lion's son) joined the Royal Navy and died in HMS *Aboukir*. Young Potsey, known to the Army as Sgt Clarke MM, joined one of the Royal Engineers' Tunnelling Companies. A 58-year old navvy from Scott and Middleton's London contract who joined to encourage younger men was sent to guard POWs in Malta. A Cwm Taff man had twenty other navvies in his Company. In Birmingham, Navvy Smith said a thousand men out of eleven hundred had joined by March, 1915. Many, he said, went into the 30th Railway Battalion.

'All our family are out at the Front at different places: brothers, brother-in-law, and nephews – nine all told,' wrote L/Cpl Fiddler Jack, late of Bungalow City, Rosyth Naval Base, to Mrs Garnett in 1915. 'Well, dear madam,' he went on, 'I wish you could send me out the shaving set that was mentioned in last quarter's Letter, it would come in very handy, as there are several old navvies in this Camp where I am; and could you beg an old accordion to pass away the evenings when we are out of the firing line? We get it a bit hot there at times, and when we come back to camp it is nothing only banging of big guns.' (He got his accordion. It was champion.)

'It's up to the waist in water and mud in the trenches,' another navvy wrote home, 'but that does not bother me a bit, as I have been used to that all my life.'

'We are still having very bad weather,' wrote another, 'and our trenches are in a terrible state, and we all look like navvies instead of soldiers. I, myself, am just like a lump of mud, but I often feel proud to know that I am an old navvy's son, because I know that there is not another class who have answered the call to the flag to fight for home and beauty as our navvies have done.'

'I was pleased with the parcel you sent me and my mates shared the underclothing and the twist the best way I could,' another thanked Mrs Garnett. 'My mates told me you can send some more any time. We are back from the trenches having a bit of a rest till we get strong again. We talk about working in a tunnel blasting, but that is nothing to the big guns firing all day and night over our heads, the noise is awful.' (Horizon to horizon, night was ablaze with gun-light as the guns stood firing wheel to wheel along the Western Front.)

'I have seen some rough times in England and Wales, I was at the Dock Disaster, Newport, Mon, 2nd July, 1909,' wrote another navvy, 'but I have seen worse than that since I have been out here. People in England may read the papers while the print drops off, but they will never realise what we have gone through and *stuck it out*.'[1]

'Dear Madam, I am at present in hospital and I should be very pleased if you could send me a little tobacco, or put me in touch with some friend who could oblige me. It is a bit hard on us when we are in hospital, as they stop your pay until you rejoin your regiment,' wrote an old gangerman, late of the Newport widening. 'I should be pleased if you would send me the Quarterly Letter also, as I should like to know how things are going off on the Public Works. Hoping you will excuse me writing you and you will oblige an old warrior, as I have not got many friends.'

'There's nothing like being a free man,' said a navvy on the North Sea Patrols. 'I'm more for roaming the country than being fastened to one job, any how, I shall stick it like a brick as long as it's for the King and Country.'

'Well, dear Mrs Garnett,' wrote home another old navvy, 'I'm going to tell you there were thirteen of us listed together, but only twelve of us came to the Front. Half was in the Dardenelles, one poor lad "went west" as we call it, but on our side we have only had two wounded out of our little band. Five of us are navvies, we keep jogging on along together and make the best of things, but we get no

---

1 Forty men were killed outright when the new dock entrance in Newport, South Wales, caved in. One man wasn't supposed to be there at all: he'd dropped his measuring rule and gone down to find it. Another man and a boy lay alive alongside a corpse all day and night. The timbers gave way and killed them both just as they were about to be saved.

tramps out here for the shilling. I have seen some of our Navvies' Battalion some time ago, but none that I know.'

In the Crimea the Army Works Corps had saddened the military. In the Sudan navvies did nothing to gladden the Royal Engineers. Since then the army had used local labour or its own infantry. Now however the whole of one corner of France was churned up like a huge public works site, railwayed, quarried, trenched and tunnelled. Early in 1915 the War Office began recruiting specialist labour units to handle the civil engineering work it needed to protect and supply its forward troops. Officially they were Labour Battalions, Service Battalions, or Pioneer Battalions. Mrs Garnett called them, incorrectly, Trench-Digging Battalions. Everybody else just as incorrectly called them Navvy Battalions.

In its March 1915, issue the *Navvies Letter* told its readers about the labour battalions in infantry regiments. 'To get together men of our class,' said Mrs Garnett proudly. You signed on like any other soldier for three years or the duration. You were paid like an infantryman, plus two-pence a day. Already the 18th Middlesex were mustering at Alexandra Park race track.

Some labour battalions had no navvies at all. The 19th Cheshires, its historian says, was made up of miners, novelists, cotton spinners, factory hands, farmers and music hall artistes. Between them they won five Military Medals and the Distinguished Conduct Medal repairing railway lines under fire, but still had to put up with jibes about being conscientious objectors ('do you fight with bananas?') Among Mametz Wood's shell-stripped trees they trenched down through layers of decomposing Germans buried in shallow graves. They seemed happy enough, however. Their two music hall turns (Silaborn and Rooney) wrote and acted in sketches in their own Nissen-hutted Hippodrome. For two years the battalion lived under fire around the ruins of Ypres and the wilderness of the Somme, cheerfully, ironically, whistling their theme tune: 'Oh, it's a lovely war.'

But other labour battalions, though far from being exclusively navvy-manned, did have a lot of middle-aged and even elderly navvies serving in them. (A Labour unit once played football against an infantry regiment. Neither side had proper strip, but none was needed – all the navvies were grey-haired.) All were over forty; most, over fifty; some, over sixty.

They built and ran railways and dug communication trenches like endless lines of linked graves zig-zagging and gaping across France.

They made and mended roads and filled in craters in the weird landscape (less strange to navvies, perhaps, than most). Convoluting wire, fish-hooked to catch the floundering dying and the dead; sandbags among fractured roots; trees like barked logs; gas-masked horses hock deep in muck; heaped empty rum-jars and spent shell cases; hump-backed elephant shelters on plains like steppes; shell-fall, earth-burst: through it all the old navvies, stoop-backed, shovelled away.

'Lord Kitchener himself,' said the *Staffordshire Sentinel*, 'obtained John Ward's appointment as Colonel, and got it confirmed by a Cabinet Minute, when some officers of the Regular Army opposed the appointment. Lord Kitchener was Major in General Graham's Expedition, with whom Colonel Ward served as a navvy-soldier in 1885.'

Altogether Ward personally raised four battalions, mainly from among navvies in Staffordshire:

18th (Service) Battalion (1st Public Works Pioneers), Middlesex Regiment.
19th (Service) Battalion (2nd Public Works Pioneers), Middlesex Regiment.
26th (Service) Battalion (3rd Public Works Pioneers), Middlesex Regiment.
25th (Garrison) Battalion, Middlesex Regiment.

The 18th were allocated to 33 Div, on the Somme. Just after midsummer's day, 1916 (the landscape white as winter with shell-blown chalk), the Germans obliterated part of the Division's front line near La Bassée Canal. German soldiers occupied the crater and navvies from the 18th were sent to oppose them until the infantry could be got ready. Nine old navvies were killed, nineteen wounded.

During the Battle of the Somme itself the battalion followed the Royal Welch Fusiliers into the assault on High Wood. (It was more like an overploughed field than a forest, shell-stripped bare as it was to a few lacerated poles, feathery with shredded bark.) The land rose slightly and the 18th were set to digging a communication trench back from the old woods to the low ground. They began just before dawn, delayed since midnight by a barrage, and worked till the older men dropped.

'They worked as though they were opening Piccadilly,' said an officer, 'and took as little notice of German shellfire as they would have done of the London traffic.'

The 19th Battalion went to 41 Div. In September, 1915, they were in the Battle of Flers-Caucelette, repairing roads and cable trenches on the dry plain. They were at Ypres. In 1918 they were used as infantry on the Somme before following the Army into Germany. (Long after the War, Ward's son gave the 19th's Colours to the family solicitor for safekeeping. They were put away in the cellar of the solicitor's offices and forgotten until they were accidentally found again in 1959 and given to the Regimental Museum.)

The 26th joined 27 Div in Salonika, in 1918, straight from training camp. Half were dead of disease and hardship within weeks of leaving England.

Ward himself commanded the 25th Middlesex. He was still an MP, still General Secretary of the Navvies' Union, still Treasurer of the GFTU. In 1915 he spoke at the Federation's Annual Council Meeting in the Temperance Hall, Derby, wearing his uniform with the three pips and two stripes of the half-colonel. What was happening in Flanders, he told them, was an inevitable war between societies living by different philosophies: the belief that the will of the strong is all that matters, against the belief in justice and mercy; liberalism against nationalism; Locke, perhaps, against Hegel: the idea that the state serves each bit of humanity, against the idea that people are only bits of the state.

'There are worse things than losing life,' he ended. 'Losing one's honour, one's sense of decency or self-respect, not merely as a man, but as a member of a great race and nation – that shows a moral decay which is worse than physical death a thousand times. But no matter how many Englishmen may die outwardly, spiritually they continue to live, and it's that conviction that has made me don the uniform I wear today.'

Early in 1917 he sailed for the Far East in the troopship *Tyndareus*. East of Cape Town she struck a mine very near the spot off Danger Point where in 1852 the troopship *Birkenhead* foundered. Ward mustered the battalion on deck. 'This, comrades,' he told them, 'is the hour that we ought to have lived for. Don't forget that you're members of one of the most famous regiments in the British Army. We will try to save you, but if we can't, let's agree to finish like English gentlemen.'

But they didn't finish like English gentlemen, not off the Cape. Their ship's bulkheads held until they were towed into Simon's Town harbour where they re-embarked for Hong Kong and more strange adventures. Not long after the regiment landed in China, to begin with, a case of slave-stealing came before the local court. A little girl, recently sold as a slave, had been stolen from her new owner. Ward was astounded. Slavery? In a British colony? He wrote from Mount Austin Barracks to William Appleton, Secretary of the GFTU.

Slave-owning, Ward was told, was an old Chinese custom which the British had agreed to recognise by Proclamation when they occupied the place. Even if this were true, Ward argued, it must have been a muddle-headed oversight by some Victorian clerk. No Proclamation could abrogate fundamental law.

'I offered my life, like millions of other Englishmen,' Ward wrote to Appleton, 'to defend the British State, our State, because I believed that it represented all that is best, so far, in the shape of humane government. That whatever by-products may issue from our Empire over subject races we stand for what is best, brightest, and honourable in the rule of the coloured peoples. That our Empire is a free Empire, where no slave can breathe its air. These are really things worth fighting for.'

Appleton spoke to Walter Long, the Colonial Secretary; privately, to keep it out of the newspapers and away from enemy propagandists. Long promised something would be done immediately, but Appleton was still waiting in Colonial Office corridors late into 1920. Eventually, a couple of years later, the GFTU heard the Hong Kong Government was to issue another proclamation telling everybody it was wrong to sell people.

After Russia's abrupt withdrawal from the war in November 1917 Britain and France tried to reopen an Eastern Front of some – of any – kind. Interventionists operated where they could get ashore – the Black Sea, Archangel, the Baltic coasts – except in Siberia. Only Japan was close and uncommitted enough to be able to intervene significantly in Asia but the Japanese refused to move without US approval and US approval was unforthcoming. For one thing President Wilson mistrusted Japanese motives. For another he was doubtful about diverting any effort from the Western Front.

In March 1918, the Bolsheviks let their Czech ex-prisoners of war leave Russia, journeying eastwards, circumambulating the planet, to re-engage the Germans in western Europe. In May, when over forty thousand were beaded out along the Trans-Siberian Railway, Czech troops lynched a Hungarian who threw a cast-iron stove at one of their soldiers near a place called Chelyabinsk on the steppes just east of the Urals. Moscow, regretting the decision to let them go (they were, by now, an Allied army crossing country held by counter-revolutionaries) began hindering their movement. Trotsky even ordered local soviets to stop their trains.

It was this, it seems, which finally convinced President Wilson something must be done. The US agreed to send a small force of around seven thousand men to be matched by as many Japanese. (The Japanese disembarked 72,000 troops, occupied what ground they wanted for themselves and refused to go any farther.) Ward's 25th Middlesex were the first Allied troops to land at Vladivostock, filing off the steamer *Ping Suie* in August 1918, solar topeed and kitted for the tropics, straight from Hong Kong.

'The Hernia Battalion,' some British officers in Siberia called them. 'Poor old men,' said Captain Howgrave-Graham of the 1st/9th Hampshires, the only other British battalion posted to Siberia, 'they ought never to have been sent here: they were mostly unfit when they came and are absolutely useless now.' They did well, nevertheless, given they were B-1 garrison troops graded unfit for active service in a war theatre.

Ward, always a huge man, was now a little huger, thickened around the neck and middle a little, dwarfing his middle-European allies.

For its last few hundred miles the Trans-Siberian Railway runs north/south down to Vladivostock, part of the way in the Ussuri valley where the Czechs held off an army of Bolsheviks, Hungarians and Germans. Ward went, with half his battalion and his machine gun section, to help.

Siberia that August was gaudy, the summer sky stained with colour like spilt paint. Purple daybreaks brightened to orange dawns. At times on the Ussuri bullets were thick as mosquitoes but the real mosquitoes, big as spiders, did more damage. Ward took command of the tiny Allied Front but on orders from Vladivostock was not allowed to advance. He watched the enemy openly outflanking him across the river.

But his stint as sole commander of his own little war didn't last long, since he was given to the Japanese 12th Division as soon as it reached the battlefront. The Japanese Major-General, on the other hand, had no time for a British half-colonel and a British half-battalion. Ward was told to get behind the backs of the Japanese and keep out of the way.

Then early one morning, the Japanese Liaison Officer handed

him a note: a general offensive was to be launched in just over an hour, four miles away. Politically it was the correct thing to do: the Japanese were duty bound to tell the commander-in-chief of their ally's forces that a major battle was about to begin. Militarily, they thought Ward had no chance of cluttering up a purely Japanese victory by intruding unwanted allied troops into what was to be a purely Japanese affair. On the other hand, they hadn't properly taken into account Ward's blimpish stubbornness. The Czech, Japanese and Cossack troops under his command refused to get out of bed, but in less than half an hour his own battalion was marching up the Trans-Siberian Railway to war. They reached the battlefield half an hour late, but still in time for the fighting: in fact a soldier of the Middlesex Regiment started it prematurely when he accidentally fired his rifle.

The Allies – a whole Japanese Division and half a British battalion – advanced on a twelve mile front, Ward's men in their own private battlefield in scrub and cornland on either side of the railway track, self-chosen because it was the only space unfilled by Japanese, who thought it too dangerous. Ward stepped out along the middle of the sleepers, directing his troops like a ganger. 'It was,' he said, 'just ding-dong open fighting, wonderfully spectacular in character.'

Yet in a way they were also curiously detached from the battle, prodding at it from the outside, never really being let in. They did fusilade one armoured train – but its six-inch gun was fitted so high it fired harmlessly over their heads. Another, which they ignored (thinking it empty), porcupined with rifles and Magyars as soon as they were out of the way. Japanese quickly swarmed all over it pitchforking Hungarians out of the windows on bayonets.

The battle ended at the railway station in Kraevsk after another brief encounter with an armoured train. The train steamed off. The officers' breakfast steamed on a stove. Ward and some of his men ate it. The Japanese had six hundred casualties: the British, nil.

'This small minor action,' Ward wrote later, 'proved to be one of the most decisive of the war, as it destroyed the whole Terrorist army east of the Urals.'

After that he served as a kind of Military Governor for a time, holding court like a medieval baron, sole judge of everything from murder to who owned what, until in October, 1918, he was ordered to Omsk, the Siberian capital, half a hostile continent away. Everybody was his enemy, even his friends. At Manchuli he wrested railway coaches from his Japanese allies whose intention he believed was to discredit the British by making him travel in a cattle truck. At Chita they stole a locomotive, his men holding cocked rifles at the driver's head. Ward rode the tender, spattered with hot ash from the smoke stack.

Omsk he found to be a village of wooden huts interspersed with globed churches grouped around a ponderous Government House. He didn't stay long. Soon after they got there he and his battalion were off again, escorting Admiral Kolchak, Minister of War, across the Urals to the Volga battlefields where the Czechs dragged the tail of their army into Siberia, fighting off the Bolsheviks by the river. Then back in Omsk in mid-November a gang of Cossacks kidnapped half the Government, leaving the rest to elect Kolchak Supreme Ruler under Ward's machine guns. When everything is disintegrating, he said later, even the smallest core of single-mindedness and certainty can save an entire society. His regiment, he believed, was that core of certainty in Omsk that winter.

Early in 1919 (hiding from blizzards cold enough to freeze your eye fluids), Ward toured the Trans-Siberian railway speaking to meetings of workers, persuading them to support Kolchak as he had once persuaded gangs of navvies to join his union. His hecklers were less gentle than the Staffordshire men of 1906. Middle class revolutionaries, he called them: slouched hatted, unshaven shop-keepers, teachers, doctors, who kept their grip on the community by murdering anybody, worker or bourgeois, who disagreed with them.

In May, soldiers of the 2nd Siberian Cossack Regiment elected him to the rank of Ataman, a kind of chief, in a long ritual on the treeless steppes, pressed flat by a weight of sky. They were all giddy with vodka and wild whirling Cossack dances: stirred by marching tunes and sad, fierce, troubled Cossack songs.

In May, also, he was ordered home. It was around the time of the Red Army offensive which broke Kolchak's forces and forced him into a long eastward retreat along the Trans-Siberian railway, which the Czechs still held and which they ran primarily to extricate their own Legion from Asia. Alongside the railway ran the *trakt*, the old Trans-Siberian highway, now deep in snow and broken regiments, deserters, running peasants and lost children. The Bolsheviks shot Kolchak in February, 1920, at Irkutsk on the frozen banks of the Angara, a river which in summer flows into sea-sized Lake Baikal. They slid his corpse down a snow slide into the water through a hole in the ice.

On the Western Front the guns had long gone quiet, the men of the labour battalions long gone home. As well as infantry regiments, the Royal Engineers had also recruited navvies, as early as March 1915, into their own Labour units which came complete with missionaries, sent to war by the Navvy Mission with the Army's approval. They wore khaki, but with 'Navvy Mission' in place of regimental flashes on their shoulder straps. (What's the Royal Navy doing at the Front, soldiers kept asking.)

Missionary Wilkinson was with the 1st Labour Battalion, RE; Holden with the 5th; Leach, the 7th; Creber, 8th; Avery, 9th; Milner with the 10th. For them it was not unlike at home: catching men drumming up, preaching, reading, teaching in the evenings, except you didn't stand bare-headed at prayer on the Western Front, particularly near observation balloons where shrapnel fell like splintered iron rain.

'Navvies pure and simple,' said an officer describing his new RE recruits, 'builders' labourers, shipwrights, rough carpenters, old sailors, thatchers.' They worked behind the front line army making and repairing roads and railways, digging trenches, making corduroy roads from logs to haul guns out of mud. Part of the 8th Battalion quarried rock at night (even a small crater needed three tons of stone to fill it). The rest of the battalion worked the forests near Rouen.

For nearly two years the 2nd Battalion stayed in one place while Divisions and Corps came and went all around them. They felled timber, built and ran sawmills, quarried stone, built bunkers and roads and ran light railways. By May 1917 over half their original thousand were dead. (For every fifty casualties a navvy battalion suffered by enemy action, they lost another two hundred to illness and work accidents. Not unlike at home.)

By the end of the 1916 the Royal Engineers had eleven Labour Battalions, the infantry had thirty, while the Army Service Corps had thirty-one Labour Companies. That December a Directorate of Labour was set up to regroup them as Companies in a new Labour Corps. The 1st Labour Battalion, RE, for instance, became 701 Company, Labour Corps; the 2nd Battalion, 702 Company; the 3rd, 703. The new regiment had its own badge: a spade and rifle crossed over a pick beneath a wreath topped by a crown. Motto: Labor Omnia Vincit – work overcomes all. Each Company was five hundred and thirty-six men strong. By Armistice Day the Labour

Corps on the Western Front numbered around a hundred and twenty-five thousand men. Not many of *them* were navvies, though the unofficial name – Navvy Battalion – still stuck.

The 1918 German offensive caught 707 Coy in a massive crossfire. Their mission hut exploded. A shell-burst killed Pioneer Jackson and wounded two others. For four days they lay under Royal Navy guns in the rear, German guns in front. 21 Company lost its gramophone and its little library. 21 Company's commanding officer lost his pet canary. Later the 707th dug themselves into a deep maze of dugouts they called Underground City.

That Labour Corps men were killed by artillery, not rifle fire, was one of their problems. Technically they were not front line troops and so were ineligible for leave. 'We are still pegging away', said Missionary Milner, 709 Company, in 1917. 'The attempt to grow leave tickets in our gardens was a failure.'

'I received your PC at one of our saps, where two of our boys are buried down below', L/Cpl Fiddler Jack wrote to Mrs Garnett in 1916. 'They have been down there nearly three months now, it was no use trying to get them out as they were killed outright. I'm going to make a head cross in memory of them.' Fiddler Jack, who was with a Clay-kicker Company, made all his unit's crosses from old bits of timber they used as side-trees in the headings.

Clay-kickers were first raised by Empire Jack Norton Griffiths, baronet, Member of Parliament, wartime Colonel and pre-War colonial adventurer. (He also raised the 2nd King Edward's Horse from among fellow-imperialists.) He was Boy's Own Paper material, a man fulfilled by war and empire. By 1914 he was prospering after a dusty life on the veldt, in the bush, in the outback: tall, tanned by the never-setting colonial sun. He was both buoyant and flamboyant: he *never* gave in to adversity and drove through the sludge of the Western Front in his wife's chocolate-coloured Rolls. He had commanded Scouts in the Matabeleland-Mashonaland and Boer Wars. He had been in the Royal Horse Guards. Briefly he had been a sheep farmer, gold prospector, diamond prospector, South African company promoter and Empire-wide public works contractor.

In 1914 he had a contract, one of many, to lay pipes in Manchester. In Manchester, pipes were laid by threading them through burrows bored through the subsoil. For this they used clay-kickers: clay-caked men who worked worm- or mole-like in burrows barely big enough for a man.

Each miner sat leaning backwards on a cross-shaped back-rest and kicked at the working face in front of him with a grafting tool, a shovel-like claw fitted with two kicking pegs on the haft. His muckshifter lay close by, scrabbling the spoil back down the burrow. They were more like burrowing animals excavating by claw than human miners. In fact they called themselves 'moles'. Moles, thought Empire Jack, were just what this war needed. The idea, first devised by the Germans, was to clay-kick your way under the enemy's trenches, pack the end of the burrow with ammonal, then blow them all to smithereens.

Clay-kickers were first drawn from their Manchester burrows on February, 17th, 1915, and set down the war-holes of France only hours later. They were a strangely soiled, shuffling, unsoldier-like bunch, unloved by the respectable regular army. The Royal Engineers kitted them out at its Chatham Depot, armed and instantly despatched them. Hours later in France the Army as instantly disarmed them for its own good. As a rule tunnel tigers spent a week between peacefulness and Flanders. (Tom Cusack, National Organiser of the Navvies' Union, was with the unit which blew the first big crater on the Somme.)

Underground was where the war of movement was, a few feet a day in three-foot burrows. Both Armies were terrified of the enemy underfoot. It made your soles ache waiting for them to detonate their mines, splinter your leg bones, and explode you tumbling in the air with the uplifted landscape. Mines went up like momentary loose-soiled mountains.

'If you know of any good tunnellers,' a navvy-sapper wrote home to Mrs Garnett, 'tell them it's up to them to come and help us out here. The money is pretty good and age no matter. One man here is fifty-eight, and a sapper now.'

'The work is very hard, as in any tunnel,' he went on, 'we are as busy as bees, and also dangerous, as we have not got a fighting chance. There's always the possibility of the Germans being first, when by the pressure of a button up goes McGinty, and there you are, but we always look on the best side of course.'

'We have a rough time out here,' said Fiddler Jack, 'but we're a bit rough ourselves, and we keep a good heart.'

Chapter 22

Ending

When we first shifted up to Haweswater from Ewden they were all navvy people but later you got a lot of unemployed from West Cumberland. The money was never good enough for navvy people any road, and any road there weren't many navvy people about any more.

They were a bad lot working up there, though, the unemployed. They hadn't much class.

They had just started when we shifted to Haweswater, the huts weren't all up anyhow, and I started as a timberman and finished up as a ganger. Ten pence an hour for men when they started. Timbermen used to get eleven pence. Gangers only got twopence more. They didn't give them much.

During the Slump I was in the tunnel driving a heading into the valve shaft. One and threepence an hour, timbering, by then. When I was six foot in a Union feller comes along and says I was entitled to one and six. So I got one and six. I knocked the heading through the muck until I got to rock and then Jameson, the chief engineer, fetched me away from there to go down on the dam, excavating. I was made gangerman then. It was me and my gang what got the biggest part of the foundations out. Rotten rock, a lot of it, too. Terrible stuff.

It was a good job if it wasn't for that bloody click that got up there. They'd put years on you. They weren't workmen. You had to regulate them all the time.

After the rage of the guns there was a bottomless quiet about places like Ewden valley, a deep silence that ached, a homecoming to make men cry, standing on the hillside outside the old stone village of Bolsterstone, the valley green below, house smoke idling up from the gabled huts. A stone farm-house stood on its own hill on the hill over the valley. There were quite gentle crags and whole woods of trees unlacerated by gunfire. Ewden Beck flows into the Don, but close as it is to Sheffield it is quiet.

Navvies coming home went back to what public works were restarted and to what fresh beginnings were made, but their old ways were collapsing beneath their boots. Nobody *became* a navvy after 1914: recruiting stopped when war started. Navvying was killed by new machinery, bureaucracy and a lack of big new public works.

New machinery was least harmful: it may never have mattered at all if it hadn't been for the other two. Navvies learned to cope with steam machinery and could have done so again with diesel and petrol. There was more to being a navvy than swinging a pick. To be a navvy was to be a special man, belonging to a special community. Navvying *was* a community, not just a way of doing work.

Bureaucracy was worse, circumscribing people as it did with its dole money, means tests, its prying, its bits of paper. Bureaucracy has no place for free paperless men. No place for penniless Lincoln Tom. No room, either, for tramp-navvies: priggish civil servants now often decreed who'd work on public works and who wouldn't. In the summer of 1927 an ear-ringed ganger was unearthed, crying, behind a tree at a Cardiff relief work scheme. Stiff-collared clerks in the Labour Exchange had picked him his gang, a hand-dog, under-muscled bunch. 'Not a man jack of them,' sobbed the ganger, 'is strong enough to dig the skin off a rice pudding.'

Worst was the Slump. There *was* no work. The *Quarterly Letter* opened 1932 with a list of sixteen jobs: six on dams, ten on railways (and one of *them* was a pedestrian subway at Paddington station). Back in the '80s it began with incomplete lists of fifty big railway jobs, twenty-odd big dams, and massive dock works. All navvy-intensive affairs.

In 1919 the Navvy Mission and the Navvies' Union renamed themselves, in accordance with new realities. The Mission became the Industrial Christian Fellowship, its work now in factories where it had gone during the War, not with the diminishing navvy. The Union became the Public Works and Constructional Operatives' Union, open to a whole swathe of trades: navvies, tunnel miners, pit and well sinkers, blackgang men, timbermen, platelayers, pipelayers and jointers, pipedrivers, concreters, asphalters, scaffolders, gangers, timekeepers, builders' labourers, brickfield men and cement and lime workers.

Membership of the old Navvies' Union held steady throughout

most of the war until suddenly it climbed to 11,000, its highest ever, in 1918. The new Public Works' union kept on climbing as well until it, too, peaked at around 18,000 at the end of 1919. From then on it was all decay and disintegration: sometimes precipitate, sometimes slow. In 1929 the Transport and General Workers' Union poached an entire North Staffordshire branch without the executive in London knowing a thing about it.

The Transport and General, in fact, had been recruiting navvies for some time, without really understanding them. (Muckshifters, they knew, were navvies' labourers – but they found they were also semi-skilled men in their own right and therefore no labourers at all.) They recruited Tom Cusack from the Public Works' Union in 1928 to be their District Organiser in Stoke where he was a town councillor. With him he took the credit for winning the boot money dispute in the Mersey tunnel where the old navvy muck-shifter was lost in a welter of grummetters, telephone men, tool and bolt carriers, pit bottom men, crab-fixing-labourers, and labourers-clearing-up. Tom Cusack died early in 1929.

In the summer of 1933 the Public Works' Union – all one hundred and fifty of them – transferred to the Builders' Labourers' and Constructional Workers' Society which, in 1952, amalgamated with the Amalgamated Union of Building Trade Workers which, in 1971, merged with UCATT. (In 1920 some break-away members of the Navvies' Union joined with the National Association of Builders' Labourers to become the Altogether Builders' Labourers' and Constructional Workers' Society which, in 1934, merged with the TGWU.)

John Ward came home from Siberia, hating totalitarianism and even more politically independent than before. 'The War killed party for me', he declared. 'England and its people, the great race and the Empire to which we all belong is the only thing that really matters now.' Russia, China, the Royal Air Force and Hong Kong now matched his pre-War concern with the African colonies, the Army, and his never-ended feud with the Admiralty. He rarely spoke in the House. He spoke longest during the Workmen's Compensation Bill debate, 1923. It was November. A general election was close. 'Don't let us leave the thing half finished in the last days of our life,' he pleaded with the Commons. 'Usually people do justice at that moment if they never did it at any other time.'

In 1922 he was taken ill at the League of Nations Assembly in Geneva and came home to have a bone removed from his face. He was still General Secretary of the Public Works' Union, still Treasurer of the General Federation of Trade Unions, but his union was in decay, the Federation was in decay, and he was getting old. Old and ill. Old and moderate, scorned by sneering young extremists. He had a heart attack at the 1925 GFTU annual meeting in Blackpool. Next year his wife died. In 1928 his son, Dr Larner Ward, accidentally scratched himself with a scalpel as he dissected a corpse at the King Edward Hospital, Ealing. Infection killed him. 'I am awaiting the end,' Ward wrote to a friend as his son lay dying, 'almost bereft of reason, that a brilliant young life should be so sacrificed at the dawn of its day.'

Lady Cynthia Mosley, Oswald Mosley's wife, took his Stoke-on-Trent seat from him in 1929. Now he sixty-five, not too sorry to go home to Hampshire where he had a house he called Omsk, a jumble of stucco and clapboard, between Appleshaw and Wey-hill, the place where he had learned to read half a century before. He even rode to hounds, in a car. He had come a long way from the ploughboy of the '70s, the navvy of the '80s, the radical of the '90s. He died at Christmas time, 1934.

(Omsk was later occupied by a recluse, a rector's daughter. The house lay shuttered in a wilderness of hawthorn, bramble and garden flowers run wild.)

In December, 1919, the Industrial Christian Fellowship brought out what was meant to be the last *Letter* (and even then it was addressed to 'Industrial Workers Everywhere'). It was a little premature: the navvy was not yet dead. The old *Letter* was re-issued in 1922, running without another break until 1933 when it closed for good.

Mrs Garnett edited her last *Letter* in December 1916, sharp and biting as ever ('some mean skunks never contribute a penny, though they always expect a *Letter* given them'). She had first bought her shovel, she said, in 1872 when she took a Christmas tree to the Lindley Wood children. Now those children were old, or dead. 'I always loved you,' Pincher King, once a nipper at Lindley, now an old man in Australia, wrote to her, 'though I was a rough lad. I couldn't help it, so keep smiling.'

'For the navvies,' she once said of herself, 'I have sacrificed ease, health, money, and other things which I love and enjoy. I have given all I had to give. It is love's work, and love is the pay.' She died in March, 1921.

A plaque to her memory was unveiled in Ripon Cathedral in 1926 and a memorial fund was opened in her name. Dan Munro of the Ewden valley dams was the first beneficiary. He got an artificial foot.

Navvy – now Daddy – Smith was sent to Luton in 1926, lost and lonely. His work with the Industrial Christian Fellowship took him only into factories, though in 1928 he did make a trip to Tilbury docks. 'It was like old times,' he said, 'to be among a few navvy friends again.' He died in Luton, in 1932.

Patrick MacGill went back to writing, fictionalising and rejuvenating Moleskin Joe as the hero of a novel. The book opens in 1914 with a dam burst. Moleskin falls in love with the girl who saves him. He goes off to the War and comes home determined to find her. His money runs out and he sets up a moonshine still in the hills around Kinlochleven with the gentrified son of a ganger. The boy has already seduced the woman who saved Moleskin but in the end he gets his deserts and Moleskin gets the girl.

'Times are not what they were', says one of the characters in the book.

'And the old buck-navvies are off the map,' says Moleskin. 'I was at the old kip-shops in Newcastle, Manchester, Bradford, and they're not there. And there ain't so many o' them at this skinny job.'

MacGill survived the death of the navvy, survived the next War, and died in 1962.

Navvies, always isolated by fear and contempt, were now isolated by their own decay. The roaring and the riot were over. They were like relics, they were so few.

Young men from Haweswater rode in long-nosed buses down to Penrith on Saturday afternoons to taste small-town teas. They drove home tipsy in the still, light-fading evenings, cuddling girls with thighs like feather beds, the bus lurching between high uncut hedges, changing down through the gears on the steepening hills, to the dam: the last big navvy job. On their way they crossed the Eden, only yards from where navvies had rioted in 1846, a few miles downstream from where they killed a man at Armathwaite in 1870.

After 1943 half their village had gone. Trees, a wood of them, grow where the huts were. In the woods, like rows of orderly tumuli, are their foundation mounds.

Rough times, though. A rough affair.

Bibliography and Sources

BIBLIOGRAPHY

Quarterly Letter to Navvies 1878–1893
Quarterly Letter to Men on Public Works 1893–1933
Annual Reports, Navvy Mission Society
Annual Meeting Speeches 1904–1914, Navvy Mission Society. All
  held by the Industrial Christian Fellowship, St Katherine Cree,
  Leadenhall Street, London EC3

Report from the Select Committee on Railway Labourers, printed
  by order of the House of Commons, 28 July 1846

*Papers Read Before the Statistical Society of Manchester on the
  Demoralisation and Injuries Occasioned by the Want of Proper
  Regulations of Labourers Engaged in the Construction and
  Working of Railways*, Edwin Chadwick, Manchester, 1846

First Hand and Contemporary Accounts
Anon. *Death or Life*, 1864
Barrett, Daniel William. *Life and Work Among The Navvies*, 1880
Conder, Francis. *Personal Recollections of English Engineers*, 1868
Cresswell, Henrietta. *Winchmore Hill, Memories of a Lost Village*,
  1912
Fayers, Thomas. *Labour Among the Navvies*, 1862
Garnett, Elizabeth. *Our Navvies*, 1885
Kennedy, Duncan. *The Birth and Death of a Highland Railway*
  (John Murray), 1971
MacGill, Patrick. *Gleanings from a Navvy's scrapbook*, 1910
MacGill, Patrick. *Songs of a Navvy*, 1912
MacGill, Patrick. *Children of the Dead End*, 1916

Marsh, Catherine. *English Hearts and English Hands*, 1858
Mayhew, Henry. *London Labour and the London Poor*, Vol 3, 1967
Munby, George. *Former Days at Turvey*, 1908
Palk, William. *A Glance at the Navvies*, 1859
Taylor, John. *Poems, Chiefly on Themes of Scottish Interest*, 1875
Taylor, W. T. *The Life and Work of the Late William Taylor, the Navvy*, 1892
Tregelles, Anna Rebecca. *The Ways of the Line*, 1847

Later Accounts
Handley, James *The Navvy in Scotland* (Cork UP), 1970
Klingender, Francis. *Art and the Industrial Revolution*, 1947

Canals

First Hand and Contemporary Accounts
Cole, William. *A Poetical Sketch of the Norwich and Lowestoft Navigation Works*, 1833. Held by Lowestoft Central Library
Leech, Sir Bosdin. *The History of the Manchester Ship Canal*, 1907
Pinkerton, John. *Abstract of the Cause Just Arbitrated between the Birmingham and Birmingham and Fazeley Canal and John Pinkerton*, 1801. Held by Birmingham Central Library
Shaw, Stebbing. *A Journey to the West of England in 1788*, 1789
Southey, Robert. *Journal of a Tour in Scotland in 1819*, 1929
Tatham, William. *Political Economy of Inland Navigation*, 1799
Young, Arthur. *A Six Months Tour Through the North of England*, Vol 3, 1771

Later Accounts
Bick, David. *The Hereford and Gloucester* (The Pound House), 1979
Booker, Frank. *Industrial Archaeology of the Tamar Valley* (David & Charles), 1971
Broadbridge, S. R. *The Birmingham Canal Navigations*, Vol 1, 1768–1846 (David & Charles) 1974
Burton, Anthony. *The Canal Builders* (Eyre Methuen) 1972
Cameron, A. D. *The Caledonian Canal* (Terence Dalton), 1972
Clew, Kenneth. *The Kennet and Avon Canal* (David & Charles), 1969
Denney, Martyn. *London's Waterways* (Batsford), 1977

Faulkner, Alan. *The Grand Junction Canal* (David & Charles), 1972

Gladwin, D. D. *The Waterways of Britain* (Batsford), 1976

Hadfield, Charles. *The Canals of the West Midlands* (David & Charles), 1966

Hadfield, Charles. *The Canals of South West England* (David & Charles), 1967

Hadfield, Charles. *British Canals* (David & Charles), 1969

Hadfield, Charles. *The Canal Age* (David & Charles), 1969

Hadfield, Charles. *The Canals of South and South East England* (David & Charles), 1969

Hadfield, Charles. *The Canals of Yorkshire and North East England* (David & Charles), 1972

Hadfield, Charles, and Biddle, Gordon. *The Canals of North West England* (David & Charles), 1970

Hadfield, Charles, and Norris, John. *Waterways to Stratford* (David & Charles), 1962

Handford, Michael. *The Stroudwater Canal* (Alan Sutton), 1979

Hanson, Harry. *Canal People* (David & Charles), 1978

Household, Humphrey. *The Thames and Severn Canal* (David & Charles), 1969

Lindsay, Jean. *The Canals of Scotland* (David & Charles), 1968

Masefield, John. *Grace Before Ploughing* (Heinemann), 1966

Russell, Ronald. *Lost Canals of England and Wales* (David & Charles), 1971

Stevens, Philip. *The Leicester Line* (David & Charles), 1972

Vine, Paul. *London's Lost Route to Basingstoke*, (David & Charles), 1969

Vine, Paul. *The Royal Military Canal*, (David & Charles), 1972

Ward, John Robert. *The Finance of Canal Building in Eighteenth Century England* (OUP), 1974

Railways

First Hand and Contemporary Accounts

Booth, Henry. *An Account of the Liverpool-Manchester Railway*, 1831

Brees, Samuel Charles. *Railway Practice*, Appendix, 1839

Francis, John. *History of English Railways*, Vol 2, 1851

Lecount, Peter. *The History of the Railway Connecting London and Birmingham*

Walker, James Scott. *An Accurate Description of the Manchester-Liverpool Railway*, 1830

Williams, Frederick. *The Midland Railway*, 1886

Williams, Frederick. *Our Iron Roads*, 1888

Later Accounts

Abbott, R. D. (ed). *The Last Main Line* (Leicester Museums), 1960

Barker, T. C., and Robbins, Michael. *A History of London Transport* Vol 1 (Allen & Unwin), 1975

Coleman, Terry. *The Railway Navvies* (Pelican), 1965

Collins, Michael. *The Railway Age*, 1962

Dow, George. *Great Central*, 2 Vols (Locomotive Publishing Co.), 1959

Houghton, F. W., and Foster, W. H. *The Story of the Carlisle-Settle Railway*, 1965

Lloyd, Roger. *Railwayman's Gallery*, 1953

Thomas, Ronald. *The Liverpool and Manchester Railway* (Batsford), 1980

Dams

Bateman, John La Trobe. *History and Description of the Manchester Waterworks*, 1884

Bowtell, H. D. *Reservoir Railways of Manchester and the Peak* (Oakwood), 1977

Harwood, Sir John James. *History and Description of the Thirlmere Water Scheme*, 1895

Index of Register of Dams International Commission on Large Dams (British Section: Institution of Civil Engineers)

Smith, Norman. *A History of Dams* (Peter Davies), 1971

Docks and Ports

Broodbank, Sir Joseph. *History of the Port of London*, 1921

Pudney, John. *London's Docks* (Thames & Hudson) 1975

Wren, Wilfrid. *Ports of the Eastern Counties* (Terence Dalton), 1976

Tunnels

The Blackwall Tunnell (articles reprinted as a booklet by London Magazine, 13 May 1897)

Gripper, Charles. *Railway Tunnelling in Heavy Ground*, 1879

Lampe, David. *The Tunnel* (George Harrap), 1966

Sandstrom, Gosta. *The History of Tunnelling*, 1964

Sims, Frederick Walter. *Public Works of Great Britain*, 1838

Sims, Frederick Walter. *Practical Tunnelling*, 1896

Walker, Thomas. *The Severn Tunnel*, 1890

Biographies

Bellamy, Joyce, and Saville, John. *Dictionary of Labour Biography* vol 4, 1972

Chown, Leslie J. *Sir Samuel Morton Peto, Bt MP*, 1943

Dewey, Joseph. *The Life of Joseph Locke*, 1862

Dictionary of National Biography

Helps, Arthur. *The Life and Labours of Mr Brassey*, 1872

Hobson, G. A. *Life of Sir James Falshaw*, 1905

McDermott, Frederick. *Life and Work of Joseph Firbank*, 1887

O'Rorke, L. E. *The Life and Friendships of Catherine Marsh*, 1917

Rolt. L. T. C. *Thomas Telford* (Penguin), 1979

Smiles, Samuel. *Lives of the Engineers*, Vols 1–5, 1874

Thomas, Ivor. *Top Sawyer: A Biography of David Davies of Llandinam*, 1938

Chapter 15: War

Carter, Ernest. *Railways in Wartime*, 1964

Henry Clifford VC, His Letters and Sketches from the Crimea (Michael Joseph), 1956

Russell, William H. *The War*, 2 Vols, 1855

Sandes, W. C. *The Royal Engineers in Egypt and the Sudan*, 1937.

Sterling, Anthony. *The Highland Brigade in the Crimea*, 1895

Wrottesley, George. *Life and Correspondence of Field Marshal Sir John Burgoyne, Bart.*, 2 Vols, 1873

Chapter 17: Strikes, Truck, Cash

Brassey, Thomas. *Work and Wages*, 1873
Burnett, J. *A History of the Cost of Living* (Penguin), 1969
Hilton, George. *The Truck System*, 1960
Pelling, Henry. *History of British Trade Unionism* (Penguin), 1963
Prochaska, Alice. *History of the General Federation of Trade Unions from 1899 to 1980*
Redford, Arthur. *Labour Migration in England 1800–1850* (Manchester UP), 1964

Chapter 21: Great War

Barrie, Alexander. *The War Underground*, 1962
Fleming, Peter. *The Fate of Admiral Kolchak* (Rupert Hart-Davis), 1963
Grieve, W. G., and Newman, K. B. *Tunnellers*, 1936
McGill, Patrick. *The Great Push*, 1916
Official History of the War (Military Operations France and Belgium), 1916 *Work of the Royal Engineers in the European War, 1914–1919.* (a) Work under the Director of Works (France), (b) Miscellaneous, (c) Military Training
Thomas, T. C. *With a Labour Company in France*
Ward, John. *With the Die-Hards in Siberia*, 1920
Wyrall, Everard. *The Die-Hards in the Great War*, 2 Vols, 1926

General

Armytage, W. H. G. *A Social History of Engineering* (Faber & Faber), 1976
Derry, T. K., and Williams, Trevor. *A Short History of Technology* (OUP), 1975
Hoskins. W. C. *The Making of the English Landscape* (Hodder & Stoughton), 1977
Oxford History of England:
  (a) Watson, Steven J. *The Reign of George III 1760–1815*
  (b) Woodward, Sir Llewellyn. *The Age of Reform*, 1815–1870
  (c) Ensor, Sir Robert. *England 1870–1914*

Pannell, J. M. *An Illustrated History of Engineering* (Thames & Hudson), 1964

Thompson, E. P. *The Making of the English Working Class* (Pelican), 1979

Fiction

Burton, Anthony. *The Navigators* (MacDonald and Jane's), 1976
Farrer, Henrietta Louisa. *The Navvies*, 1847
Garnett, Elizabeth. *Little Rainbow*, 1877
McGill, Patrick. *Moleskin Joe*, 1923

SOURCES

The source of much of the material should be clear from the text. If the name of a single-work author (like Barrett, or Anna Tregelles, or Katie Marsh) is mentioned in the text, the title of the book can be picked out from the bibliography. Similarly, in this list of sources, authors' names on their own or abbreviated titles, refer to works in the bibliography.

NL is short for *Navvies' Letter*; NMS for Navvy Mission Society; ICF for Industrial Christian Fellowship; BL, British Library; PRO, Public Record Office; NAM, National Army Museum; ILN, *Illustrated London News*.

Chapter 1: The Chew Valley Dam

Notice of Tommy Tucker's death is from NL 123, March 1909.

Chapter 2: In Brief

MacGill spoke of women shunning navvies like lepers in *Children of the Dead End*. The Aclands are from NL April 1924.

Chapter 3: Strangers

The Old Blackbird story is from *Our Navvies*, as are the stories of the deserted wives' two weeks grace, and the boys who ran away, and the early motherhood of girls. Little Rainbow is from *Little Rainbow*.

'Sudden Death' etc is from *Our Navvies* and *Annual Meetings Speeches*. Red Neck Hunns is from *English Hearts*. The man who said breaking the teetotal was the reason navvies relapsed is from *Death or Life*. That drink selling in huts was the only way to make a profit is from *Our Navvies*. Mrs G said piecework caused heavy drinking in NL 12, June 1881. Coltings are from Barrett. The furniture van raid is from Leech.

The truck-brothel is from Conder. What happened at the Summit is from Chadwick's *Papers*. The woman who knew nothing but work and wickedness and the story of Polly are from *Our Navvies*. Sarah and Chimley Charlie are from *Ways of the Line*, as is Miss Tregelles's brush with Lincoln and his wife.

Peto told the 1846 Committee about navvy hospitality. William Grime, moocher, is from NL 89, Sept 1900. Mrs G's attack on the shilling is from NL 9, Sept 1880.

Tramps and Lanarkshire's Chief Constable are from *Minutes of Evidence Taken by the Departmental Committee on Vagrancy*, Vol 2, *Accounts and Papers* Vol CIII, 1906 (BL Official Publications). This is also the source of the story about the tramps' warehouse on the MSC. Corwen's tramp problem is from the *Liverpool Echo* 17 Feb 1912. How Moleskin and MacGill mooched their way to Kinlochleven is from *Children of the Dead End*.

Mrs G said there was now less honour among them than formerly in NL 37, Sept 1887. The improvement at Chew is from the 34th *Annual Report*, 1911–12. John Burns's speech in praise of navvies is from NL 122, Dec 1908.

Chapter 4: The Sloping Lodger

The names navvies had for themselves is from the NL, Palk, word of mouth.

Nicknames are from Smiles, Fayers, Barrett, *Our Navvies*, *Our Iron Roads*, *Death or Life*, NL, and word of mouth. Nippers' tea making habits are from Kennedy. Mrs G's scorn of slopers is from NL.

How navvies dressed in the 1830's is from Smiles's *Stephensons*, in the 1850s from *ILN*, at Winchmore Hill from Henrietta Cresswell, and at Lindley from *Our Navvies*. Mrs G reminisced about navvy dress in NL 177, Sept 1907. The Forkstrong ad. is from the *Journal of the National Union of Gasworkers*, 1923.

Stoicism at Cowburn is from *High Peak: Places and Faces*, by Keith Warrender (published by the author). The story of the horse that fell with the staggers was told to the 1846 Committee. Other stoicism stories are from *Our Iron Roads*, as is the story of the greyneck, the navvy, and the landlady (a different account appears in Lecount).

Most of the jokes are from the *Navvy's Guide*. The other side of the story of the navvy who told the boss to go to hell is from Leech.

The man who told the Rev Sargent his wife had gowns enough for life is from the 1846 Committee. The man who thought it a navvy's duty to spend like an ass is from NL 30, Dec 1885.

The story of the Dearne and Dove feast is from Hadfield's *Canals* where the source is given as the *Doncaster Gazette* 13 Nov 1801. The Elan valley feast is from the *Montgomery and Radnor Echo*. Navvy opinion of Westmorland and navvy smoking habits are from Fayers.

Chapter 5: Bumpsticks

MacGill and the death upon the railway is from *Children of the Dead End*. The statistics comparing navvy mortality to that of soldiers in the Napoleonic War are from Chadwick's *Papers*. The comparison with the Boer War is from *Annual Meeting Speeches* (Sir John Jackson). Statistics elsewhere are either from Mrs Garnett or have been worked out from the dead and hurt lists published by the NMS.

The Sapperton accident is from the *Gloucester Journal* 22 Jan 1787: that at Strood is from Simm's *Public Works*. What happened at the Eston cutting is from *Our Navvies*. The London-Birmingham men with smallpox thick upon them is from Chadwick's *Papers*. Cholera at Woodhead is from John Dransfield's book *History of Penistone*, 1906. Epidemics on the Dore-Chinley are from NL 55, March 1892. Typhoid and whooping cough on the Great Central are from NL 74, Dec 1896.

The mass-accident at Ince is from the *Daily Graphic* 20 July 1891 et seq.

The Didcot-Newbury hospital is from *Our Navvies*. Hospitals on dams are from NL 25, Sept 1884. The MSC Accident Service is from Sir Harry Platt's article *Canal Accident Service* in the *Port of Manchester Review*, 1968.

Soup kitchens on dams are from various editions of the NL. That people were dying of hunger at the Vrynwy dam is from the *Shropshire and Montgomeryshire Post* 20 March 1886.

Distress at Hull is from the *Hull Packet* 18 July 1884 et seq, and NL 25, Sept 1884, and NL 27, March 1885. The whole story is retold in Mrs Sleight's obituary, NL 81, Sept 1898, which is also the source of Walker's observation. What happened at Tilbury is from the East and West India Dock Company's *Minute Book* No 50.

The Rainy Day Fund was suggested in NL 27, March 1885. What happened to it is from NL 28, June 1885. What happened on the Christchurch-Bournemouth is from NL 29, Sept 1885. What happened at Blackheath is from NL 120, June 1908.

What happened when the NMS delegation met John Burns is from NL 123, March 1909. Material about the 1907 Bill is from *Parliamentary Papers: Bills, Public* 1907 IV, 915. The Bishop of London and the Society for the Suppression of Vice is from the London Dock Company's Court of Directors' *Minute Book*, 1804. Navvy attitude to work relief schemes is from the *Report of the Royal Commission on the Poor Laws and Relief of Distress*, 1909.

Katie Marsh asked and answered her question in *English Hearts*. Brassey asked and answered his in *Work and Wages*. The man who expected to die in a hedge bottom is from NL 83, March 1899. Telford's recommendations are from PRO RAIL 808/1. That Firbank's men need not fear white hairs is from NL 33, Sept 1886. Walker's Fragments are from Leech. The man who prized loyalty is from the *Ship Canal News* 1 Feb 1891. Sam Hall is from the same source, 22 Oct 1889. The Craven well-sinkers are from *Our Navvies*.

The idea of navvy pensions was floated in NL 99, March 1903. How much the fund had paid by 1916 is from NL 154, Dec 1916. Mrs G's tirade against the firms who did not pay is from NL 114, Dec 1906.

The navvy who said our chaps are very good is from NL 83, March 1899. The wife who sold fly papers is from Fayers. Richard Smith, genuine case, is from NL 131, March 1911. Charlie Ward is from NL Jan 1930.

Blind Billy is from *Our Navvies*. Annie Phelps is from NL 123, March 1909: NL 136, June 1912: NL 138, Dec 1912: and NL 144, June 1914.

Chapter 6: Beginnings

Walker said he became a navvy on the Bridgewater in Pinkerton's *Abstract of the Cause*. Richard Pearce spoke to the 1846 Committee. The origins of men on the Liverpool-Manchester is from J H Clapham, *An Economic History of Modern Britain: The Early Railway Age*, 1820–50. The original source is a pamphlet written by the L&MR rebutting criticism made in the October, 1832, edition of the *Edinburgh Review*. The pamphlet is called *An Answer by the Directors of the L&MR to an Article in the Edinburgh Review*. Mylne is from Brees.

The contractor who compared navvies to dogs spoke to the 1846 Committee. That the great agricultural slump of the 1880s was a navvy-recruiter is from an article John Ward wrote for *Justice*, one of a series called *Sketches of Labour Life*, 16 and 23 June 1888.

Soldier and Jethro Bird are from NL 21, Sept 1883. Mrs Hunter and the Oxford double-first is from *Our Navvies*. The inebriate surgeons and the mud-drowned footmen are from ILN 30 Dec 1854. Gulson's prying is from PRO MH 32/28. How the Poor Law drove men into navvying is from the *Second* and *Third Annual Reports of the Poor Law Commissioners – Parliamentary Reports* Vol XXIX part 1, 1836: and Vol XXXI, 1837. Halstead's problems are from the *Second Annual Report*, *Appendix B*, page 242. Muggeridge and the domestic migration scheme are from the same *Appendix*, page 417. Hemel Hempstead's pauper gang, and the paupers on the Newcastle-Carlisle, are from Brees.

Sir Charles Morgan and Mr Dent were reported in *The Times* and *Morning Chronicle* 11 April 1793. Mr Courtenay was covered only by that morning's *Times*. The percentage of Irish navvies is from the *Census of Ireland* 1841, *Parliamentary Papers* 1843, Vol XXIV.

The paucity of Irish navvies, compared to Irish soldiers, is from the *ILN*. Complaints that the Irish took over some jobs are from various *Annual Reports* of the NMS. The origins of the men at the Knaresborough viaduct are from J A Patmore *A Navvy Gang of 1851 – Journal of Transport History*, Vol 5, 1969. The analysis of the

Census Returns is from D Brooke's *Railway Navvies on the Pennines – Journal of Transport History*, Vol 3, 1975.

Six-Fingered Jack is mentioned in the NL: the black navvy who died above the Elan is from the *Montgomery and Radnor Echo*. The black man at Ballaculish is from Kennedy.

The fact that Irish navvies were mainly Catholic Ulstermen is from the 1846 Committee. MacGill's experiences are from *Children of the Dead End*. McDonough's complaint appeared in the *Liverpool Mercury* 8 Nov 1839. The Lancaster-Carlisle riot is from the *Lancaster Gazette* 29 Sept 1838. English navvies' conviction that the Irish undercut wages is from the *Liverpool Journal* 12 Oct 1839.

Carlyle's preference for Irish navvies is from a letter to Gavan Duffy (dated 29 Aug 1846) as reprinted in R W Wilson's *Genesis and Growth of the Caledonian Railway* in the *Railway Magazine*, June 1907.

The Sheriff of Edinburgh spoke to the 1846 Committee. The bilingual Scotsmen at Kinlochleven are referred to in a booklet put out by the British Aluminium Corporation. The recruiting of Scottish labour for the Lancaster canal, through ads. in north of the Border papers, is from the *Lancaster Canal Committee Book*, 23 Oct 1792.

Welsh-language bookselling at Vyrnwy is from the NL. The battle of Webb's ear is from the *Chester Courant* 10 June 1846. The Penmaenmawr and Bangor riots are from the same newspaper, 27 May and 3 June 1846.

Chapter 7: The Clockwork Shovel

Brassey's timekeeper's remarks are recorded in *Work and Wages*. Hekekyan Bey's are from his *Journal*, BL Add Mss 37448. Navvies abroad are from *Our Iron Roads*, Smiles, and Helps.

The canal cutter's daily 12 cu yds is from Tatham. Early railway daily workloads are from Brassey, as is the amount shifted in the Victoria Dock. Ward's 24 tons is from his *Justice* article, already referred to.

Cutting and embanking is from various sources – Chadwick's *Papers*, the 1846 Committee, *Our Iron Roads*, Brees, and Kennedy. Fayers told the story of the horses which unhitched themselves.

Southey's remarks are from his *Journal*. The MSC barrow runs are from Leech. The burning bank at Wolverton is from Lecount.

Brindley's dump boat is from Young's *Tour*. Turn-up trucks on the Caledonian are from Cameron.

Numbers of dams are from the *Register of Dams*. Other dam material is from Smith's *Dams*. Chadwick's report is from *Sanitary Condition of the Labouring Population of Great Britain*, 1842. Knighton reservoir is from PRO RAIL 808/1.

Details of the Vyrnwy dam are from *The Engineer, Supplement*, 15 July 1892. The toad anecdote is from D W L Rowland's *History and Description of Llanwddyn and Lake Vyrnwy*. The toad on the Birmingham is from Lecount. The Belsize tunnel toad is from MacDermott's *Firbank*. The pterodactyl is from *The Unexplained* Vol 1, No 8.

What it was like in the Wapping tunnel is from James Walker. (Blasting in the same tunnel is from John Raistrick's *Notebook* (13 Jan 1829), University of Liverpool MSS Dept, but here taken from Thomas's *Liverpool and Manchester Railway*. The history of gunpowder is from Sandstrom. The rock ganger who blew away his waistcoat is from Kennedy, as is the clearing of drill holes. Tunnelling techniques are from *Practical Tunnelling*, *Our Iron Roads*, and *Severn Tunnel*. The method used at Curdworth is from *Abstract of the Cause*: at Blisworth from *The Grand Junction Canal*. Most of the material on Brunel's Rotherhite tunnel is from Lampe. Most of the material on the Blackwall is from *The Blackwall Tunnel*.

What happened at Strood is from Simm's *Public Works*. Shaft sinking and surveying at Sapperton is from Household. Sea compasses in the Wapping are from Walker. Brindley's spoons are from *The History of Inland Navigation*, Anon, 1766. What happened at Kilsby is from *Our Iron Roads*, and Smiles's *Stephensons*. John Byng's adventures are from the *Torrington Diaries*, Vol 1, 1934. How much Sapperton miners brought down at a firing is from Simeon Moreau's book *Tour to Cheltenham Spa*, 3rd Edition, 1788. What happened under the Severn is from Thomas Walker.

Mechanisation on the Hereford and Gloucester and Gloucester and Berkeley is from PRO RAIL 836/3 and 829/3. What happened on the Caledonian is from Southey, Cameron, Rolt's *Telford*, and the 3rd *Report of the Caledonian Canal Committee*.

The early, perhaps earliest, use of steam to haul material on public works is from the London Dock's Committee of *Treasury Minute Book*, 1803. The Marine Society's complaint is from the *Court of Directors' Minute Book*, 1804. The use of a beam engine to turn a mortar mill and the proposal to drive piles by steam are from the West India Dock Company's *Minute Books*, 1801–2.

William Cole's poem is *A Poetical Sketch of the Norwich and Lowestoft Navigation Works*, 1833. There's a copy in the Lowestoft Central Library.

The crane on the Mid-Level Sewer is from Helps. Ward said invention had revolutionised navvying in his *Justice* article, already mentioned. He talked about Lincoln Wills in the same story. Mrs G's recollections of Denshaw and navvy physique is from NL 117, Sept 1907. Brassey on physique is from *Work and Wages*. Why the NL changed its name is from the 16*th Annual Report*, 1893. Machinery on the MSC is from Leech.

Chapter 8: Sod Huts and Shants

The South Devon's huts are from the 1846 Committee, those on the Edinburgh-Hawick from the *Scottish Herald*, 4 to 25 April 1846, and those on the Kettering-Manton from Barrett. Ward's mushroom picking is from the *Staffs Sentinel* 25 Oct 1924.

The Lune engineer's Shade is from PRO RAIL 844/240. The *York Courant* ad. is from the 10 Nov 1772 edition. Hutting on the Stroudwater is from Handford's *Stroudwater* and ultimately the Gloucestershire Record Office. Huts on the Gloucester and Berkeley are from PRO RAIL 829/4. The Tunnel House is mentioned as being expressly built for the tunnellers in the *Gentleman's Magazine* No 56, part 2, 1786. It, and the Daneway Arms, are also referred to by Household. All material about the Worcester and Birmingham is from PRO RAIL 886/4.

Dandy Dick is ultimately from an article Dandy himself wrote in *Household Words*, as retold here by Barrett.

Huts at Lindley Wood are from Evans's article in *The Quiver*, 3rd Series, Vol 12, 1877, and *Our Navvies*. Sudbrook is from Walker's *Severn Tunnel*. His cottages at Eastham are from the *Ship Canal News* 26 May and 15 June 1889. Elan's lay-out and amenities are from the *Public Works Magazine* 15 March 1904. The drinking rules at Elan and Lindley are from papers held by the ICF library. Grizedale is from the *Blackpool Herald* 17 May 1904. The self-shooting at Elan is from the *Montgomery and Radnor Echo* 24 Sept 1898.

Hovels on the Water Orton-Kingsbury are from NL 186, Jan 1927. Ward's exchanges with Lloyd George are from *Parliamentary Debates* Vol 152, 1906. Trouble at Brooklands is from Dr Reginald Ferrar's *Report to the Local Government Board on the Accommodation of Navvies at the Brooklands Race Track, Parliamentary Papers* Cd 3694 LXVIII 1907. The announcement of the new House of Commons Standing Orders is from *Parliamentary Debates* Vol 29, 1911. Ward and the Ashford Common dam is from Vol 157, 1922.

Chapter 9: Cat-Eating-Scan to Half-Ear Slen

All material from the NL.

Chapter 10: Impact

The London-Birmingham men who tore kittens apart are from *Death or Life*. Mrs G stated her conviction that nobody so improved their country as navvies in NL 5, Sept 1879. "Rattle his Bones" is from NL July 1931.

The numbers of men working on various jobs are from printed sources, except the Worcester and Birmingham – PRO RAIL 886/4 – and the Chester, PRO RAIL 816/2.

The description of runaway navvies from the Staffs and Worcester is from Hanson's *Canal People* where the source is given as *Aris's Birmingham Gazette* 1 June 1767. The Chesterfield's dictat is from PRO RAIL 817/1. What happened to Hereford and Gloucester absconders is from PRO RAIL 836/3 and 829/3. Gentleman Dick's poaching is from PRO RAIL 886/4.

That 50,000 men built the earliest railways is from Redford. The 1870s' estimates (40,000) are from *The Quiver*, 3rd Series, Vol 12, 1877. The 90,000 up-date is from the *Wandsworth Observer* 15 June 1889. The Local Government Board's figures are from Dr Reginald Ferrar's *Report to the Local Government Board on the Accommodation of Navvies at the Brooklands Race Track, Parliamentary Papers* Cd 3694 LXVIII 1907. The highest figure, 170,000, is from *Evidence Before the Royal Commission on the Poor*

Law, already mentioned.

The tale of the corrupted females is from the 1846 Committee. Ward claimed navvies were the world's best poachers in his *Justice* article, already referred to. Sir William Wake's losses are from the 1846 Committee, as is the story of the Northamptonshire butcher. Gaffer Brown is from NL 11, March 1881. The Bedfordshire poachers are from *Our Navvies*.

Burgess's poem is from the *Oldham Chronicle* 22 Jan 1881.

Wordsworth's sonnet, *On a Projected Kendal and Windermere Railway*, is from his collected *Works*. Ruskin's quotation is from *Works of John Ruskin*, 1907. How the National Trust was founded is from B L Thompson's book *The Lake District and the National Trust* and Henry Fedden's *The Continuing Purpose*. The Rev Armstrong's lament is from R M Robbins — *A Middlesex Diary*, printed in the *Transactions of the London and Middlesex Archaeological Society*, X 1, 1954. Dickens wrote of the Camden Town in *Dombey and Son*. Masefield wrote of the Hereford and Gloucester in *Grace Before Ploughing*. What happened to Winchmore Hill is from Henrietta Cresswell.

Chapter 11: Moleskin Joe

The conversion of Red Bill Davis is from NL 169, Oct 1922. Otherwise most of the chapter is from *Children of the Dead End*.

Chapter 12: The Making of Hawick

Mostly from the *Hawick Advertiser* 7 Sept 1859 et seq.

Chapter 13: The Long Drag

The *Midland Railway* and *Our Iron Roads* are important sources. The *Daily News* items were printed on 26 and 29 October 1872. Pollens's party and the man who drowned in the Blea Moor tunnel are from *Chambers's Journal* 15 March 1873. Rioting at Armathwaite is from the *Carlisle Patriot* 21 Oct and 4 Nov 1870, 6 Jan 1871.

Chapter 14: Riot

Mrs G's plea not to cross a threshold red with blood is from NL 106, Dec 1904.

Trouble at Tidworth is from the *Salisbury Times* 9 Sept 1904 et seq. Rioting at Barrow on Soar is from the *Gentleman's Magazine* Aug 1795. Ned the Navigator is from *The Times* 15 Feb 1805. The Fighting Field at the Redmires dam is from Warrender's *High Peak*, already referred to.

The "D" for Deserter story is from *English Hearts*. Electioneering riots on the Lancaster are from PRO RAIL 844/241. Peto and the Norwich riots are from the *Norfolk Chronicle* 20 July 1874 et seq and *The Times* 28 July 1847.

The Hereford and Gloucester's problems are from PRO RAIL 836/3. Riots on the Dearne and Dove are from Hadfield's *Canals* where the source is given as the *Yorkshire Gazette* 17 Jan 1795. The Leicestershire riots are from the *Leicester Journal* 3 April 1795 and from Stevens's *Leicester Line* where the *Leicester Herald* 3 April 1795 is given as another source. The Sampford affair is from the *Annual Register* April 1811 and the *Taunton Courier* 2 May 1811. The occupation of Bardney is from James Padley's book *Fens and Floods of Mid-Lincolnshire*, 1882.

The American Tavern incident is from NL 15, March 1882 and *the Hull Packet* 30 Dec 1881. Trouble on the Leeds-Thirsk is from the *Halifax Guardian* 10 June 1846 and the *Manchester Guardian* of the same day. Trouble at Lupton is from the *Kendal Mercury* 15 Sept 1890.

The Glasgow murders are from *The Times* 15 Dec 1840 et seq. The hanging is from *The Times* 19 May 1841. The Penrith riots are from the *Carlisle Patriot* 13 Feb 1846 et seq. Hobday's trial is from the same paper, 27 Feb 1846. Murder and riot at Gorebridge was mentioned to the 1846 Committee and was fully reported by the *Scottish Herald* 28 Feb 1846.

The battles on the Chester-Birkenhead are from the *Liverpool Journal* 12 Oct 1839 and the *Manchester Guardian* 16 Oct 1839. The man who thought the English out-fought the Irish with fists is from the *Dumfries Standard* 25 Feb 1846. Maurice Dowling spoke to the 1846 Committee.

Fighting the Belgians is from the *Sussex Advertiser* 5 Sept 1866 et seq. Rioting at Kinghorn is from *Fifeshire Journal* 14 May 1846. The AWC fight at Penge is from *English Hearts* and O'Rorke's *Life*.

The assault in Newhaven is from the *Sussex Advertiser* 20 Oct 1866. The killing at East Coker is from the *Yeovil Telegram* 27 March 1862 et seq. Lovett's trouble in Marlborough is from NL 104, June 1904. The goings-on at Hapton are from the *Manchester Guardian* 19 Sept 1846.

The battle for the Gravesend-Rochester is from the *Maidstone Journal* 28 Jan and 4 Feb 1845, and Conder. The Battle of Mickleton is from the *Railway Times* 26 July 1851 and the *ILN* of the same date. The killing at Seathwaite is from NL 105, Sept 1904 and the *North Western Daily Mail* 26 July 1904 et seq.

Chapter 15: War

Bagshaw's letters are from NAM 6112–35–1. The effect of the Napoleonic War on canal prices is from Hadfield and Lindsay.

The recruiting of paid-off soldiers on the Lancaster is from PRO RAIL 844/264. The press gang in London is from the East India Dock Company's *Minute Book*, 1803–5. Thatcher's ad. in the *Kentish Gazette* appeared on 6 and 9 Nov 1804. Evidence of labour shortages on the Kennet and Avon is from PRO RAIL 842/10. What happened on the London Dock, and subsequently, is from Broadbent and both the London Dock *Committee of Treasury Minute Book* (1803) and *Court of Directors' Minute Book* (1804). The Royal Military Canal is from Vine.

The recruiting of navvies for the Crimea is from *The Times* 23 Dec 1854 et seq: the *ILN* 9 Dec 1854 et seq: and the *Chelmsford Chronicle* 8 and 14 Dec 1854. Shipping movements to the Crimea are from the *ILN* 30 Dec 1854.

What happened in the Crimea is from the *ILN* and – above all – from Russell's reports to *The Times* as published in his book, *The War*.

The composition of the navvy corps is from PRO WO 28/245. The stolen bullock is from Burgoyne's *Life*. The navvy who was flogged for the honour of his country is from Sterling. The railway accident is from *The War* and Fayers.

The account of the AWC is largely from *The War* and *English Hearts*.

That navvy non-combatants may have been Paxton's idea is from G F Chadwick *The Army Works Corps in the Crimea, Journal of Transport History*, May 1964. Doyne is from PRO WO 28/263.

The AWC's composition is from PRO WO 28/230. The Doyne v Beatty argument is from Chadwick's article in *JTH*, listed above, as are the stories of road repairing under fire, and the AWC as a back-up gang for naval divers. General Simpson's complaint is from the *Panmure Paper*.

What happened to the Commissariat Detachment is from PRO WO 28/262. Doyne's lack of authority to punish offenders, from NAM 6807-380-25. The General Order threatening to stop the navvies' gratuities is from the same pouch.

Doyne's letter to Paxton, putting his side of the case, is from NAM 6807-142-25.

Bagshaw's name was still on the pay lists, PRO WO 28/228. Crankey Oxford's death is from NL 73, Sept 1896. Mr Spowant's request is from PRO WO 25/3861.

The account of the Sudan railway is from three sources- the *Navvy's Guide*, Sandes's book, and two articles in the Royal Engineers' *Journal*: Vol 15, 1885, by Capt H G Kunhardt, and Vol 16, 1886.

The sailing of the *Osprey* is from NL 27, March 1885. Deaths in the Sudan are from NL 28, June 1885. Moorley's death is from NL 29, Sept. 1885.

Chapter 16: Hagmasters and After

The Union's opinion of butty messes is from the *Guide*. Jones at Sapperton is from the *Proceedings of the Cotteswolds' Naturalists Field Club*, Vol 5, 1870. Jones on the Chesterfield is from PRO RAIL 817/1. Jones v the Thames and Severn in Chancery is from PRO C 33/488, 21 March 1795, page 285d. Jones at Blisworth is from the *The Grand Junction Canal*. The volcano image is from the *Gentleman's Magazine*, Vol 56, part 2, 1786.

Pinkerton's clashes with Millar are mainly from PRO RAIL 844/240. The turning of Barrow Beck into the canal is from PRO 844/263. Pinkerton on the Barnsley canal is from PRO RAIL 806/3, and W N Slatcher, *The Barnsley Canal: Its First Twenty Years*, *Transport History*, Vol 1, 1968. Pinkerton's earlier life is mainly from his own *Abstract of the Cause*. What happened on the Erewash is from PRO RAIL 828/1. At the Dudley Tunnel, PRO RAIL 824/3. That he had legal troubles left over from the Basingstoke canal is obvious from internal evidence in PRO RAIL

844/241. Trouble on the Birmingham-Fazeley is from PRO RAIL 810/5, and *Abstract of the Cause*. Pinkerton's jailing is from PRO RAIL 810/43. The fact that faults on the canal were not rectified until the 1820s is from PRO RAIL 810/12.

Telford's contractors are mainly from Rolt and PRO RAIL 808/1. Ward's *Rude Reality* was serialised in the *Navvy's Guide*. How Wythes got rich is from McDermott's *Firbank*. How people based tenders on 'formulae' is from the 1846 Committee.

The song about Brassey is from NL 116, June 1907. How mid-century contractors bought contracts is from Harold Pollins, *Railway Contractors and the Finance of Railway Development in Britain*, parts 1 and 2, *Journal of Transport History*. What Peto did at Lowestoft is mainly from Wren. Walker's life is mainly from the NL.

Chapter 17: Strikes, Truck, Cash.

Strikes on the Lune are from PRO RAIL 844/240. Sir Charles's despair is from *The Times* and *Morning Chronicle* 11 April 1793. The Slamannan and Edinburgh strike is from the *Falkirk Herald* 12 March 1846. The Thirlmere strike is from the *Manchester Guardian* 22 Feb 1886. The Hereford and Gloucester's objections to its employees setting up shops is from PRO RAIL 836/3. The Woodhead chit was shown to the 1846 Committee. Truck at Woodhead is from Chadwick's *Papers*.

The Riley v Warden case is from 2 *Exch* 59 (BL Official Publications). Truck at Grimsby is from the *Wolverhampton Chronicle* 22 May 1850.

Peto's strictures on employing unmoneyed men, and Brunel's anti-truck clauses, are from the 1846 Committee. Peto's statistics are from *Parliamentary Papers: Reports from Committees: Payment of Wages*, 1854, Vol XVI.

Earnings on the Bridgewater are from Mallet. The doubling of canal prices in the Napoleonic War are from Hadfield and Lindsay. The Royal Military Canal is from Vine. Wages in Bristol are from the *Kentish Gazette* 6 and 9 Nov 1804. George Stephenson on the cost of good navigators, and Palmer on what he paid them, is from Brees. Cost of living comparison are from Burnett.

The weekly wages table is from Brassey. Ward claimed wages had been reduced, and that contractors swindled piecemen, in his *Justice* article, already mentioned. The first firms to pay seven pence an hour are from the *Daily Dispatch* 22 April 1913. Wages at Rood End Lane are from the *Blackpool Gazette News* 17 Nov 1917. How the Conciliation Board worked is from *The Record* (journal of the Transport and General Workers' Union) March 1928. That union's success at Harwich is from the same source. Comparable yearly earnings are from Burnett. The settlement at Hurstwood is from the *Lancashire Daily Post* 11 Dec 1920.

Problems on Firbank's contract are from Brassey.

The wages riot at Rotherham is from the *Leeds Mercury* 13 Oct 1838. The Clamerous navvies at Stratford are from Hadfield's *Waterways to Stratford*. What happened on the Huddersfield Narrow is from PRO RAIL 838/2. The runaway hagman on the Basingstoke is from the *Reading Mercury and Oxford Gazette* 22 Dec 1788. The Leeds and Liverpool runaway is from PRO RAIL 846/40.

Chapter 18: The Navvies' Union

Most of the material on the union's early days are from the *Navvy's Guide*. Ticket navvies are from NL 43, March 1889. The work list idea is from NL 65, Sept 1894.

Biographies of Humphreys and Hall are from the *Guide*. Material on Cusack is from his obituary in the *Staffs Sentinel* 21 Feb 1929 and the TGWU's *The Record*. How he met Ward is from a private letter Ward wrote to the editor of the *Staffs Sentinel* (dated 8 March 1929) now in that newspaper's library.

Cox told navvies to stop drinking in NL 48, June 1890. NMS denial of a low-wage policy is in the next issue. Mrs G hoped landladies would give Cox a cup of tea in NL 44, June 1889.

The 1 March mass meetings in Manchester and London are from the (Salford) *Reporter* 7 March 1891, and the *Middlesex County Times* 7 March 1891. The strike/lock-out on the MSC is from the *Guide*, which quoted the other Manchester papers. Mrs G's comments on the *Guide* are from NL 58, Dec 1892. The 1892 strike and violence on the Ship Canal are from Leech.

The *Labour Leader's* attack on Ward is in the 21 Sept 1906 edition.

Statistics about union membership are mainly from the GFTU's *Quarterly Reports*. Ward and the founding of the GFTU is from the *Report of the 30th TUC* 1897.

Chapter 19: John Ward

Ward's early life is mainly from an article, *The Rise of a Ploughboy*, he wrote for *Pearson's Weekly* 15 March 1906. More material is from the *Staffs Evening Sentinel* 13 Sept 1933 (seen in galley form in the newspaper's offices) and 25 Oct 1924. Yet more material is from Ward's *Justice* article, already referred to. MacGill's quote is from *Gleanings from a Navvy's Scrapbook*.

The Trafalgar Square affray is from *The Times* 5 Nov 1886 et seq and (and mainly) *Justice* 13 Nov 1886 et seq. Ward's trial is from *The Times* 15 Nov 1886. The second, peaceful, rally is from *The Times* 22 Nov 1886.

What Ward thought as a young man is from two pamphlets: *Socialism, the Religion of Humanity* and *England's Sacrifice to the God Mammon* (1888–90). Copies of both are held by the General and Municipal Workers' Union (Woodstock College, Surbiton).

Ward's arguments in the School Board election are from his electoral address, a copy of which is also held by the GMWU. Who won and who lost is from *Justice* 1 Dec 1888. Ward and the Wandsworth Vestry is from the *Wandsworth Observer* 17 May 1890 et seq. The pamphlet he wrote with George Fisher is called *How the Wandsworth Charities were Stolen*, 1890, a copy of which can be read in the BL. Details of the LCC elections are from *The Times* and the *Wandsworth Observer* 12 March 1892 et seq.

Ward's speeches to the TUC are from the *Staffs Sentinel* 5 Sept 1902, and 10 Sept 1904.

The *Staffs Sentinel* covered his election campaign 3 Jan to 16 Jan 1906. Ward in Parliament is from *Parliamentary Debates*: his King's Speech reply is from Vol 152, 1906. He asked for a minimum wage at Rosyth in Vol 153, 1906. The Admiralty said the Rosyth contractors were paying a fair wage in Vol 23, 1911. The debate on the amendment to the West Killingholme Pier Bill is from Vol 42, 1912.

Reactions to the Fair Wages Clause at Blackwall is from *The Blackwall Tunnel*. Where Ward sat and what he looked like in the House are from Sir A. Griffith-Boscawen's *Memories*, 1925.

Chapter 20: Churching the Ungodly

The Ward quotation is from his *Justice* article, already referred to. Munby is from *Former Days at Turvey*. Jenour, Thompson and Sargent spoke to the 1846 Committee. Mrs G's belief that laws should be based on the laws of Christ is from NL 61, Sept 1893.

The *Letter's* change of name is from the *16th Annual Report*, 1893. That people read them, like the Chinese, back to front is from NL 4, June 1879. Mrs G asked how many bundles of meat had been carried off in NL 12, June 1881. The drunkard who cut his throat is from NL 100, June 1900. W-P- is from NL 42, Dec 1888. The song is from NL 8, June 1880.

The founding of the NMS is from NL 3, March 1879, and *The Quiver*, 3rd Series, Vol 12, 1877. The founding of the CEU is from NL 19, March 1883: NL 20, June 1883: NL 137, Sept 1912. A copy of the leaflet, *Navvies and Their Needs*, is bound in with the first and second editions of the *Letters* in the ICF library.

The Dean of Ripon's comments are from: *The Church's Work Among the Navvies, Being a Paper Read Before the Church Congress, held at Sheffield, October 3rd, 1878, by the Very Rev W H Fremantle (Dean of Ripon)*. A copy can be found between the first and second editions of the NL in the ICF Library.

Mrs G reminisced about the Mission's early troubles in NL 117, Sept 1907.

NMS office space in London is from *16th Annual Report*, 1893. Katherine Sleight's story is from NL 81, Sept 1898. Navvy Smith's is from NL 170, Jan 1923: and NL 188, July 1927. Tom Cleverley's is from NL 171, April 1923, and *Annual Meeting Speeches*.

Navvy Smith's belief that Christianity *and* Labour changed public works is from NL 170, Jan 1923.

Chapter 21: The Great War

MacGill at Loos is from *The Great Push*. Letters from navvies are from various editions of the NL. The story of the 19th Cheshires is from *With a Labour Company in France*. Kitchener's involvement with Ward's Lt-colonelcy is from the *Staffs Sentinel* 19 Dec 1934 — as is the story of the *Tyndareus*.

What happened to the Middlesex battalions is from the regimental journal *The Die-Hards*, Vol XIII No 8 and Vol XIV No

3, as well as Everard Wyrrall's history, and the official history of the war. Ward's reflections on what the war was about are from GFTU *Proceedings and Reports* July 1915/June 1916. Slavery in Hong Kong is from the same source, July 1921/June 1922. Ward in Siberia is from his own book and from Fleming's *Kolchak*.

Missionaries at war are from NL 151, March 1916. The RE officer's comments on his men's origins are from NL 157, Sept 1917. The raising of the Labour Corps is from PRO WO 107/37.

Tunnelling Companies are from the NL, *Tunnellers*, *The War Underground*, and from the Royal Engineers' own publications.

Chapter 22: Ending

The new scope of the Public Works Union is from its *Handbook*, 1919. Membership figures are from the GFTU's *Quarterly Reports*. The TGWU's raid on the Staffordshire branch is from GFTU *Proceedings and Reports* July 1928/June 1929. What happened to the Public Works Union after 1933 is from the TUC's *Historical Index*. Cusack and the Mersey tunnel is from the TGWU's *The Record* March 1929. His death is from the same source and from the *Staffs Evening Sentinel* 21 Feb 1929 and a private letter (dated 8 March 1929) which Ward wrote to the *Sentinel's* editor and which is now in the newspaper's library.

Ward's plea to the House during the Workmen's Compensation debate is from *Parliamentary Debates* Vol 168 1923. His son's death is from a letter Ward wrote to the editor of the *Staffs Sentinel* (dated 20 Sept 1928) now in the newspaper's library. His own death is from the *Staffs Sentinel* 19 Dec 1934, the *Andover Advertiser* 21 Dec 1934, and *The Times* 20 and 22 Dec 1934.

The renaming of the NMS is from NL 163, March 1919. Mrs G's last letter is NL 154, Dec 1916. Her lifelong devotion to navvies is from NL 81, Sept 1898. Her death and the plaque in Ripon Cathedral is from NL 185, Oct 1926. Navvy Smith's death is from NL July 1932.

MacGill's novel is called *Moleskin Joe*.

Index

103, 109, 111
rope-running **59–60**, 82
Royal Engineers 156–7, 217, 224–6
runners out 54

Scottish navvies 48, 51, **52**, 114, 121,
    133, 135–6, 205
Settlements: Birchinlee 80; Carlisle-
    Hawick line 108; Carlisle-Settle
    line 115–19; Eastham 79; Elan 78–
    80; Kinlochleven 100–5; Lindley
    Wood 78; Sudbrook 78
sewage 34, 39, 61, 67, 71, 88, 182
Sick Clubs 15, 38, 43, 210
sickness **37–8**, 112–13, 116–17; sta-
    tistics **37**, 224
shaft sinking 65, 68, 108
Sleight, Katherine 39, 202, 211
sloping 25–6, 83–8 *passim*, 170
soup kitchens 21, 38–9
strikes: Crimea 147, 154; Lancaster
    canal 167–8; Liverpool docks 198;
    Manchester Ship Canal 185–6,
    187 fn; Rosyth 199; Severn tunnel
    167;   Slamannan-Edinburgh-
    Glasgow line 168; Thirlmere dam
    168
Sudan 156–7, 189–90

taskers 158, 159–60
Telford, Thomas 41, 52, 158, 162,
    164
Tidworth 124–5, 141, 159
tigers 2, 49, **55**, 64, 65–8, 120, 123,
    226
timbering 54, **55**, 225, 227
tipping 13, 54, **59–60**, 118, 121
tip wagons 59, 60 fn
tobacco 32
toe-the-line fighting 125–6
tommy 25; amounts eaten 31–2, 93,
    116; cooking 73, 75–6, 100, 119;
    eating habits 56, 112–3
tommy tickets 169–70
trade unions 177, 179–80, 194–5,
    228–9
tramping 2, 8, 9, 13–21, 98

Tregelles, Anna 12, 13–15, 16, 125,
    126, 171–2, 202
truck 169–74
tunnelling 3, 36, **64–9**, 108, 119–20,
    159–60, 225–6, 227
Tunnels: Abbot's Cliff 66, Blackwall
    38, 67, 198 fn; Blea Moor 118–20;
    Blisworth 65, 160; Bugsworth 28;
    Cowburn 28, 66; Cowley 163;
    Curdworth 65, 162; Dudley 161;
    Greywell 90, 161; Harecastle 68,
    90, 162; Hirwaun 3; Kilsby 68;
    Llangyfellach 10–11, 35, 82–3;
    126, 130; Lunedale (pipe track) 2,
    36; Mersey 229; Netherton 65,
    90; Oxenhall 70; Patricroft
    (drainage) 159–60; Rotherhithe
    (Brunel's) 27, 66, 166; Sapperton
    34, 67, 68, 74, 160; Severn 66, 69,
    78, 167; Strood 34, 67, 140;
    Thames (subway) 66; Totley 37,
    66, 182; Wapping (Liverpool-
    Manchester) 64; Watford 75–6;
    Whitrope 108–14 *passim*; Wood-
    head (Summit) 5 fn, 12, 34, 170;
    Woodhead (second) 37, 165
turn-outs 37, 54

Unemployed Workmen's Act 22, 40

wages 1, 57, 170–1, **174–8**, 227; Fair
    Wages Clause 198–9
Walker, Thomas 39, 42, 78, 163, 166,
    167, 181, 183
walking ganger 1, 86 fn, 186
Ward, John 6, 31, 57, 71, 72, 74, 163,
    176, 179; founding Navvies' Un-
    ion 181–8; *passim*; early life 189;
    Sudan 157, 189–90; early politics
    190–2; Wandsworth Vestry 192–
    3; 1906 General Election 194–7;
    in Parliament 81, 197–9, 229;
    Great War 218–23; post-War
    229–30
wagon filling 54, **56–7**, 164
Welsh navvies 48, **52–3**, 63
women (navvy) 9, 12–15, 32, 49, 75–

261